THE EVERYDAY ART OF
GLUTEN-FREE

**125 SAVORY AND SWEET RECIPES
USING 6 FAIL-PROOF FLOUR BLENDS**

THE EVERYDAY ART OF
GLUTEN-FREE

125 SAVORY AND SWEET RECIPES USING 6 FAIL-PROOF FLOUR BLENDS

KAREN MORGAN
BLACKBIRD BAKERY

PHOTOGRAPHS BY KNOXY KNOX

Stewart, Tabori & Chang | New York

Published in 2014 by Stewart, Tabori & Chang
An imprint of ABRAMS

Text copyright © 2014 Karen Morgan
Photographs copyright © 2014 Knoxy Knox

Library of Congress Control Number: 2014930929

ISBN: 978-1-61769-060-0

Editor: Holly Dolce
Designer: Danielle Young
Production Manager: Katie Gaffney

The text of this book was composed in Brandon Grotesque and
Proxima Nova.

Printed and bound in the United States

10 9 8 7 6 5 4 3 2 1

Stewart, Tabori & Chang books are available at special discounts
when purchased in quantity for premiums and promotions as well as
fundraising or educational use. Special editions can also be created
to specification. For details, contact specialsales@abramsbooks.com
or the address below.

THE ART OF BOOKS SINCE 1949
115 West 18th Street
New York, NY 10011
www.abramsbooks.com

THIS BOOK IS FOR EVERYONE, GLUTEN-FREE OR NOT, WHO LONGS
TO CRACK THE GLUTEN-FREE CODE AND LEARN HOW TO MASTERFULLY
BAKE AND COOK AS A CHEF FOR THE MODERN AGE.

CONTENTS

INTRODUCTION

In the summer of 2006, I got off a train in Nans-Sous-Sainte-Anne, France. I'd come to do a guest stint as baker and pastry cook at a boutique hotel, A l'Ombre du Château. Unlike the other visiting chef engaged for that season, I hadn't trained at La Varenne, or any other cooking school. Still in my twenties, I came armed only with what I'd taught myself about cooking, a stack of boxes with CULINARY LIBRARY Sharpied on their exteriors, and a good supply of the American audacity Europeans love to laugh at (but quietly envy).

"In the shadow of the château," as the hotel's name translates, I served up my takes on French classics. At the close of each evening, the hotel's patrons requested that I step out of the kitchen into the dining room, where I was greeted with applause. Many times, shocking at first, I got a standing ovation. This enthusiastic reception confirmed that I'd pulled off what I'd come to do: fool some pretty savvy customers. I'd been carrying out a stealth operation just as shadowy as the hotel's name. All those raved-about delicacies I'd been making? They were gluten-free. The boxes I'd shipped in were filled not with cookbooks and gastronomical references, but with my arsenal of wheat-free flours.

My greatest satisfaction came in hearing, again and again, that my pastries and cakes were not merely *as good as* those the patrons knew from other kitchens, but were in fact *better*. In gluten-free cooking, in those early days, this was not merely unheard of—it was believed to be impossible. I'd taken the guest shot at the hotel looking for an unbiased verdict, understanding that the best way to get it was to put my recipes forward without the "gluten-free" label.

Since the blind test had vindicated my methods, I went ahead and confessed. The hotel's owner expressed both astonishment and admiration. Word got out, and more taste-testers arrived to find out for themselves. They all posed the same question: What was my secret?

The only answer I could muster at the time probably sounded evasive: "Endless trial and error." Every cake, pie, loaf, tart, roll, and brioche my fans marveled at was the endpoint of countless experiments conducted back home, as I'd zeroed in on the just-right combinations of ingredients to adapt the classics. Getting to that sublime first bite, my family, friends, and I had to grimace through a baker's dozen of rubbery, crumbling, adobe-brick or hockey-puck attempts. Each recipe, once perfected, involved multiple flours, meals, and starches in place of plain old all-purpose wheat flour.

So my secret was that of many other kids who cut their teeth on the streets: dogged experimentation and a stubborn refusal to give up until I got exactly what I was after. Whenever I tried to describe how I came to a gluten-free adaptation of a time-honored favorite, I sounded, even to myself, like a mad scientist. It wasn't until I began teaching regularly that I realized how complicated my process really was and vowed to make my discoveries accessible to the home chef. So, I gave myself a new challenge: figure out the method to my madness.

Thankfully, my remaining time in France got me going on the right track. I can't remember the day, but in my memory, the breakthrough came as a cumulative realization. The hotel's kitchen maintained a supply of flours I had no use for. Each time I stepped into the pantry to restock from my well-hidden boxes of gluten-free alternatives, those conventional flours stared back at me. This was not just one bin labeled FLOUR, or even two, but more than a dozen—each containing a different flour prized for its individual characteristics. Eventually, I got it. And it hit me like a tuning fork struck right on my head. Of course! There is no such thing as "all-purpose" flour, unless your purposes begin with making Play-Doh and end with hanging wallpaper.

Even when working with flours made from wheat alone, French cooks and bakers rely on a range, each having a density, texture, flavor, and aroma that make it best for distinctive uses. One flour suits baguettes, while another works for choux paste; a self-respecting *boulangerie* makes its croissants with a particular flour, grown and milled to pretty exact specifications. "Specific and important," a phrase I'd heard repeatedly among the native chefs, started to make sense.

My own experience had, in fact, shown me the same thing. Gluten-free cooking, at its best, relies on specific flours for specific purposes. Precision in these choices has to be extra high, as tolerances, once we leave gluten behind, are low. A tablespoon more or a tablespoon less of the single-grain flour going into a yeast-raised wheat bread won't make a huge difference. But a tablespoon's variation in sorghum flour used in a gluten-free combination with rice flour and tapioca starch has a huge impact on what comes out of the oven. Minor changes swing the balance between delicate crumb and "Mmm . . . chewy . . . like damp cardboard."

Back at home in the United States, I stared at what was on the shelves of the grocery store—dozens of brands of the same "all-purpose" wheat flour and "all-purpose" gluten-free options. All-purpose gluten-free flours work well for *some* uses, but not *all*, as their name suggests. They might make a great cookie, but produce horrible bread, which certainly is not okay. The all-purpose label has to do with how food products are manufactured and marketed, not with how good food is made. I read up on how the demands of industrial baking prompted North American wheat growers to pump up the grain's gluten, to nearly double what nature and traditional farming had settled on. The need for "all-purpose" fueled an epidemic of gluten intolerance. That's another story—but if you're curious, you can read more about it in the Pantry section's survey of ingredients that most effectively replace gluten (see page 215).

But back to the cool limestone cave beneath A l'Ombre du Château: I did have a method, I saw, and a very simple one at that, but it would take me seven years to boil it down to something I could teach and put in a book.

I spent much of that time up to my elbows in more experimentation. Thankfully, my mad-scientist days are behind me—at least for now—and I'm happy to say that as a result, *you* can skip the endless approximations and tragic mistakes and get right to the good stuff. I worked out my six blends—Biscuit, Donut & Fritter, Pie & Pasta, Cookie Jar, Cake & Muffin, and Bread & Pizza. They're combinations of flours ideally suited to each of the major sections of baking and cooking. Each blend is tailored to a given range of American classics, but they also work extremely well for all manner of international baked goods and main dishes, too. So no matter what level of culinary genius you may happen to be at, these blends will come to life in your hands. They're the starting point for this book and anchor all its recipes.

As you make your way through the blend recipes, you may notice that their individual metric equivalents aren't exactly equal to the numbers in the conversion charts. This is because different brands of gluten-free flour and starch have different metric weights. The numbers in the ingredient list reflect the specific brands I use at Blackbird Bakery, while the conversion chart is based on an average metric weight for the gluten-free flours and starches involved.

Each blend introduces a chapter of recipes, showing the variety of the blend's applications. The recipes move generally from simple to complex, within each section and throughout the book. While the aim is to show how versatile these blends can make your gluten-free kitchen, the recipes are also those nominated as my greatest hits by the people I cook for—my friends, family, and customers. I'm proud of my gâteau St. Honoré, but I haven't included it; it's just not as close to my heart as my Jelly-Filled Donuts (page 74), Batter-Fried Chicken (page 59), Chicken-Fried Steak (page 52), Macaroni & Cheese (page 67), Gumbo (page 71), Apple Slab Pie (page 103), and Cake-Style Ice Cream Sandwiches (page 181). In the pages that follow, you'll even find my spins on the Hostess Cupcake (page 177) and Pop-Tarts (page 88).

My ambition for this book is to show everyone that we can go home again, gluten-free, to the foods that make us nostalgic and give us the greatest comfort, and make them even better than before.

In addition to learning how to make a variety of cookies, pies, cakes, and breads, the best ravioli ever, and those brand-name favorites I mentioned, you'll learn how to put together a set of basic doughs, batters, and sauces that can open the way to limitless adaptations of your own. I've laid claim to some of the most important French culinary landmarks that figure in all manner of homey comfort foods. My classic white sauce, or béchamel (page 50), can be the starting point for your shrimp Alfredo or your mother's cheese soufflé, as well as my mac & cheese. Maybe what you're after is your grandmother's white lasagna, and this béchamel is perfectly suited for that, too. You'll get to know basic bread and cookie doughs that also have various classic applications. The blend that makes my tempura and calamari batter so good will work out great for your battered eggplant and fish 'n' chips, too.

As you get to know this book, its blends, batters, doughs, breadings, fry-coatings, and sauces, think of your own recipe collection and the ones you want to adapt to be gluten-free. The recipes that follow embrace the most basic foods of all sorts, not just things that go onto cookie sheets and into loaf pans. I purposefully included a swath of the everyday dishes that represent the American melting pot, the comfort foods that remind us of who we are and where we came from, so the blends can strut their stuff and show you the ropes not just of gluten-free baking, but of *everyday* gluten-free cooking.

Now, a couple of tips on how you'll get the most out of my approach:

Having worked things out for myself by *doing*, I'm a big believer in rolling up my sleeves and going right into the kitchen. I learn the theory best when I'm engaged in hands-on practice and encourage you to do the same. Browse through the recipes that use each blend and choose some foods you want to make for yourself, your family, and your friends. The ingredient lists and methods are recipe-focused, not gluten-free philosophy classes. But the introductions to the blends and the pantry section at the back of the book (page 215) provide a good deal of information on the ingredients, tools, and techniques called for in the recipes. You'll also find references that take you to tips and tricks in the pantry, intros, and sidebars. Hop around, from Biscuit Blend to Pie & Pasta, from breakfast foods to main-dish dinners and desserts, and from hands-on experience of what these blends do to notes on the personalities of the flours they bring together. My aim has been to let information percolate through the hands-on process, bringing us all a bit further out of the gluten-free dark ages with each turn of the spoon.

All that being said, I'm not out to incite a free-for-all in the kitchen! A vital keyword is *specific*. Trust me when I tell you that I'm not exaggerating how many glitches I had to inflict on people to get these recipes right. So let me urge you to make them, at first, as they're written, so you get a direct feel for how and why I chose each specific and important approach. Once you've got an experience of the ratios and proportions the blends use and how the flours combine with other ingredients, you'll be equipped to make adjustments as you see fit. And by combining intuition and expertise, you'll likely jump from my recipes into adaptations of other old favorites you're jonesing for.

The real revelation for me, over these experimental years, is that gluten-free doesn't have to take the fun out of food or cooking. After trying your hand at a few breads, treats, and dishes across the range of blends, "I wish I could make *that*" won't play in your mind like a mantra anymore. Instead, you'll live by the motto that guided me through my early disasters, into my nervy covert ops in France, and on to the success (and loyal fans) I enjoy at Blackbird Bakery: "I can make *that* gluten-free!"

BISCUIT BLEND

The Biscuit Blend was engineered for everything that is made at the beginning of the day, and it combines flours and starches with both quick breads and yeast-risen pastries in mind. Raised either with baking powder and soda, or with yeast, the flours play together to give the ideal physical characteristics for everything that screams "Breakfast." When I was able to master both quick breads and yeast-risen pastries with this blend, however, I realized it was silly to stop at breakfast, so I included some classic soft dinner rolls and hot dog buns to show you that this blend is quite the workhorse.

Of all the blends in this book, you will see that the Biscuit Blend has the greatest range in terms of what you can make with it. Here, the brown rice and glutinous rice flours contribute a lightness commonly achieved by using cake flour. Together with the sorghum flour, they ensure that the finished baked good will have the texture of a quick bread, not a brick bread.

THE RECIPE

1¾ cups plus 2 tablespoons plus 1 teaspoon (220 g) glutinous rice flour

1 cup plus 1¼ teaspoons (126 g) cornstarch

1 cup (125 g) extra-fine brown rice flour

1 cup (108 g) tapioca starch

1 cup (108 g) sorghum flour

6 teaspoons (18 g) guar gum

SPECIAL EQUIPMENT
Digital scale

The Biscuit Blend, like each blend in this book, is assembled with at least one complete protein grain (in this case, sorghum flour), a variety of starches, and guar gum. Each of these flours and starches plays a critical role by lending their various flavors, textures, and constituent characteristics, which are usually "activated" after liquids have been added. Each of the blends has a different ratio of these various ingredients so as to ferret out the very best in their specific purpose. The names of the blends define what they are ideal for and the specific section of cookery that they satisfy.

For me, the most important ingredient in all the blends is the guar gum. Most gluten-free bakers prefer xanthan gum, but I have never used the stuff. It's made from a toxic bacteria that has been scientifically proven to cause tissue death in infants and the terminally ill. Unfortunately, the binding function of xanthan gum has been essential to successful gluten-free baking. The good news? Guar gum does the same thing without the scary toxic bacteria profile and provides volume where xanthan gum does not. I call guar gum the magic rubber band of gluten-free baking because it replaces the elasticity of the gluten protein.

For more information on the individual flours, starches, and other ingredients in the blend, see the Pantry section on page 215.

MAKES 6 CUPS (705 G), ENOUGH FOR 6 BATCHES OF BISCUITS OR 3 LOAVES OF BASIC QUICK BREAD

Using the spoon-and-sweep method, measure (or, for absolute precision, weigh using a digital scale) each ingredient into a large bowl. Whisk together and then sift the mixture into a separate large bowl. Repeat several times so the flours, starches, and guar gum are uniformly distributed throughout.

Below is the approximate weight of the blend, by volume for use in doing your own adaptations:

EACH	OF BLEND WEIGHS APPROXIMATELY
1 tablespoon	6.5 g
¼ cup	26 g
⅓ cup	35 g
½ cup	52 g
⅔ cup	70 g
¾ cup	78 g
1 cup	104 g

THE DOUGH

REFRIGERATION MAY BE REQUIRED

Always read the recipe all the way through before beginning. Many gluten-free doughs require rest in the fridge to make them the very best they can be, so if the recipe calls for a time-out in the fridge, follow the instructions to the letter.

FOLDING MATTERS

Folding means combining ingredients while retaining the air in the mixture. For example, fluffy beaten egg whites, full of the air that has been incorporated during beating, are often folded into batters to lighten them. The Buckwheat Blini (page 20), made with the Biscuit Blend, require careful folding to keep them light.

I recommend using a wooden spoon instead of a rubber or plastic spatula to fold egg whites into the other ingredients. When used for folding, spatulas have a tendency to mash or flatten the dough or batter and let the air out of beaten egg whites. Mashed and flattened is not what you want; your goal is to keep the dough light.

The key to folding is exaggeration. Don't just scoot your spoon around the dough—get it way down to the bottom of the bowl, gently lift the dough and fold it over itself, rolling the spoon as you fold. (Think about turning a crank—the spoon is the crank, and the dough or batter is the gear being spun by the crank.) Rotate the bowl and repeat until the ingredients are incorporated.

If a certain degree of folding is required, the recipe will say so—for example, you might be told to "fold the egg whites into the batter until no white streaks remain" or "fold in the dry ingredients until just incorporated." The thing to remember is the air! Fold those egg whites until no white streaks remain, but don't squash the air out of them. Fold in those dry ingredients, but don't over mix them so they choke the lightness out of the dough.

Need some practice? I recommend trying your hand at the blini or the Boston Cream Pie (page 170) to master folding in beaten egg whites. No matter what, always remember it takes time to master anything so don't be hard on yourself. We all have to fall down so we can get back up.

DON'T BE TOO KNEADY

Kneading means working or mixing a dough by pressing, folding, and turning it on a lightly floured surface. In traditional baking, kneading is essential to activate the gluten protein in a dough. Thankfully, we don't have to worry about activating gluten (and indeed, are in trouble if there's gluten present)—so our doughs require very little kneading, saving time and elbow grease. In this chapter, you'll be instructed to knead the yeast-risen Biscuit Blend doughs to get the dough to the ideal texture so you can properly shape it into its respective forms. I always tell my students that over-kneading gluten-free dough is like adding too much salt; overkneading will result in too much flour being incorporated into the dough, and the moment this occurs, that delicate texture you're looking for will turn into below-code concrete—yes, it's soft, but it's not exactly tender. The same thing goes for salt—you can always add more, but once it's too salty, you're pretty much done for.

When a recipe requires kneading, like the Clover-leaf Dinner Rolls (page 33) pictured here, first dust the counter with additional Biscuit Blend or a bit of glutinous rice flour, then take the dough and lightly coat it with the blend or flour so it won't stick to your hands. Form the dough into the shape the recipe calls for, either a disk or a rectangle. Working on the dusted surface, fold the dough toward you and press down and forward, gently stretching the dough outward without tearing it. Rotate the dough 90 degrees and repeat, folding and turning, maintaining a smooth disk. This makes one "turn." The recipe will indicate for how long you should knead the dough, either for a number of "turns," so a certain consistency is reached ("until smooth"), or for an amount of time. Your goal is to eliminate stickiness and make the dough very pliable. As you can see, one turn massively improves the dough. Look at that elasticity!

ROLLING

Rolling out your dough should be done on a lightly floured work surface with a lightly floured rolling pin, while applying steady, even pressure.

There are several types of rolling pins: I prefer a French rod-style pin, which is a long wooden cylinder, thinner than a roller-style pin and without handles. This type of pin allows me to feel much more directly how the dough is taking shape as I roll, and it's easier to tell if I'm applying even pressure. I can roll the pin under my hands and even along the underside of my forearms, which is a great way to get intimate contact with your dough and has become my preferred technique for perfectly even rolling.

To roll out your dough, first give your rolling pin and work surface a dusting of Biscuit Blend or glutinous rice flour. Form the dough into a disk and set it on your dusted work surface. Gently roll the dough from the center toward the edge of the disk, always rolling outward. I call this "planing." If you've ever watched a carpenter plane a piece of wood—they always begin by moving in one direction first. When the dough looks level, then begin working the pin back and forth. Turn the dough 45 degrees after each pass of the rolling pin. This helps keep the rolling even and lets you ensure the dough is not sticking to your work surface. If it does stick a little, use a bench scraper to gently lift the stuck-on portion and then dust your work surface with a bit more flour or blend. Repeat the rolling and turning until the dough is the thickness or shape indicated by the recipe.

COTTAGE CHEESE PANCAKES

If there is one pancake for which I just *might* forsake all others, it's not the fluffy, big-as-your-face buttermilk number that pancake chains swear by. It's this one, with delicate curds that melt and string apart on the fork and in the bite. A wooden spoon is a must in this recipe; a mixer shreds the cottage cheese curds, makes the mixture too homogenous, and results in denser pancakes.

MAKES EIGHT 4-INCH PANCAKES

In a large bowl, sift together the Biscuit Blend, oat flour, sugar, baking powder, and salt.

In a separate bowl, whisk together the eggs, milk, oil, and vanilla. Pour the egg mixture into the dry ingredients and, using a wooden spoon, mix until they are just smooth. Gently fold in the cottage cheese. At this point, the batter can be held in the refrigerator in an airtight container for up to 3 days. It will thicken as it chills; bring it back to the desired consistency by beating in a tablespoon or two of milk.

Set a griddle or skillet over medium heat. If the pan is not seasoned, give it a light coating of oil as it heats (or if you're going hard-core all-American, slick the pan with bacon grease or butter).

Using a ¼-cup (60-ml) measure, begin forming pancakes on the hot griddle, leaving at least 1 inch (2.5 cm) between each pancake. Cook them for 90 seconds or so, until small bubbles form on the surface of the pancakes and begin to pop. The holes should close slowly; if they stay open, the pancakes are getting overdone, so reduce the heat to medium-low. Flip the pancakes and cook them for 90 seconds to 2 minutes more. Repeat until all the batter has been used, adding more oil or bacon grease to the griddle as necessary to keep the pancakes from sticking.

To serve, transfer the pancakes directly from the griddle to a warmed platter or individual plates, with toppings and butter served alongside. Alternatively, you can hold the pancakes on a platter in a 175°F (80°C) oven, covered loosely with foil. Leftovers will keep well in an airtight container in the refrigerator for up to 4 days. Reheat them, loosely wrapped in foil, in a warm oven. You can make the batter up to three days before you make the pancakes—just store it in an airtight container in the refrigerator until ready to use. Keep in mind that the refrigerated batter will thicken up so just add a tablespoon or two of milk and you're good to go.

¾ cup (78 g) Biscuit Blend (page 13)

¼ cup (21 g) gluten-free oat flour (see Note)

2 tablespoons sugar

1 teaspoon double-acting baking powder

¼ teaspoon kosher salt

2 large eggs

¼ cup (60 ml) milk

¼ cup (60 ml) grapeseed oil or pure olive oil, plus more for the pan

1½ teaspoon pure vanilla extract

½ cup (120 ml) large-curd cottage cheese

Bacon grease, for the pan (optional)

OPTIONAL TOPPINGS:

Maple syrup, preserves, lemon juice, confectioners' or granulated sugar, *baci* filling or Nutella, applesauce, pear sauce, berry compote (and don't forget butter!)

NOTE: For the fall, swapping chestnut flour for the oat flour is stupendous. Or, if you can't tolerate oats, even gluten-free varieties, use ¼ cup (22 g) almond flour in place of the oat flour, or use a full cup (104 g) of the Biscuit Blend. If you use almond flour, your pancakes will be slightly more fragile but just as delicious.

BUCKWHEAT BLINI

6 tablespoons (39 g) Biscuit Blend (page 13)

¼ cup (32 g) buckwheat flour

2 teaspoons sugar

¼ teaspoon baking soda

¼ teaspoon kosher salt

½ cup (120 ml) 2% milk

2 large eggs, separated

½ cup (1 stick / 113 g) unsalted butter, melted

TOPPINGS:

Crème fraîche and caviar (optional)

Smoked salmon (optional)

Minced red onion or shallot

Small lemon wedges

Food snobs, rejoice! Even Vladimir Putin isn't served better blini than these. The classic chassis for caviar of all grades, blini are every bit as good with smoked salmon or lox and accompaniments. Since buckwheat flour doesn't sift well, be sure to use a whisk to combine the dry ingredients for these little pancakes, and remember—folding the egg whites in *slowly* is the key to keeping the blinis' texture nice and light (for tips on folding, see page 15).

(And in case you're feeling fancy, a dozen blini will accommodate a 1-ounce / 30-g jar of caviar.)

MAKES TWENTY-FOUR 2-INCH (4-CM) BLINI; SERVES 6

In a large bowl, whisk together the Biscuit Blend, buckwheat flour, sugar, baking soda, and salt.

Stir in the milk and egg yolks all at once and whisk until the batter is very smooth. Add 4 tablespoons (60 ml) of the melted butter and whisk well to combine. The batter will thicken up, which is exactly what you want.

In a separate bowl using a clean whisk, or a stand or hand mixer fitted with the whisk attachment, beat the egg whites until they are frothy and glistening, but not dry. You want them firm enough that when you lift the whisk, the meringue forms a peak like a soft-serve ice cream cone. (If the egg whites are overbeaten, the blini won't get the right lift.)

With a wooden spoon, gently fold the egg whites into the batter until you no longer see flecks of white.

If necessary, reheat the remaining 4 tablespoons (60 ml) melted butter until the butterfat and milk solids separate. Using a spoon, skim the foamy top off the butterfat. The clear, yellow liquid that's left is clarified butter. Dip a pastry brush in the clarified butter, avoiding the milk solids that fall to the bottom. Brush the butter onto a griddle or a heavy-bottomed skillet and set the pan over medium heat.

Spoon 1-tablespoon portions of the batter onto the hot griddle, leaving a good 1 inch (2.5 cm) of space around each. Cook them for 90 seconds per side; adjust the heat, if necessary, so they're cooking at close to that rate. Repeat until all the batter has been used, brushing more butter onto the griddle as necessary to keep the blini from sticking.

Serve the blini directly from the griddle, with crème fraîche and caviar or smoked salmon alongside. Either way, be sure to serve them with garnishes: minced red onion or shallot, chives, and small lemon wedges. If you're feeling like showing the Kremlin how it's done, go for all of the above. These keep beautifully in the refrigerator, tightly wrapped, for up to 3 days.

TEXAS BREAKFAST TACOS

FOR THE TORTILLAS:

2¼ cups (234 g) Biscuit Blend (page 13), plus more for dusting

1 teaspoon kosher salt

½ teaspoon baking powder

1½ tablespoons lard (rendered pork fat)

FOR THE FILLING:

1 tablespoon unsalted butter (grapeseed oil and olive oil are also good)

8 large eggs

Kosher salt and freshly ground black pepper

8 slices peppered bacon, cooked until semi-crisp

1 cup (225 g) Monterey Jack or Asiago cheese

1 cup (240 ml) pico de gallo (or whatever salsa claims your affections)

These tortillas are good simply warmed in a dry skillet and eaten with a side of charro beans, or with a dab of butter, but are extra delicious when loaded with classic breakfast taco fillings. Make a double batch of the tortillas here for quesadillas (see the variation, below), enchiladas, or whatever you like. You can substitute vegetable shortening for the lard, but the flavor just won't be the same.

For the best results, let the dough rest for at least 30 minutes before using.

MAKES 8 TACOS

Make the tortillas: In a large bowl, whisk together the Biscuit Blend, salt, and baking powder. With your fingertips, work in the lard until the mixture resembles damp cornmeal.

Using a wooden spoon, briskly stir ¾ cup (180 ml) water into the dry ingredients. The dough will be very thick—it should come together into a ball and be barely stir-able.

Lightly dust your work surface with Biscuit Blend. Turn out the dough onto the dusted surface and knead it with the heel of your hand until it is smooth (this should take about eight turns). The dough should feel warm to the touch.

Form the dough into a ball, wrap it in plastic wrap, and let it sit on the counter for at least 30 minutes.

Divide it into 8 equal-size balls. Lightly dust the dough with additional Biscuit Blend or glutinous rice flour. Place each ball between two pieces of plastic wrap and, using a tortilla press or a rolling pin, flatten the dough into a round about 1⁄16 inch (2 mm) thick. (Flattening the dough on a wooden cutting board with a wide, flat-bottomed pan also works well, but will give the tortillas an irregular shape.)

Set a large nonstick skillet or griddle over medium heat. Get the surface hot enough that a bit of water dripped onto the surface forms droplets that jump around as they evaporate.

Set a tortilla on the hot cooking surface. Let it settle onto the metal a bit, but don't press down on it. Cook it for 1 to 2 minutes per side, until both sides have the trademark brown "done" spots, and the texture is firmed but pliable. Keep the finished tortillas warm by wrapping them in a clean kitchen towel or on a heatproof platter in a low oven.

Make the filling: In a separate griddle or skillet, melt the butter over medium heat. When the butter foams, add the eggs and cook, stirring to scramble them, until they are set but not dry. Turn off the heat as soon as you can no longer see any wet spots—they'll continue to set off-heat. Season them with salt and pepper.

To serve, spoon a generous scoop of eggs into one of your hot tortillas, followed by a slice of the cooked bacon, a handful of cheese, and a spoonful of pico de gallo. Fold and serve.

These tortillas are best the day they are made.

VARIATION: Quesadillas

Heat a dry griddle or skillet over medium heat. Lightly toast a tortilla in the pan. When the first side is warm, flip it and spread ½ cup (55 g) shredded cheese (Monterey Jack, mozzarella, or queso blanco are best, or a combination of all three) evenly over the toasted side. Top with a second tortilla, and keep toasting until the cheese starts to melt. Flip it to get the second side brown. Transfer the quesadilla to a plate and cut it into triangles. Repeat with the remaining tortillas and cheese. Serve them hot, with salsa and sour cream and sprinkled with cilantro.

WAFFLES

My mom never used seltzer in her waffles, but it is essential for this gluten-free version. The fizz gives a delectable light-on-the-inside, crisp-on-the-outside texture. Divine for breakfast and devilishly good with fried chicken (especially Batter-Fried Chicken, page 59), these waffles dare you not to enjoy them.

Waffles are at their best the moment they come out of the iron. But if you've got to get a bunch made up before serving, keep the first batches warm in a 300°F (150°C) oven, on a metal tray, haphazardly stacked so they have airspace and don't steam one another. These freeze beautifully, too, double-wrapped, for up to a month. The best way to reheat them is in the toaster, just like Eggos. And that's all that *this* waffle and the commercial kind have in common.

MAKES 8 WAFFLES

Preheat a waffle iron.

In a large bowl, whisk together the Biscuit Blend, powdered buttermilk, sugar, salt, and baking soda. If the buttermilk powder has become the least bit clumpy, press it through a sieve using the back of a spoon. If it's silken smooth, just whisking the dry ingredients together is sufficient.

In a separate bowl, whisk together the sour cream, eggs, oil, and vanilla until they are smooth. Using a wooden spoon, stir the sour cream mixture into the dry mixture until you have a uniform batter. Whisk in the seltzer. From here, move fast so the seltzer doesn't lose its bubbles.

Brush a bit of the melted butter onto the plates of the hot waffle iron. Ladle about ¼ cup (60 ml) batter onto the iron to fill the plates three-quarters full. Close the waffle iron and cook according to the manufacturer's instructions. (Alternatively, watch the steam escaping from the iron. Once the steam has diminished to a bare vapor, the waffle is ready.) The cook time for most waffle irons is 3 to 5 minutes, and the finished waffle should be golden brown and release easily from the plates of the iron. Repeat with the remaining batter.

Serve the waffles immediately, hot off the iron.

2 cups (208 g) Biscuit Blend (page 13)

½ cup (34 g) powdered buttermilk

1½ tablespoons sugar

½ teaspoon kosher salt

½ teaspoon baking soda

½ cup (120 ml) sour cream

3 large eggs

¼ cup (60 ml) vegetable oil

2 teaspoons pure vanilla extract

1¼ cups (300 ml) plain seltzer water

2 tablespoons unsalted butter, melted

OPTIONAL TOPPINGS:

Whipped cream and berries

Butter and maple syrup

Confectioners' sugar and cinnamon

Preserve whipped cream cheese

NOTE: Try substituting ¼ cup (26 g) tapioca starch for the Biscuit Blend for an even lighter version.

LATKES

2½ cups (400 g) coarsely shredded peeled potatoes

2 tablespoons grated white onion

2 tablespoons (13 g) Biscuit Blend (page 13)

½ cup (120 ml) peanut oil, for frying

2 large eggs

1½ teaspoons kosher salt

½ teaspoon freshly cracked black pepper

TOPPINGS:

Sour cream

Chives

Applesauce or pear sauce

Potatoes themselves are naturally gluten-free, but traditional latke recipes call for wheat flour, bread crumbs, or matzo meal to hold the pancakes together. Here, we skirt the issue by using the Biscuit Blend as a binding agent. For these potato pancakes, russets, Yukon Golds, and jumbo bakers like Idahos are the best varieties to go with. Red Bliss and waxier types of potatoes have a tendency to fall apart instead of forming the crispy pancakes you're looking for. When forming and frying, go for latkes that are a bit free-form, and don't worry about dangling strands of potato and onion—they give the latke that perfect outer crunch.

MAKES SIX 3-INCH (7½-CM) LATKES

Wrap the shredded potatoes in a tea towel or a double layer of cheesecloth and squeeze out any excess moisture.

Place the potatoes in a large bowl, add the onion, and toss to combine. While tossing, sprinkle the Biscuit Blend over the potato-onion mixture to lightly and evenly coat it.

In a large skillet (big enough to accommodate three or four 3-inch / 7½-cm latkes without crowding), heat the oil over medium heat. Line a platter with a brown paper bag or paper towels.

In a small bowl, whisk the eggs with the salt and pepper and pour them over the potato mixture. Using a wooden spoon, stir until they're just combined; the mixture should still be a bit runny rather than pasty.

Immediately begin frying so the potatoes keep the proper consistency. Spoon about 2 tablespoons of the latke mixture into the hot oil and immediately flatten it with the back of a spoon or spatula to be about ½ inch (12 mm) thick. Repeat to form a few more latkes, but be sure not to crowd the pan.

Cook the latkes for 2 to 3 minutes on the first side, until golden brown, then flip and cook the second side for no more than 2 minutes, until equally golden and crisp. Using a spatula, transfer the latkes to the lined platter to drain any excess oil; flip them after a few seconds to drain the other side. Repeat until you have used all of the potato mixture.

Serve the latkes immediately with sour cream, chives, apple or pear sauce, or all of the above. (Pear-ginger sauce is delish, and as far as I know, kosher.)

The latkes will keep, tightly wrapped, in the refrigerator for up to 3 days. They can be reheated in the oven, but won't regain that right-out-of-the-pan crispness.

RICOTTA CHEESE PUFFS

Serve these cheese puffs in a basket, warm, alongside soups, salads, and light meals. They're particularly good with gazpacho, the soup that thinks it's a salad. Or just eat them as a snack, hot from the oven.

Freezing the puffs before baking them is critical to getting the right texture, so don't cut corners and skip their chill-out time.

MAKES 12 PUFFS

In a large bowl, whisk together the Biscuit Blend, baking powder, salt, and pepper. Using a pastry cutter or a firm, dry whisk, cut in the butter until there are no longer any visible lumps of butter and the mixture resembles damp cornmeal.

Add the ricotta and eggs and stir them vigorously with a wooden spoon until the batter is thick and smooth. Add the cheese and parsley and stir until they are just incorporated.

Line a baking sheet with parchment paper or a Silpat. Using a 1½-inch-(4-cm-) diameter ice cream scoop, drop portions of the batter onto the baking sheet, leaving a couple of inches between each. Transfer the baking sheet to the freezer and freeze the batter for at least 30 minutes and up to 1 hour.

Preheat the oven to 450°F (230°C).

Transfer the frozen ricotta puffs to the oven and bake them for 10 to 12 minutes, until the tops and edges of the puffs are golden brown. Allow the puffs to cool on the pan for 5 minutes before serving or transferring them to a wire rack to cool completely.

The puffs are best the day they are baked, but are still delicious on day three. Be sure to store them in an airtight container. I like to warm them gently in the oven, loosely tented with aluminum foil.

½ cup plus 2 tablespoons (65 g) Biscuit Blend (page 13)

½ teaspoon baking powder

½ teaspoon kosher salt

¼ teaspoon freshly ground black pepper

1 tablespoon unsalted butter, diced and kept cold

½ cup (120 ml) whole-milk ricotta

2 large eggs, beaten

⅓ cup (40 g) grated extra-sharp cheddar

1 tablespoon finely chopped fresh parsley

Nonstick cooking spray (optional)

ALL-AMERICAN ICE CREAM CONES

1¾ cups (182 g) Biscuit Blend (page 13)

¾ cup (150 g) caster or superfine sugar

⅛ teaspoon kosher salt

¾ cup (6 oz / 170 g) vegetable shortening

4 large eggs

1 teaspoon grated lemon zest

1 tablespoon fresh lemon juice

1 teaspoon grated tangerine or orange zest

1 tablespoon fresh tangerine or orange juice

2 teaspoons pure vanilla extract

1 teaspoon gluten-free vodka, like Tito's Handmade Vodka (optional)

NOTE: For this and other recipes involving the mixer, I like to drape a kitchen towel over the top of the mixer bowl when I'm making the dough so the ingredients don't billow out like a mushroom cloud.

Nothing says summer like an ice cream cone, and since anything in a cone is pretty fabulous, be sure to check out the variations for some versatile savory and sweet twists on both the cone and filling. The vodka gives each cone an extra-crispy texture, causing it to surrender the moment it comes into contact with your teeth. As an extra treat, dip the ends of the cones in melted dark chocolate after they have been formed and cooled. The chocolate will seal the cones and prevent drips—and it tastes pretty great, too—I mean, who doesn't remember eating Drumsticks on a hot summer day?

Making these cones might sound involved, but it's not. It just takes a fair number of words to describe a process that's really both simple and fun. In fact, kids love shaping the cones, so if you have a few running around, recruit them as helpers. If you have a pizzelle iron, this is the time to use it!

MAKES 12 CONES

In the bowl of a stand mixer fitted with the paddle attachment, combine the Biscuit Blend, sugar, and salt and mix until they are well combined. Add the shortening and mix on low speed until you no longer see lumps and the mixture resembles damp cornmeal. With the mixer on medium speed, add the eggs, waiting until the first is incorporated before adding the next. The dough should be wet and tacky, sticking to the sides of the bowl and the paddle.

Add the citrus zests and juices and ¼ cup (60ml) water and continue to mix the dough on medium speed, scraping down the sides of the bowl with a spatula as necessary. Add the vanilla and vodka and mix until they are just incorporated.

Cover the mixer bowl with plastic wrap and refrigerate it for at least an hour; overnight is optimal. At this point, the dough will keep in the refrigerator for up to 3 days.

If you want close-to-perfect, uniform cones, roll a piece of heavy-gauge paper into a cone to tape on the inside of a prepared cone so it holds the shape. Cut the open end so it is level and will stand on end with the point up. (If you want to go assembly-line, make three or four paper cones.)

If you have an electric pizzelle iron, heat it according to the manufacturer's instructions. Otherwise, grease a broad, flat skillet lightly or spray it with nonstick cooking spray and set it over medium heat. Grease the outside of the bottom of a heavy-bottomed 6-inch (15-cm) saucepan, too.

CONTINUED

Scoop a rounded tablespoon of the dough onto the pizzelle iron or skillet. If using an iron, close it to flatten the dough nice and thin, and cook the dough for 2 to 3 minutes. If using a skillet, scoop the dough onto the hot surface of the skillet and immediately press it flat with the bottom of the saucepan. Cook the dough for 90 seconds, then lift off the saucepan, flip the dough, and replace the saucepan. Cook it for 1 minute or so more, until just golden.

Shape the cones as they come off the iron or skillet. Allow them to cool just enough that you can handle them, but still hot enough so they're soft. Lay the unrolled cone on a flat surface. Set the paper cone mold on top, with its tip just inside the circle's edge, and the mold lying across the middle of the circle. Roll the dough around that form, so the two sides close. Hold the cone for about 30 seconds, so it keeps its form, then set the cone and mold upright on the open end and set them aside to cool completely while you bake the next scoop of dough. Repeat until you've used all the dough.

The cones will keep in an airtight container at room temperature for up to a week.

VARIATION: Mexican Chocolate Cones
These are a great treat with a rich chocolate ice cream. Add ¼ cup Dutch cocoa powder, ½ teaspoon ground cinnamon and ⅛ teaspoon cayenne pepper to the dry ingredients. Omit the lemon zest and juice, increase the vodka to 1 tablespoon, and add 3 tablespoons water.

VARIATION: Ceviche Cones
To the dry ingredients, add 2 tablespoons masa harina, ⅛ teaspoon cayenne pepper, and ½ teaspoon dried cilantro (or 1 tablespoon minced fresh cilantro, but it won't keep its vibrant color); reduce the sugar to ¼ cup (56 g) and increase the salt to ½ teaspoon. From the wet ingredients, eliminate orange zest and juice, increase the vodka to 1 tablespoon, and add 3 tablespoons of water.

Serve these with a communal bowl of fresh ceviche, so each person gets to make her/his own ceviche cone. Alongside, have bowls of garnishes: lime wedges, minced fresh cilantro, diced avocado tossed with lime juice, and finely minced fresh hot red or green chiles.

VARIATION: Pizzelle Cookies
Add a splash of anise extract to the batter when you incorporate the wet ingredients. Instead of forming the dough into cone shapes, leave them flat after you have cooked them. These are divine with preserves.

CRÊPES SUZETTE

What's more solidly good-old-USA than this dessert? It hasn't been seen in France for over a century, but it's a fancy treat that to the 1950s generation here meant swank dining. (Flaming optional.) If you aren't feeling that nostalgic, they're also good the way Europeans like them today— see the variations. (A food processor works well, but a blender's easier for this recipe.)

MAKES TWELVE 8-INCH (20-CM) CRÊPES; SERVES 6

Make the crêpe batter: In a small bowl, whisk together the Biscuit Blend, sugar, and salt. Transfer them to a blender and add half of the milk. With the blender on low speed, add the remaining milk, the eggs, melted butter, Grand Marnier, and zest. Raise the speed to medium and mix until the batter is very smooth. (At this point, you can refrigerate the batter in the blender cup, covered, for up to 2 days.)

Make the sauce: In a saucepan, combine the sugar and 3 tablespoons water and set the pan over medium heat. Heat until the sugar has dissolved and then continue to cook until the sugar begins to caramelize. When the caramel is medium-brown, stir in the orange juice; cook until the mixture is bubbly. Remove the pan from the heat and add the Grand Marnier. Using a long kitchen lighter, ignite the liqueur and let the flame burn out. Add the orange zest and sections and toss to coat. Set the sauce aside.

Make the filling: In the bowl of a stand mixer fitted with the paddle attachment, whip the butter until smooth, then add the marmalade and mix until just combined. Set aside.

Cook the crêpes: Preheat the oven to 200°F (90°C). Whisk the batter briefly. If it has thickened and isn't at the "running batter texture," lighten it with a couple of tablespoons of water, whisking until very smooth. (This usually isn't necessary until day 2 in the fridge.)

In an 8-inch (20-cm) skillet or crêpe pan, melt about 1 teaspoon of clarified butter over medium heat. Measure out 3 tablespoons (45 ml) of the batter and pour it into the pan, tilting the pan so the batter evenly coats the bottom. Cook it for 1 to 2 minutes, until the crêpe is golden brown and has a lacelike edge, then carefully flip it over and cook it for 30 seconds more. Transfer the finished crêpe to a heatproof platter and place it in the warmed oven. Repeat with the remaining batter, adding more butter to the pan as needed to prevent the crêpes from sticking.

CONTINUED

FOR THE CRÊPES:

¾ cup plus 1 tablespoon (84.5 g) Biscuit Blend (page 13)

1 tablespoon sugar

¼ teaspoon kosher salt

1¼ cups (300 ml) whole milk

4 large eggs

4 tablespoons (½ stick / 56 g) unsalted butter, melted

1 tablespoon Grand Marnier or Cointreau

Finely grated zest of 1 orange

FOR THE SAUCE:

½ cup (100 g) sugar

1 cup (240 ml) orange juice

2 tablespoons Grand Marnier

Finely grated zest of 1 orange

2 oranges, peeled and sectioned (without the membrane; just the flesh of the fruit)

FOR THE FILLING:

4 tablespoons (½ stick / 56 g) unsalted butter, softened

½ cup (120 ml) orange marmalade

Clarified butter or ghee, for the pan

To serve, lay a crêpe on a warmed plate and spread it lightly with some of the orange marmalade butter. Roll or fold the crêpe into a triangle. Repeat with the remaining crêpes. Divide them among six individual plates and spoon the sauce over them, plating 2 to 3 orange sections per serving.

Leftover crêpes will keep, wrapped in plastic, in the refrigerator for up to 4 days. Freezing them is not recommended.

VARIATION: Simple Crêpes

Try the crêpes simply rolled with the orange butter filling only, or with butter and cinnamon-sugar; a smear of Nutella; or with butter, sugar, and lemon juice.

VARIATION: The Dutch Way

Omit the orange zest from the batter and replace the Grand Marnier with vodka. Serve the crêpes open-faced topped with melted Gruyère and crumbled crunchy bacon—and maybe set a fried egg on top. (Or if you're really ambitious, a 110-minute egg.)

CLOVERLEAF DINNER ROLLS

This versatile dough can be used for both sweet and savory baked goods (like Monkey Bread, page 36, and Parmesan-Sage Pull-Apart Bread, page 36). It needs to rest in the refrigerator for at least 4 hours, so be sure to plan ahead. The rolls are best enjoyed the day they are baked.

MAKES 8 ROLLS

In the bowl of a stand mixer fitted with the paddle attachment, combine the Biscuit Blend, sugar, yeast, and meringue powder and mix them on low for 30 seconds. Turn off the mixer.

In a saucepan, heat ½ cup (120 ml) of the milk over low heat. When the milk begins to steam, remove the pan from the heat. Stir in the remaining ½ cup (120 ml) milk. The mixture should be a bit warmer than bath water, but not hot—otherwise, it will kill the yeast.

Add the milk along with the eggs, honey, oil, vanilla, and 10 tablespoons (150 ml) water to the dry ingredients and mix on high speed for 1 minute. Add the salt and continue mixing on high for 3 minutes more. Finally, add the diced butter and mix on high until you can no longer see any lumps of butter. The dough should be quite thick at this point, sticking to the sides of the bowl and the paddle.

Lightly butter a bowl. Set the dough into the bowl, cover it with plastic wrap, and refrigerate it for 4 hours (see Note).

Preheat the oven to 400°F (205°C).

Lightly dust your work surface with Biscuit Blend. Knead the dough until it is very smooth, but give it no more than eight turns. Divide it into 24 pieces, each roughly 2 tablespoons in volume (weighing about 50 g). Dust your hands with Biscuit Blend and form each piece of dough into a ball. Set 3 balls into each cup of a nonstick muffin tin (if it's not nonstick, grease the cups with butter first). Using a small spoon, drop a few drop-lets of water at the point where the three pieces of dough meet. This will help the sections fuse while they bake.

Reduce the oven temperature to 350°F (175°C). Bake the rolls for 25 to 30 minutes, until they puff up into a clover shape and their tops are pale gold.

Serve warm. Store leftovers in an airtight container in the refrigerator for up to 3 days, or freeze them for up to 1 month.

6 cups (624 g) Biscuit Blend (page 13), plus more for rolling (see Note)

⅔ cup plus 2 tablespoons (155 g) sugar

3½ teaspoons gluten-free active dry yeast

1½ tablespoons meringue powder

1 cup (240 ml) whole milk

4 large eggs

¼ cup (60 ml) honey

3 tablespoons vegetable oil

1 tablespoon pure vanilla extract

4½ teaspoons kosher salt

3 tablespoons unsalted butter, plus more for the bowl

NOTE: Letting this dough rise for more than 8 hours can lead to a raw flavor. For best results, the magic time seems to be 4–6 hours.

NOTE: If you don't have extra Biscuit Blend for dusting, use glutinous rice flour instead.

KOLACHES

The kolache, a small hybrid of a tart and a filled pastry, is a standard on the dessert tables at Central European weddings. This treat, a variation of the Cloverleaf Dinner Roll dough, was a favorite during my childhood and formative years, but seems not to be so well known outside the South and Midwest. Whenever we would drive to Dallas to visit my grandparents, we always stopped at the Little Czech Bakery in West Texas, where they are famous for their kolaches.

The traditional jams used for filling are apricot, plum, cherry, strawberry, and blueberry. Kolaches are best enjoyed the day they are baked.

MAKES 24 KOLACHES

Preheat the oven to 400°F (205°C).

Line two jelly-roll pans or rimmed baking sheets with Silpat mats or parchment paper.

Lightly dust your work surface with Biscuit Blend. Knead the dough until it's very smooth, but give it no more than eight turns. Divide it into 24 pieces, each roughly 2 tablespoons in volume (weighing about 50 g). Dust your hands with Biscuit Blend and form each piece of dough into a ball. Place the dough balls 3 inches (7.5 cm) apart on the prepared pans and press them flat with the bottom of a drinking glass with a 2½-inch (6-cm) base. You should have a raised ¼-inch (6-mm) edge around the perimeter of each pressed ball of dough. (If you have an heirloom kolache press, use that.) Fill the dent in the dough with about 2 teaspoons of jam.

Reduce the oven temperature to 350°F (175°C). Bake the kolaches for 20 to 25 minutes, until the edges have puffed and doubled in size and the filling is bubbly.

The kolaches will keep in an airtight container in the refrigerator for up to 2 days.

Biscuit Blend (page 13), for dusting

1 recipe Cloverleaf Dinner Roll dough (page 33), refrigerated for 4 hours

Jams, for filling

PARMESAN-SAGE PULL-APART BREAD

4 tablespoons (½ stick / 56 g) unsalted butter

10 fresh sage leaves

1 recipe Cloverleaf Dinner Roll dough (page 33), prepared without vanilla extract, refrigerated for 4 hours

1 cup (225 g) shredded Parmesan

Kosher salt and freshly ground black pepper

This is a savory version of traditional monkey bread. I like to make my sage pull-apart bread in a Savarin pan. If you have one, use it—it makes for a gorgeous presentation.

MAKES 1 LOAF

Preheat the oven to 400°F (205°C). Line a plate with paper towels and butter a Savarin pan, a 9-inch (23-cm) Bundt pan, or a loaf pan (or set aside a nonstick pan).

In a small saucepan, melt the butter. When it foams, add the sage leaves and sauté until they are just beginning to brown on their edges. Using a slotted spoon, gently transfer the leaves to the lined plate and reserve the butter.

Prepare the dough as above, but roll the balls of dough in the sage butter and then in the Parmesan until they are well coated. Place them in the pan, lining the bottom in a single layer. Dust them with salt and pepper. Repeat until all the dough has been used, seasoning each layer with salt and pepper.

Reduce the oven temperature to 350°F (175°C). Bake the bread for 25 to 35 minutes (40 minutes if you are using a loaf pan), until it has risen and the Parmesan is golden brown. Unmold the bread onto a serving plate and enjoy pulling it apart!

VARIATION: Monkey Bread

And for the traditionalists, here's the sweet and breakfasty pull-apart pastry.

1 cup (156 g) golden raisins

½ cup (110 g) light brown sugar

½ cup (100 g) granulated sugar

1½ teaspoons ground cinnamon

1 recipe Cloverleaf Dinner Roll dough (page 33), refrigerated for 4 hours

½ cup (1 stick / 113 g) salted butter, melted and kept warm

MAKES 1 LOAF

Preheat the oven to 400°F (205°C). Butter a 9-inch (23-cm) cake or Bundt pan with butter (or set aside a nonstick pan).

In a medium bowl, stir together the raisins, sugars, and cinnamon. Lightly dust your work surface with Biscuit Blend. Knead the dough until it's very smooth, but give it no more than eight turns. Divide it into 24 pieces, each roughly 2 tablespoons in volume (weighing about 50 g). Dust your hands with Biscuit Blend and form each piece of dough into a ball. Roll each ball of dough in the melted butter and then in the cinnamon-sugar mixture until well coated. Place them in the pan, touching.

Bake the bread for 25 to 35 minutes, until it has puffed up and the sugar is melting. Unmold the monkey bread onto a serving plate and pick away.

BLACKBIRD BAKERY'S CLASSIC CINNAMON ROLLS

Getting this dough's consistency right had me tearing my hair out when I wasn't bouncing beady-eyed, vulcanized cinnamon rolls off the kitchen wall. The missing link turned out to be resting the dough overnight in the fridge. This chilly time-out lets the yeast develop in slow motion, keeps the air bubbles small, and gives the finished rolls the ideal soft-but-stretchy cinnamon-roll texture.

If you'd like to serve these hot for breakfast or brunch, make the dough the night before. They're also extra-good if you can find and use Vietnamese (Saigon) cinnamon.

MAKES 9 PERFECTLY SPIRALED 2½- TO 3-INCH (6- TO 7.5-CM) BEAUTIES

Make the rolls: In a small saucepan, warm the milk to bath temperature and set it aside to cool slightly. (The ideal temperature to activate the yeast is 92°F / 33°C.)

In a large bowl, whisk the eggs and beat in the sugar until dissolved.

In the bowl of a stand mixer fitted with the paddle attachment, or in a food processor fitted with the S-blade, combine the Biscuit Blend, potato starch, meringue powder, and yeast. Mix on low or pulse until they are well blended. Add the salt and mix just until combined.

With the stand mixer on the lowest setting, add one-third of the egg mixture to the dry ingredients, followed by one-third of the milk mixture. Repeat until both mixtures have been incorporated and the dough is well combined. Scrape down the sides of the bowl and then mix on high for 2 minutes more. The dough should be thick enough that a finger pressed into the surface leaves an indentation that stays.

With the mixer on medium speed, add the butter a few cubes at a time and mix until you can no longer see any clumps and the dough is smooth.

Very lightly grease a large bowl with butter. Form the dough into a ball and place it in the bowl. Cover it with plastic wrap and refrigerate the dough overnight.

Assemble the rolls: Preheat the oven to 350°F (175°C). Grease a glass bowl with 1 tablespoon of the butter.

In a small bowl, whisk the sugars and cinnamon together and set them aside. Melt the remaining 4 tablespoons (55 g) butter; remove it from the heat but keep it warm.

CONTINUED

FOR THE ROLLS:

⅔ cup plus ¼ cup (225 ml) whole milk

4 large eggs

⅔ cup (130 g) sugar

3½ cups (364 g) Biscuit Blend (page 13), plus more for rolling

⅓ cup (42 g) potato starch

1 tablespoon meringue powder

1 tablespoon gluten-free active dry yeast

1 teaspoon kosher salt

6 tablespoons (84 g) unsalted butter, diced, plus more for the bowl

TO ASSEMBLE:

5 tablespoons (70 g) salted butter

1 cup (200 g) granulated sugar

½ cup (110 g) packed light brown sugar

2½ teaspoons ground cinnamon

FOR THE GLAZE:

1 tablespoon salted butter

1½ cups (150 g) confectioners' sugar

2 tablespoons milk

½ teaspoon pure vanilla extract

Dust your work surface with Biscuit Blend. Turn out the dough, cold from the fridge, and knead until it is smooth, about ten turns. Shape the dough into a rectangle or oblong and roll it out to 14 by 16 inches (35.5 by 40.5 cm). Using a pastry brush, spread the melted butter over the dough, leaving a ¼-inch (6-mm) border from the edge of the dough, until it is glossy. Avoid leaving any dry spots. Sprinkle the dough evenly with the cinnamon-sugar.

Starting at a long edge, roll the dough rectangle into a tight cylinder, turning the edge a bit at a time. If the dough sticks to your work surface, use a bench scraper to free it and dust the surface with just a bit more Biscuit Blend. Transfer the dough cylinder to a tray or cutting board and freeze it for 15 minutes.

Cut a 12-inch (30.5-cm) strand of unflavored dental floss or fine white thread and use it to cut the dough into thirds, then cut each third into thirds again so you have 9 rolls.

Set the cut rolls in 3 rows of 3 in the prepared pan, leaving ¼ inch (6 mm) between each.

Bake the rolls for 30 minutes. They are done when they have tripled in size and are golden brown, with cinnamon-sugar bubbling up from the spirals at the top and the bottom.

Make the glaze: Cut the butter into the confectioners' sugar by kneading it into the sugar with your fingertips. When you can no longer see any lumps of butter, whisk in the milk and vanilla. If the glaze is still quite thick, whisk in 1 tablespoon of water, then more if needed. Drizzle over the cinnamon rolls immediately.

Let the cinnamon rolls cool for at least 15 minutes before you chomp into one; the sugar is molten-lava hot.

The cinnamon rolls will keep in an airtight container in the refrigerator for up to 3 days. They freeze well for up to 3 months, double wrapped to prevent freezer burn.

VARIATION: Sticky Buns

Double the quantity of cinnamon-sugar, reserving half and using the remainder to fill the rolls. Melt an additional ¼ cup (55 g) salted butter and pour it into the pan. Sprinkle the remaining cinnamon-sugar over the butter followed by 1 cup (100 g) chopped pecans before arranging the rolls in the pan. Bake as directed above.

LAURA'S BALL PARK DOG

It was none other than my foodie friend Laura DesEnfants that recommended that I go old-school and try using a potato-based dough to achieve that trademark hot-dog bun texture. This dough works for both of the tailgate classics: hot dog or hamburger. The difference is simply the shape and the end-use. With dogs, be sure to get gluten-free (many common brands contain wheat either in the meat or the casing).

MAKES 6 HOT DOG BUNS (150 G/EACH)

Make the buns: In the bowl of a stand mixer fitted with the paddle attachment, or in a food processor fitted with the S-blade, combine the Biscuit Blend, potato flakes, dry milk, meringue powder, sugar, and yeast and mix them well.

Add the oil, honey, eggs, and 1½ cups (360 ml) lukewarm water and mix until the dough is very thick. Add the salt and continue mixing the dough on high until it is no longer lumpy, about 3 minutes. The dough is ready when it is clinging both to the paddle and the sides of the bowl and is slightly tacky to the touch.

Very lightly grease a large bowl with butter. Turn the dough into the bowl, jostle the bowl to coat the dough in the butter, then cover it with a kitchen towel and let it rise in a warm place for 20 minutes. Cover the bowl with plastic wrap and let the dough continue to rise in the fridge until nearly doubled in volume, at least 2 to 3 hours. For the best results, I don't recommend proofing this dough beyond 6 hours.

Preheat the oven to 400°F (205°C). Line a baking sheet with parchment paper.

Dust your work surface with Biscuit Blend. Turn the risen dough out of the bowl and knead it until it is elastic and smooth. Divide the dough into 8 pieces (about 150 g each) and shape them into hot dog buns (or hamburger buns)—remember that they'll double in size as they bake, so don't make them too big! Set them side by side, edges touching, on the prepared baking sheet.

Reduce the oven temperature to 375°F (190°C) and bake the buns for 18 to 20 minutes, until they are golden brown. Let them cool, then separate the buns by tearing or cutting them along the seams.

To serve, broil or grill the hot dogs and serve them on the buns with the condiments of your preference.

The buns will keep beautifully in a plastic bag at room temperature, perhaps in a breadbox, for up to 3 days. They can be frozen, double wrapped, for up to 1 month.

FOR THE BUNS:

3 cups plus 2 tablespoons (328 g) Biscuit Blend (page 13), plus more for dusting (see Note)

⅔ cup (35 g) instant potato flakes

¼ cup (30 g) nonfat dry milk

1 tablespoon meringue powder

1 tablespoon sugar

2 teaspoons gluten-free instant yeast

2 tablespoons oil

2 tablespoons honey

2 large eggs

2 teaspoons kosher salt

8 gluten-free hot dogs

Condiments of your preference

NOTE: If you don't have extra Biscuit Blend for dusting, use glutinous rice flour instead.

LOBSTER ROLLS

2 (1½-pound / 680-g) lobsters

1 (3-ounce / 85-g) bag of Zatarain's Crawfish, Shrimp, and Crab Boil seasoning

Kosher salt

2 lemons, halved

8 Laura's Ball Park Dog buns (page 41)

½ cup (120 ml) gluten-free mayonnaise

2 stalks celery, diced

1 tablespoon thinly sliced fresh chives, plus more for serving

1 teaspoon chopped fresh dill, plus more for serving

¼ teaspoon freshly cracked black pepper

Juice of 1 lemon

Although I love a good hot dog, I can't think of a more indulgent summer treat than a lobster roll. The food snob in me just can't see a summer go by without one. For the best results, boil the lobster yourself, and for no more than 9 to 10 minutes so the flesh is delicate and flavorful.

SERVES 6

Boil the lobsters in a large covered stockpot with the crab boil seasoning, salt, and lemons, as instructed on the box of crab boil seasoning.

When the lobsters are cool enough to handle, carefully remove the flesh, leaving the claw meat whole. Cut the remaining flesh into large dice.

In a large bowl, stir together the mayonnaise, celery, chives, dill, pepper, and ½ teaspoon salt. Add the lemon juice and then fold in the lobster. Adjust the seasonings to taste.

Split the buns vertically from the top down. Spoon a generous amount of lobster salad into each bun and garnish with additional dill and chives. Serve one bun per person.

JAMES BEARD'S FOURTH OF JULY HAMBURGER

If there was ever an expert on hamburgers, it was James Beard. Not only was he single-handedly responsible for the marriage of food and television, but he is the godfather of American cuisine. Beard's *American Cookery*, published in 1972, is so influential that it deserves a footnote in almost everything on the topic that's been written since. As far as I know, he was fine with gluten, but I think he'd have liked the idea of making every day Independence Day for his GF fans.

To say he mastered the art of the hamburger is an understatement, and this recipe is a tribute to his spirit of fun in the kitchen. Beard detested a slice of processed cheese on top of his burger, so he opted to put "real grated cheddar cheese" inside. The result is mind-blowing. And if you're in the mood for Sloppy Joes? This bun is the perfect delivery vehicle.

SERVES 6

Make the buns: Preheat the oven to 400°F (205°C). Grease a baking sheet.

Lightly dust your work surface with Biscuit Blend. Turn the dough out and knead until it is elastic and smooth. Divide the dough into 6 pieces and shape them into hamburger buns. Arrange them on a baking sheet, with their edges just touching.

Reduce the oven temperature to 375°F (190°C) and bake the buns for 18 to 20 minutes, until they are golden brown. Let them cool, then separate the buns by tearing or cutting them along the seams.

Make the burgers: Heat a grill to cook over medium-high heat or set an ungreased skillet over medium-high heat.

In a large bowl, combine the ground beef with the cheese, onion, Worcestershire, salt, garlic powder, and Tabasco. Using your hands, mix until just combined. Do not overwork the meat or it will be tough.

Form the beef mixture into 6 patties, at least 1 inch (2.5 cm) thick, wrapping an ice cube into the center of each patty. (The melting ice keeps the burger moist.)

Lightly dust the outside of each burger with salt and pepper. Grill or fry them to your desired doneness, 5 minutes per side for medium-rare.

As the burgers cook, split and toast the buns. Serve the burgers on the toasted buns with the works.

FOR THE BUNS:

Biscuit Blend (page 13) or glutinous rice flour, for dusting

1 recipe Ball Park Dog dough (page 41), refrigerated overnight

FOR THE BURGERS:

2 pounds (910 g) ground top round

1 cup (225 g) grated cheese (Mr. B liked extra-sharp cheddar or Gruyère)

¼ cup (59 g) grated onion

2 tablespoons Worcestershire sauce

1 teaspoon kosher salt, plus more as needed

1 teaspoon garlic powder

½ teaspoon Tabasco sauce

8 small ice cubes (or halved full-size ice cubes)

Freshly ground black pepper

FOR "THE WORKS":

Slices of tomato, lettuce, onion, and pickle

Plenty of mayonnaise, ketchup, and mustard

DONUT & FRITTER BLEND

I designed the Donut & Fritter Blend to be the go-to solution for all manner of frying applications, such as my Batter-Fried Chicken (page 59) or Chicken-Fried Steak (page 52), *and* for making choux paste, the classic cooking heavyweight used to create cream puffs, profiteroles, éclairs, and savory delectable treats like April Bloomfield's Cheese Beignets (page 80). It also functions beautifully as the go-to flour blend for making dark roux (see Mrs Elie's Creole-Style Gumbo, page 71) and the béchamel needed for the Leo's Mac 'N' Cheese (page 67). Yes, the sky's the limit.

THE RECIPE

2½ cups plus 1½ tablespoons (320 g) cornstarch

1 cup plus 2 tablespoons plus 1 teaspoon (128 g) tapioca starch

⅓ cup plus 2 tablespoons (80 g) potato starch

½ cup plus 1 tablespoon plus 1 teaspoon (64 g) sorghum flour

8 teaspoons (24 g) guar gum

The blend is very starch heavy—and for good reason. If you look at Asian cooking, you will notice that nearly all of their fried foods are made or battered with cornstarch because starches crisp up exceptionally well in hot oil. Making the blend capable of transforming into choux paste, however, demanded that more flavor and texture be added. For this, I looked to sorghum. And of course, guar gum is included so the choux will hold its shape and not collapse after it is removed from the oven. This blend is very simple, so to achieve the built-in versatility, pay careful attention to the tips and techniques on the following pages.

For more information on the individual flours, starches, and other ingredients in the blend, see the Pantry section on page 215.

MAKES 5½ CUPS (616 G), ENOUGH FOR 8 BATCHES OF CHOUX PASTE

Using the spoon-and-sweep method, measure each ingredient into a large bowl. Whisk together and then sift the mixture into a separate large bowl. Repeat several times. Since you are working with so many different starches, you really need to sift and whisk the blend several times to ensure an even distribution of all the ingredients.

The approximate weight of the blend, by volume (for use in doing your own adaptations):

EACH	OF BLEND WEIGHS APPROXIMATELY
1 tablespoon	7 g
¼ cup	29 g
⅓ cup	40 g
½ cup	57 g
⅔ cup	75 g
¾ cup	85 g
1 cup	112 g

THE DOUGH

DON'T FOLD IT, DON'T ROLL IT

In most of the recipes using the Donut & Fritter Blend, the blend just needs to be whisked with other ingredients—folding and rolling aren't required.

A word of caution: Don't use the Donut & Fritter Blend for dusting doughs made with other blends. If used to knead and roll any dough, it will add a tough exterior to the finished goods.

BATTERING AND BREADING

The combination of starches in this blend make it particularly good for getting a delicious crust on fried foods. Many recipes in this chapter call for *battering* or *breading* with a mixture made with the Donut & Fritter Blend. Battering calls for an item to be dipped in a liquid or semi-liquid mixture and then fried,

forming a crispy shell on the food. Breading calls for an item to be dusted with or rolled in a dry mixture; sometimes, this is done in a sequence with a liquid, such as egg or milk. This produces a crispy crust, which can be thin (such as for Chicken-Fried Steak, page 52) or thick (such as for Cornflake Chicken Nuggets, page 54).

For frying, first bring a quantity of oil up to temperature in a heavy skillet, saucepan, or deep-fryer. This is a time when a deep-fry thermometer (or a candy thermometer) is essential to your success, so I strongly encourage you to invest in one. Keeping the oil at a steady temperature, usually 350°F (175°C), is the key to perfectly fried fare, and without a thermometer, this is extremely difficult to do. If you are either battering or breading food for frying, make sure to pat the item completely dry. You want the

blend to stick to every last inch of that chicken leg or thigh, and the same goes when you are dipping corndogs into batter. (The only exception to this rule is the fried calamari on page 57. The milk in which you soak the calamari packs the squid rings with a flavor and tenderness you don't want to pat away.)

For battering, whisk the batter together as directed in the recipe. Make sure the food to be battered is well dried, then dip it into the batter and let any excess drip off. Usually, the battered food should be placed directly in the hot oil.

For breading, place the blend (seasoned, if called for in the recipe) in one bowl or shallow dish and any wet ingredients (such as eggs or milk, or sometimes both) in separate bowls or dishes. Dip the food to be breaded in each bowl individually, in the order indicated by the recipe. It's a good practice to work with just one hand so the other stays clean, in case you need to adjust the stove (or answer the phone!).

After battering or breading, fry the food at the oil temperature indicated in the recipe. The length of time may be less for some recipes, like the jelly-filled donuts, than for traditional fried donuts, but this will only bring you enjoyment more quickly.

ROUX AND BÉCHAMEL

A *roux* is a thickening agent made with flour and a fat, usually butter or oil. And a *béchamel* is a white sauce made by stirring milk (or sometimes stock) into a roux. In this book, both roux and béchamel are made using the Donut & Fritter Blend.

To make a roux, you first melt a quantity of fat in a saucepan. Then, flour is added and whisked until free of lumps. The roux is then cooked for a time to remove some of the raw taste of the flour. The length of time the roux is cooked will depend on what type of roux you are making: white, blond, or brown. In this book, a white roux is used for Leo's Mac 'n' Cheese (page 67), and a brown roux for Mrs. Elie's Creole-Style Gumbo (page 71). Try those recipes out if you'd like to test your hand at making roux—you'll feel French in no time.

To turn your roux into a basic béchamel, after cooking the roux to the desired color, whisk in milk or stock. The mixture might clump up at first, but continue whisking and the lumps will dissolve, forming a smooth, thick sauce that you'll probably recognize from making lasagna (didn't know that was a béchamel, eh?). For the ideal basic béchamel or roux, you really need to use a whisk instead of a wooden spoon. This is essentially the same rule of thumb for making traditional béchamel and roux, but you will need to work faster with the gluten-free version to keep the blend from clumping. The great news is that once the milk or stock is added, you can whisk all the clumps out without a problem. So, if you see a clump or two form, fear not—like anything else in life, the more you do it, the better you will be, and that silly bit of fear will evaporate.

CHOUX PASTE

Choux paste (in French, *pâte à choux*) is a pastry dough that starts in a saucepan. Classic choux paste is made with butter, water or milk, flour, and eggs. My gluten-free version is a bit different and involves a slightly different technique than a classic choux.

To make choux paste, in a saucepan, melt butter with half-and-half, water, salt, and sugar and bring the mixture to a boil. Stir in the Donut & Fritter Blend with a wooden spoon until the mixture forms a ball and a thin film forms on the saucepan. In a bowl, sprinkle the eggs with baking powder and whisk them. (This step is crucial to your success—the chemical reaction between the baking powder and the albumen in the egg enables the choux to rise in the oven and maintain its shape after baking.) Transfer the dough to a food processor, add the egg mixture, and process until a nice thick paste has formed.

The finished choux paste can be piped, spooned, and baked in pretty much any way you see fit—try making Churros (page 72) or Cream Puffs (page 76) to see how it's done. The baking temperature is a constant 425°F (220°C) and the finished pastry should be golden, puffy, and firm to the touch.

Another wonderful characteristic of gluten-free choux paste is you can make it up to a couple of days in advance and still get the same fabulous results. If I'm going to be piping the choux paste, I like to place it in a prepared pastry bag before refrigerating it.

CHICKEN-FRIED STEAK

FOR THE STEAKS:

4 top round sirloin steaks, pounded to a ¼-inch (6-mm) thickness

¼ cup (35 g) seasoned salt (I use Lawry's)

2 cups (224 g) Donut & Fritter Blend (page 47)

¼ teaspoon cayenne pepper

¼ teaspoon freshly ground black pepper

2 large eggs

½ cup (120 ml) milk

¼ cup (60 ml) peanut oil, for frying

FOR THE GRAVY:

¼ cup (29 g) Donut & Fritter Blend (page 47)

1 cup (240 ml) milk

Kosher salt and freshly ground black pepper

NOTE: Any leftover steaks will keep, well wrapped, in the refrigerator for a couple of days. They may not reheat terribly well; warm them in a moderate oven, wrapped in foil, for about 10 minutes, if you'd like. The gravy can be stored in an airtight container in the refrigerator for up to 1 week and reheated in the microwave or in a small saucepan on the stovetop.

Chicken-fried steak—a confusing name for a straightforward dish—is an American classic. "Chicken-fried" refers to the method used for breading and frying the thin cuts of steak, similar to how you would prepare fried chicken. Any good, leanish steak, not too thick, fits the bill; you don't want a cut for roasting or stewing. You can buy top round or sirloin pre-tenderized and hammered into the steaks, saving you elbow grease and the trouble of finding your meat mallet.

Serve this with mashed potatoes and something green to balance everything out!

SERVES 4

Make the steaks: Pat the steaks dry with a paper towel and generously dust both sides with the seasoned salt. Set them aside.

In a shallow bowl, whisk together the Donut & Fritter Blend, cayenne, and pepper. In a separate shallow bowl, beat the eggs and milk together.

Heat the oil in a large skillet, cast iron if you have one, over medium-high heat, until it registers 350°F (175°C) on a deep-fry thermometer. While the oil comes to temperature, toss the steaks in the dry ingredients to coat them, then dunk them into the egg mixture, letting any excess drip back into the bowl, and then finally dip them back into the dry mixture. (This gives the steaks a good coating that will work as a batter.)

Place the battered steaks in the skillet without crowding and fry them to your desired doneness, 90 seconds to 2 minutes per side for medium. For medium-rare, press the steaks with a finger and pull them from the pan if the indentation rebounds slowly. If you want well-done meat, keep the steaks cooking until they can't be indented at all. Medium's in the middle—you can press the meat with a fingertip but the indentation springs back right away. Transfer the finished steaks to a platter while you make the gravy.

Make the gravy: Discard all but 2 tablespoons of the oil from the skillet. Whisk in the Donut & Fritter Blend, stirring until the mixture thickens to a paste. Whisk in a bit of the milk, so the paste begins to smooth out. Keep whisking in the milk, a couple of tablespoons at a time. Once the paste has thinned to a liquid, whisk in the remaining milk and cook just until the gravy begins to thicken; remove it from the heat. Taste and adjust the flavor with salt and pepper.

Serve the steaks with the gravy on top or in a bowl alongside.

CORNFLAKE CHICKEN NUGGETS

2 cups (56 g) gluten-free cornflakes (sweetened with honey)

⅓ cup (40 g) Donut & Fritter Blend (page 47)

¼ teaspoon freshly cracked black pepper

2 large eggs

1 teaspoon kosher salt

2 large boneless skinless chicken breasts, cut into 1-inch (2.5-cm) "nuggets"

4 cups (960 ml) grapeseed or peanut oil, for frying

Traditional nugget dipping sauces: ketchup, honey mustard, Dijon, dill mustard

NOTE: Store-bought sauces are notorious for not being gluten-free friendly, so be sure to read the labels before purchasing them. (Modified food starch is a big red flag.)

Gluten-free children of the world, your prayers have been answered—crispy chicken nuggets are once again safe to eat. But don't thank me—thank my precocious son, Leo! It was he who suggested I make my cornflake chicken into nuggets, and I've gotta say, he one-upped me there. Crunchy, with just a touch of sweetness thanks to the honey, these tender little morsels are the ultimate snack, dinner, and late-night indulgence. Ketchup required.

A thermometer is an absolute must for this recipe and to get any consistently crispy, fully cooked fried foods. Without a thermometer, it's almost impossible to properly regulate the temperature of the oil, leading to major frustration, or worse, burns. Remember that as you add food to the hot oil, the temperature of the oil will drop, so keep an eye on the thermometer and only add a few pieces of food at a time.

MAKES ABOUT 18 NUGGETS

In a large bowl, crush the cornflakes until they're broken into bits roughly the size of small peas. (If the flakes are too large, they won't stick to the chicken as well.) Add the Donut & Fritter Blend and pepper and toss with your hands to combine with the cornflakes. Transfer the mixture to a shallow dish or pan.

In a separate bowl, whisk the eggs with the salt. Add the chicken pieces to the eggs and stir to coat them. Cover and refrigerate for 20 minutes.

Meanwhile, in a large skillet (or alternatively, in a deep fryer), heat the oil over medium heat until it registers 350°F (175°C) on a deep-fry thermometer. Line a plate with paper towels, or line a baking sheet with a brown paper bag.

One at a time, pull the chicken pieces from the egg and let the excess egg drip back into the bowl. Roll the egg-coated chicken pieces in the cornflake mixture until well coated, then drop them into the hot oil, 3 or 4 pieces at a time. Be careful not to add too many pieces to the oil at once or the temperature of the oil will drop—do not let it drop below 325°F (165°C).

Cook the chicken for 3 to 4 minutes, until it is golden brown. Using a slotted spoon or spider, transfer the fried nuggets to the towel-lined plate to drain the excess oil. Repeat with the remaining nuggets.

Eat the chicken nuggets while they're still hot, with the dipping sauces alongside. Don't worry; there won't be any left over.

HERB-FRIED MOZZARELLA STICKS

These were a childhood favorite for movie nights, and this gluten-free version brought all those late nights in front of the TV rushing back.

For the best results, pulse the gluten-free bread crumbs with the Donut & Fritter Blend in a food processor so the mozzarella sticks get that perfect crust. Deep-frying is the only way you will get the sticks uniformly golden-brown and melt the cheese just enough that they hold together. Use a slotted spoon to remove the sticks from the oil, as tongs tend to crush them.

MAKES 12 MOZZARELLA STICKS

In a food processor, combine the bread crumbs with ½ cup (57 g) of the Donut & Fritter Blend, the thyme, basil, parsley, cumin, onion powder, salt, and pepper. Pulse until the herbs have been finely broken up. Transfer the bread crumb mixture to a shallow dish or pan.

Spread the remaining 2 tablespoons Donut & Fritter Blend on a small plate.

In a shallow bowl, whisk the eggs with 1 teaspoon water until they are smooth and well combined.

Meanwhile, in a large skillet (or alternatively, in a deep fryer), heat the oil over medium heat until it registers 325°F (165°C) on a deep-fry thermometer. Line a plate with paper towels, or line a baking sheet with a brown paper bag.

One at a time, roll the mozzarella pieces in the Donut & Fritter Blend on the plate to evenly coat them. Next, dip the pieces into the egg, letting any excess egg drip back into the bowl, then roll them in the bread crumb mixture, being sure to coat the ends well. Repeat, dipping the breaded mozzarella into the egg and then in the bread crumbs so each piece has two layers of breading. As you finish breading the mozzarella, place the pieces on a small baking sheet or plate. Transfer the breaded mozzarella to the freezer for 5 to 7 minutes to set the breading.

Carefully drop the breaded mozzarella pieces into the oil, 3 or 4 at a time so as not to lower the oil temperature, and cook until they are golden and crispy, about 1 minute. Using a slotted spoon, transfer the fried mozzarella sticks to the towel-lined plate to drain the excess oil. Repeat with the remaining mozzarella.

Serve them hot, with cocktail sauce or Grape-Tomato Sauce alongside for dipping.

1 cup (100 g) gluten-free bread crumbs (see page 197)

½ cup plus 2 tablespoons (71 g) Donut & Fritter Blend (page 47)

1 teaspoon dried thyme

1 teaspoon dried basil

1 teaspoon dried parsley

½ teaspoon ground cumin

½ teaspoon onion powder

½ teaspoon kosher salt

½ teaspoon freshly ground black pepper

2 large eggs

2 cups (480 ml) peanut oil, for frying

6 mozzarella string cheese sticks, room temperature, halved crosswise

Fried Calamari cocktail sauce (page 57) or Oven-Roasted Grape-Tomato Sauce (page 114), for dipping

NOTE: If you do have any left over (unlikely!), insist that someone eat them at room temperature. They're actually still good that way, just less stringy. But as a last resort, you can wrap them and store them in the refrigerator for up to 3 days. Reheat them on a baking sheet in a 300°F (150°C) oven for about 5 minutes.

FRIED CALAMARI (TOP)
COCONUT SHRIMP (BOTTOM)

FRIED CALAMARI

What makes these seriously crunchy—and delicious is the instant polenta. Soaking the squid in milk helps to keep the all-too-easily toughened seafood tender—the lactic acid breaks down some of the proteins. It is this pairing of opposing textures—the tenderized squid rings with the crisp polenta coating—that makes this recipe absolutely delicious.

SERVES 4 AS A HEARTY APPETIZER

Make the calamari: In a large container with a lid, toss the squid rings and baby squid with the milk, a pinch of salt, the fresh dill, and bay leaf. Cover and refrigerate them for 20 minutes.

Meanwhile, in a large bowl, whisk together the Donut & Fritter Blend, polenta, salt, pepper, and dried dill. Set them aside.

In a large bowl, whisk together the eggs and 3 tablespoons water. Set aside.

Make the cocktail sauce: In a medium bowl, stir together the ketchup, horseradish, lemon juice, Worcestershire, and Tabasco. Set them aside.

Fry the calamari: In a deep skillet (or alternatively, in a deep fryer), heat the oil over medium heat until it registers 375°F (190°C) on a deep-fry thermometer. Line a plate with paper towels, or line a baking sheet with a brown paper bag.

Drain the squid, discarding the milk, and transfer the squid to the egg mixture. Stir to coat it evenly.

A few pieces at a time, pull the squid from the egg wash, letting the excess drip back into the bowl. Toss the squid in the polenta mixture, rolling to coat the pieces completely, then transfer about ¼ cup of the battered squid to the hot oil.

Flash fry the calamari until golden brown, no more than 3 minutes. Using a slotted spoon or spider, transfer the calamari to the towel-lined plate to drain the excess oil. Repeat with the remaining squid.

Serve the calamari hot, with the cocktail sauce and lemon wedges.

VARIATION: Thai-Style Calamari

Add ⅛ teaspoon cayenne to the dry ingredients, then batter and fry the calamari as directed above. In a small bowl, combine ¼ cup (60 ml) fresh lime juice, ¼ cup (60 ml) gluten-free soy sauce, ¼ cup (49 g) sugar, 3 tablespoons fermented fish sauce (*nam pla*; optional), 1 tablespoon minced fresh cilantro, and 1 minced garlic clove and stir to combine. Add some minced, seeded jalapeño or small hot red chile, if desired, and serve it as a dipping sauce alongside the crunchy squid.

FOR THE CALAMARI:

4 squids, cleaned, not butterflied, cut into ¼-inch (6-mm) rings

4 ounces (113 g) baby squid with tentacles

½ cup (120 ml) whole milk

½ teaspoon kosher salt, plus more as needed

1 sprig fresh dill

1 bay leaf

1 cup (112 g) Donut & Fritter Blend (page 47)

½ cup (85 g) instant polenta

¼ teaspoon freshly cracked black pepper

½ teaspoon dried dill (optional)

2 large eggs

FOR THE COCKTAIL SAUCE:

1 cup (240 ml) gluten-free ketchup

2 to 3 tablespoons prepared horseradish (to taste)

1½ teaspoons fresh lemon juice

½ teaspoon Worcestershire sauce

A few drops to ¼ teaspoon Tabasco sauce (to taste)

4 cups (960 ml) peanut oil, for frying

Lemon wedges, for serving

TEMPURA SHRIMP & VEGETABLES

FOR THE DIPPING SAUCE:

¼ cup (60 ml) mirin (sweet rice wine)

¼ cup (60 ml) gluten-free soy sauce

2 teaspoons sugar

FOR THE TEMPURA BATTER:

1½ cups (169 g) Donut & Fritter Blend (page 47)

1¼ teaspoons kosher salt

⅛ teaspoon baking powder

2 large eggs

½ cup (120 ml) vodka

1 cup (240 ml) plain seltzer water

1 pound (455 g) assorted firm vegetables, such as asparagus, zucchini, green beans, broccoli, cauliflower, sweet potato, okra, turnips, and kale, cut into bite-size or two-bite pieces

4 cups (960 ml) peanut oil, for frying

1 pound (455 g) large fresh shrimp, shelled and deveined, tails left on

Grated daikon radish or red radish, for serving

The lightness in these tempura-battered shrimp comes from the combination of vodka and seltzer, which evaporates on contact with the hot oil.

SERVES 4

Make the dipping sauce: In a small saucepan, whisk together the mirin, soy sauce, and sugar. Bring them to a boil over medium heat, then remove the pan from the stovetop and allow the sauce to cool.

Make the tempura batter: In a large bowl, combine the Donut & Fritter Blend, salt, and baking powder.

In a separate bowl, whisk together the eggs, vodka, and seltzer. Whisk the egg mixture into the dry ingredients and mix until smooth. Set aside.

Bring a large pot of salted water to a boil. Fill a large bowl with ice water.

In two batches, blanch the vegetables. Green vegetables (except for kale, which does not need to be blanched) should be boiled for 1 to 2 minutes. The sweet potato, if you're using it, gets 4 to 5 minutes in the water. As you pull the vegetables from the pot, dunk them in the ice water to stop the cooking, then transfer them to a colander to drain.

Meanwhile, in a large, heavy-bottomed saucepan (or, alternatively, in a deep-fryer), heat the oil over medium heat until it registers 400°F (205°C) on a deep-fry thermometer. Line a platter with paper towels, or line a baking sheet with a brown paper bag.

Pat the shrimp and vegetables dry, so the batter will stick to them. First, fry the shrimp: Dip the shrimp into the batter, letting any excess drip back into the bowl, then put them straight into the oil. Fry them for 1 minute, or until the tempura coating is golden blond. Using a slotted spoon or spider, transfer the fried shrimp to the lined plate to drain any excess oil. Repeat the coating with the vegetables, frying them for about 2 minutes, until they are golden blond.

Serve the tempura hot, with individual bowls of the mirin-soy dipping sauce and grated daikon on the side so people can mix the radish into their sauce.

VARIATION: Coconut Shrimp

Forget the vegetables and the dipping sauce. After you have dipped the shrimp in the batter, roll them in 1¼ cups (75 g) unsweetened shredded coconut and then dip them into the batter once more. Fry as instructed above. Serve the shrimp with lime wedges, salsa, or a West Indian hot sauce.

BATTER-FRIED CHICKEN

When it comes to fried chicken, deep-frying is the only way to keep the batter where it belongs and evenly browned all over. The crust on this chicken literally shatters when you bite into it. And that's what I want inscribed on my tombstone, as it took me a *lot* of tries to get that effect.

If you don't have Southern roots, or are unfamiliar with our region's gourmet traditions, try these with Waffles (page 25), a combo that will make your head explode. Other good sides are coleslaw, Cloverleaf Dinner Rolls (page 33), and even a sprinkle of crispy fried garlic (see sidebar).

I've noticed that the brand of guar gum you use changes the consistency of this batter, and I recommend using the NOW brand here if possible. If you can't get your hands on it, just add more water and the recipe will still turn out perfectly.

If you have any leftovers, just keep them in the fridge, well wrapped, and reheat them on a baking sheet in a 300°F (150°C) oven for 5 to 10 minutes. Cold fried chicken is good, too, and room-temperature fried chicken, cut up, is a great topper for a salad.

MAKES 8 PIECES; SERVES 6 AS AN ENTRÉE

In a large container with a lid, combine the celery and carrot with ¼ cup (60 g) of the salt, the sugar, peppercorns, and 3 cups (720 ml) water and stir to dissolve the salt and sugar. Add the chicken pieces, cover, and refrigerate them for at least 1 hour, but preferably overnight. (Alternatively, combine the salt, sugar, peppercorns, and water in a saucepan and bring them to a boil for 5 minutes to intensify the flavors, then let it cool before transferring the brining mixture to a lidded container and adding the chicken and vegetables. Refrigerate as directed.)

To fry the chicken, in a large skillet (or, alternatively, in a deep-fryer), heat the oil over medium heat until it registers 350°F (175°C) on a deep-fry thermometer. Line a platter with paper towels, or line a baking sheet with a brown paper bag.

Remove the chicken pieces from the brine and pat them dry very well with paper towels. Set them aside on a platter.

In a large bowl, combine the Donut & Fritter Blend, paprika, baking powder, garlic powder, onion powder, pepper, and cayenne to taste (for a barely there vibration, use just ⅛ teaspoon). Whisk until they are well blended, cover, and let stand for at least 5 minutes. The flavors will be at their best if they have time to get acquainted.

CONTINUED

2 stalks celery with leaves, roughly chopped

1 carrot, diced

¼ cup (60 g) plus 1½ teaspoons kosher salt

⅓ cup (65 g) sugar

1 teaspoon whole black peppercorns

8 pieces chicken (a mix of breasts, thighs, legs, and wings, as you prefer)

6 cups (1.4 L) peanut oil, for frying

3 cups (336 g) Donut & Fritter Blend (page 47)

2 teaspoons paprika

½ teaspoon baking powder

½ teaspoon garlic powder

½ teaspoon onion powder

½ teaspoon freshly cracked black pepper

¼ to ½ teaspoon cayenne

FRIED GARLIC
Slice a few garlic cloves thinly and heat a few tablespoons olive oil in a saucepan over medium-high heat. When the oil is hot (a drop of water should sizzle when it hits the oil), add the garlic and fry until it is golden brown and crispy, watching carefully to make sure it doesn't burn. Remove the garlic with a slotted spoon and drain it on a paper towel–lined plate.

Divide the dry ingredients evenly into two bowls. Into one bowl, whisk 3 cups (720 ml) water and stir to combine until the batter is lump free. The batter should be the consistency of a loose custard. If it looks like thick pudding, just whisk in some additional water, a few tablespoons at a time, until you have the consistency you need.

Roll the chicken pieces in the bowl with the dry ingredients, then dunk them in the wet mixture, and finally roll them in the dry ingredients again. Place the battered chicken on a platter or large baking sheet as you coat the other pieces.

Put just a few pieces of chicken into the oil at a time, cooking big pieces together and small pieces together. This way, each batch will be finished at the same time and you won't be overcooking smaller pieces or undercooking larger ones. Keep that oil hot, so the batter fries fast and doesn't absorb the oil. Fry the chicken pieces until they're golden brown and crispy, 12 to 15 minutes for breast halves and thighs, 8 to 10 minutes for legs, and 7 to 8 for wings. Using tongs, transfer the fried chicken pieces to the brown bag or paper towel–lined platter to drain the excess oil.

Serve the chicken any old way you please!

OKIE-DOKIE ARTICHOKIE

½ cup (120 ml) lemon juice

1 bay leaf

2½ teaspoons kosher salt

8 small artichokes, trimmed and quartered, chokes removed

¼ teaspoon ground dried thyme

1 recipe Tempura Batter (page 58)

A.1. Steak Sauce, Worcestershire sauce, or ketchup, for serving

I love steamed and fried artichokes equally, and the beauty of this recipe is that you can have either, or both, depending on your menu.

MAKES 8

In a large saucepan, combine the lemon juice, bay leaf, salt, and 4 cups (960 ml) water and bring them to a boil over high heat. Add the artichokes, turn off the heat, and cover. Let them stand for 6 to 8 minutes, until the artichokes are just getting tender. Drain and let them stand in a colander to dry.

Meanwhile, in a large, heavy-bottomed saucepan (or alternatively, in a deep-fryer), heat the oil over medium heat until it registers 400°F (205°C) on a deep-fry thermometer. Line a platter with paper towels, or line a baking sheet with a brown paper bag.

Stir the thyme into the tempura batter.

If necessary, gently blot any excess water from the artichokes. Dip the artichokes in the batter, letting any excess drip back into the bowl, then transfer them to the oil and fry them until golden, 2 to 4 minutes, depending on the size of the hearts. Using a slotted spoon or spider, transfer the fried artichokes to the lined plate to drain any excess oil.

Serve them with A.1. Sauce, Worcestershire, or, for a full-on Okie experience, ketchup and banjo music.

FRIED SQUASH BLOSSOMS

Growing up in an Italian household, I got accustomed to two delicacies I really couldn't let go of once I'd gone gluten-free. The first was my grand-mother's pasta; the second, her fried squash blossoms. These delicate flowers, a natural by-product of the growth cycle of various squashes, are at their best in late spring and early summer when zucchini and other squash are coming into season.

MAKES 8; SERVES 4 AS AN APPETIZER OR SIDE DISH

Make the batter: In a large bowl, whisk together the Donut & Fritter Blend, salt, and pepper and transfer them to a shallow bowl or pan.

In a separate bowl, whisk the eggs, then whisk in the seltzer until it stops foaming.

Make the filling: In a medium bowl, combine the cheese, chives, pine nuts, honey, parsley, and salt and pepper to taste.

In a large skillet (or alternatively, in a deep-fryer), heat the oil over medium heat until it registers 350°F (190°C) on a deep-fry thermometer. Line a platter with paper towels, or line a baking sheet with a brown paper bag.

Transfer the filling to a pastry bag fitted with a plain round tip. Pipe the filling into the cups of the squash blossoms, filling them no more than two-thirds full; the filling will expand as it cooks, and you don't want it to ooze out. Gently twist the petals of the blossoms closed.

Dip the filled squash blossoms into the egg mixture, letting the excess drip back into the bowl, and then roll them in the blend mixture. Set the battered blossoms aside on a plate. To avoid crowding the pan or fryer, fry them in two batches (you don't want to lower the temperature of the oil). Fry the blossoms until they are golden brown, about 90 seconds per side. Use a slotted spoon or spider to transfer the fried squash blossoms to the lined plate to drain any excess oil.

Serve them with lemon wedges.

VARIATION: Roman-Style Fried Squash Blossoms

Omit all the filling ingredients above, and instead fill the blossoms this way: Cut a 4-ounce (115-g) ball of fresh mozzarella into 16 small rectangles, about 1 inch (2.5 cm) long and a bit less wide than the squash blossom's cup. Using 1 tablespoon of anchovy paste, spread a tiny bit on each of 8 mozzarella rectangles. Sandwich the anchovy paste with another moz-zarella rectangle. Insert one of these mozzarella-anchovy sandwiches into each squash blossom, dip, roll, and fry them as described above. Serve them with lemon wedges.

FOR THE BATTER:

½ cup (57 g) Donut & Fritter Blend (page 47)

¼ teaspoon kosher salt

Freshly cracked black pepper

2 large eggs

2 tablespoons plain seltzer water

FOR THE FILLING:

½ cup (115 g) creamy goat cheese, regular cream cheese, or ricotta

¼ cup (12 g) finely minced fresh chives, or 1 tablespoon dried

2 tablespoons pine nuts, toasted (see Note)

1 tablespoon plus 1 teaspoon honey

1½ teaspoons minced fresh flat-leaf parsley or dill, or ¾ teaspoon dried

Kosher salt and freshly ground black pepper

2 cups (480 ml) peanut oil, for frying

8 very fresh squash blossoms

Lemon wedges, for serving

NOTE: To toast pine nuts, heat a skillet over medium heat and toast the nuts by tossing them in the hot pan, or toast them on a rimmed baking sheet in a pre-heated 375°F (190°C) oven for 3 to 4 minutes, until they are golden brown. Pine nuts toast quickly due to their high fat content.

CORN DOGS

FOR THE BATTER:

½ cup (57 g) Donut & Fritter Blend (page 47)

⅔ cup (114 g) fine cornmeal

½ cup (66 g) masa harina

2¼ teaspoons baking powder

¾ teaspoon kosher salt

1¼ cups (300 ml) 2% or whole milk

2 large eggs

2 tablespoons sugar

2 tablespoons honey

8 gluten-free hot dogs

4 cups (960 ml) peanut oil, for frying

Mustard, ketchup, and/or relish, for serving (optional)

The sounds of roller coasters and the smell of funnel cake won't be far from your mind when you make these corn dogs. Best of all, no one will ever suspect they are gluten-free. (Or that a tad of sugar contributes to the beautiful color and crunch and makes them faintly sweet, just like the golden corn dogs of our youth.) This recipe batters up eight dogs, so you can serve them individually as a snack or at a tailgate, or double up and serve them as a full meal.

You'll need thick bamboo or wooden skewers for these.

MAKES 8 CORN DOGS

In a large bowl, combine the Donut & Fritter blend, cornmeal, masa harina, baking powder, and salt.

In a separate bowl, whisk together the milk, eggs, sugar, and honey. Keep whisking until the sugar has dissolved and the mixture is smooth and combined. (You'll no longer hear the scrape of the sugar against the bowl as you whisk when it has dissolved.)

Pour the egg mixture into the dry ingredients and stir them with a wooden spoon to combine. The batter should be thick—just barely pourable—with no dry patches. A few lumps are OK.

Pat each hot dog dry, and then lightly dust each dog with additional blend so the batter will stick. Spear each hot dog, end to end, with a thick bamboo or wooden skewer.

Meanwhile, in a large, heavy-bottomed saucepan or Dutch oven, heat the oil over medium heat until it registers 375°F (190°C) on a deep-fry thermometer. Line a platter with paper towels, or line a baking sheet with a brown paper bag.

Pour batter into a tall glass (at least as tall as the hot dogs) until it's three-quarters full. Dip a hot dog into the batter, coating it right up to the skewer. Draw the hot dog out, letting the excess batter drip off a bit, and then slide the dog straight into the hot oil. (The skewer can fry; it won't hurt it much.) If the corn dogs are not fully submerged in the oil, trim the skewer so they will fry up uniformly. Add more batter to the glass after dipping each dog so it is always full.

Fry the dogs a few at a time, so as not to crowd them or cool the oil, cooking them until the corn crust is brown, 4 to 6 minutes. So as not to break the crunch, use silicone-padded tongs to pull the fried corn dogs from the oil, grabbing them by the stick. Transfer the corn dogs to the lined platter to drain any excess oil.

Serve them with mustard and ketchup, for sure. Maybe relish.

HUSH PUPPIES

1 cup (165 g) corn kernels

1 recipe Corn Dog batter (page 64)

Kosher salt and freshly ground black pepper

Dipping sauces of your choice

Forget the dogs, the sticks, and the glass. But you will need a slotted spoon. Use any type of corn for this—fresh, frozen and thawed, or canned—but not creamed (most creamed corn isn't gluten-free)! Hush puppies were bred to sop up everything from tartar to barbecue sauce, but they're good with lots of condiments—even the spicy ones, like Sriracha. Just a bit of salt and pepper does nicely, too.

MAKES 12 TO 18 HUSH PUPPIES

In a large, heavy-bottomed saucepan or Dutch oven (or alternatively, in a deep-fryer), heat the oil over medium heat until it registers 375°F (190°C) on a deep-fry thermometer. Line a platter with paper towels, or line a baking sheet with a brown paper bag.

Stir the corn into the prepared batter. Scoop up heaping tablespoons of the batter and drop them into the hot oil. Fry the hush puppies until they are golden brown, 2 to 4 minutes. Use a slotted spoon or spider to transfer the fried hush puppies to the lined plate to drain any excess oil.

Sprinkle them with salt and pepper and serve them hot, just drained, with dipping sauces on the side.

LEO'S MAC 'N' CHEESE

My son, Leo, would eat macaroni and cheese every day if he had the chance, which means I end up eating it more often than I'd like to admit. So in an effort to make a gluten-free version that tastes better than the store-bought variety, I tested this recipe well over a dozen times before I perfected the taste, texture, and appearance. After that much testing, I want to emphasize that the cayenne really is a must for a trademark kick at the end of each bite. The base is a classic white sauce, or béchamel—a pan-toasted mix of flour, butter, and milk. Now Leo won't touch the (heavily processed) leading store brand. Sigh.

SERVES 4

Bring a large pot of salted water to a rolling boil. Add the pasta, stirring to make sure it doesn't stick, and cook according to the package instructions until it is al dente.

Meanwhile, make the béchamel: In a bowl, combine the Donut & Fritter Blend, salt, pepper, cayenne, and nutmeg, whisking to combine them.

In a heavy saucepan, melt the butter over medium heat. When it foams, whisk in the dry ingredients and cook, whisking continuously, until you have a thick paste, about 1 minute. Whisk in the milk, a bit at time, gradually thinning the paste to a liquid. The mixture will thicken quickly, so keep adding the milk and continue whisking until the mixture is thick and smooth. The béchamel is done when the sauce drips off the end of the whisk in a steady stream. Add more milk if needed until you have achieved this texture and thickness. Remove it from the heat. Add the cheese and whisk until there aren't any lumps, then let the sauce sit for 2 to 3 minutes so the cheese melts completely. Whisk in the sour cream.

Drain the pasta and rinse it with cold water, shaking off any excess moisture, then transfer it back to the pot in which it was cooked. Pour the cheese sauce over the noodles and stir gently until all the macaroni is evenly coated. Serve immediately.

1 pound (455 g) gluten-free macaroni

FOR THE BÉCHAMEL:

3 tablespoons (21 g) Donut & Fritter Blend (page 47)

½ teaspoon kosher salt

¼ teaspoon freshly ground white pepper

⅛ teaspoon cayenne

⅛ teaspoon freshly grated nutmeg

3 tablespoons unsalted butter

2 cups (480 ml) 2% or whole milk, at room temperature (plus more if needed)

2½ cups (300 g) grated extra-sharp cheddar

2 tablespoons (30 ml) sour cream

ASIAGO LASAGNA

FOR THE BÉCHAMEL:

¼ cup (28 g) Donut & Fritter Blend (page 47)

1½ teaspoons kosher salt

½ teaspoon freshly ground white pepper

4 tablespoons (½ stick / 56 g) butter

2½ cups (600 ml) milk

¼ teaspoon freshly grated nutmeg

2 cups (200 g) grated Asiago or Parmesan

FOR THE VEAL:

2 tablespoons olive oil or any neutral-flavored vegetable oil

¼ cup (35 g) finely grated white onion

½ teaspoon kosher salt, plus more as needed

12 ounces (340 g) ground veal or lean beef

1 teaspoon chopped fresh thyme

½ teaspoon dried oregano, or 1 teaspoon fresh

½ teaspoon ground cumin

If you aren't in the mood for the richness of this red-and-white lasagna made with an Asiago-laced white sauce, substitute the béchamel with cheese ravioli filling (page 114) for a more Spartan alternative.

The thirty-minute resting time is crucial, as it allows the lasagna to set while simultaneously sparing diners a second-degree burn to the roof of the mouth. Probably the most famous of all hot casseroles, this lasagna keeps very well in the fridge, covered, for up to a week. Freeze it like a popsicle for up to 3 months.

SERVES 8

Make the béchamel: In a bowl, combine the Donut & Fritter Blend, salt, and pepper, whisking to combine them.

In a heavy saucepan, melt the butter over medium heat. When it foams, whisk in the dry ingredients and cook, whisking continuously until you have a thick paste, about 1 minute. Reduce the heat to low and whisk in the milk, a bit at time, gradually thinning the paste to a liquid. The mixture will thicken quickly, so keep adding the milk and continue whisking until the mixture is thick and smooth. The béchamel is done when the sauce drips off the end of the whisk in a steady stream. Whisk in the nutmeg and remove from the heat but keep it warm on the stove. Add the Asiago and whisk until there aren't any lumps.

Make the veal: In a medium skillet, heat the oil over medium heat. Add the onion with a pinch of salt and sauté until it is translucent, about 5 minutes. Add the veal, thyme, oregano, cumin, and salt and cook, breaking up the meat with a wooden spoon, until it is browned. Remove it from the heat and keep it warm.

Assemble the lasagna: Preheat the oven to 350°F (175°C).

Bring a large pot of salted water to a boil. Cook the sheets of fresh pasta until they float to the top, about 30 seconds. Gently remove them from the water and drape them over the side of a large bowl to drain. (If using store-bought noodles, cook them according to the package directions.)

Spread one-third of the tomato sauce on the bottom of a 9-by-13-inch (23-by-33-cm) baking dish. Top it with a layer of noodles, followed by one-third of the veal. Spoon one-fourth of the béchamel on top of the veal and spread it evenly using the back of a spoon. Repeat this layering process until all of the ingredients have been used. Finish with a layer of pasta.

Sprinkle the top evenly with the mozzarella, then scatter the Asiago over that.

Bake the lasagna for 30 minutes, or until the cheese is browned and the sauce is bubbling up through the noodles. Remove it from the oven and let stand for 30 minutes before cutting it into squares and serving.

NOTE: For a healthier version, substitute the noodles with zucchini (4 medium squash will do) that has been sliced to $\frac{1}{16}$ inch; using a mandoline is the best way to achieve a perfect slice unless you just got your chef's knife professionally sharpened. Because the squash contain so much water, drizzle the slices with kosher salt and allow to sit for 15 minutes. Press with a paper towel to remove this drawn-out moisture. Lightly grill the zucchini on a nonstick griddle and then layer your lasagna as instructed above.

FOR ASSEMBLY:

1 recipe Homemade Egg Pasta (page 114), cut into lasagna noodles, or 1 pound (455 g) store-bought gluten-free lasagna noodles like Tinkyáda

1 recipe Oven-Roasted Grape-Tomato Sauce (page 114)

2 cups (240 g) shredded mozzarella (do not use buffalo mozzarella)

¼ cup (25 g) grated Asiago or Parmesan

MRS. ELIE'S CREOLE-STYLE GUMBO

This recipe is adapted from one by Mrs. Elie, a famous Cajun chef from New Orleans whom I read about in *Smithsonian Magazine*. Mrs. Elie was lauded for her gumbo, which, in some circles, is as prestigious an honor as being president. The key to any good gumbo is a well-blended brown roux. The Donut & Fritter Blend makes one that gives this gumbo the kind of flavor and texture that Mrs. Elie took justifiable pride in—but this one's gluten-free. Filé powder might be an unfamiliar ingredient, but don't let it intimidate you. Made from powdered sassafras leaves, filé thickens the gumbo and adds a distinct flavor, a bit like eucalyptus. Gumbo will keep for up to a week in the fridge and improves with every reheating. It doesn't freeze well, as stews based on a roux will change consistency once they've been frozen and thawed, and the seafood gets rubbery.

SERVES 6 TO 8

In a large stockpot, combine the carrot, 1 tablespoon salt, and 5 quarts (3.8 L) water. Chop the leafy tops from the celery and add them to the pot; dice the celery and reserve them for the gumbo. Bring the mixture to a simmer over low heat and simmer for at least 30 minutes.

Peel and devein the shrimp; add the shells to the pot with the stock and reserve the shrimp for the gumbo. Simmer the stock for 10 minutes more, then remove it from the heat and set it aside for 30 minutes to allow the flavors to develop. Strain the stock through a fine-mesh sieve into a bowl and discard the solids. Set the stock aside.

In a separate stockpot, brown the sausages over medium heat. Using a slotted spoon, transfer them to a bowl. Pour off the fat from the pot, leaving about 1 tablespoon. Add the okra and cook it over medium heat until it is crispy and dried, 40 to 45 minutes. Transfer it to the bowl with the sausage and set it aside.

Add the oil to the pot over medium heat. Add the Donut & Fritter Blend and whisk to combine. Cook, whisking continuously, until the paste takes on a medium-brown or mocha tint, 5 to 10 minutes.

Add the onions and cook until they are softened, then add the reserved diced celery, the bell pepper, scallions, garlic, and parsley. Cook, stirring occasionally, for 20 minutes more. Pour in the stock, whisking continuously. Add the sausage, okra, and bay leaves and simmer the gumbo for 1 hour, skimming off any fat that floats to the top.

Add the filé powder, Creole seasoning, cayenne (if using), reserved peeled shrimp, and crabmeat (but not the claw meat). Cook them for 10 minutes more, then add the crab claw meat and cook the gumbo for just a few minutes more to get the crab claws hot. Season the gumbo with salt and pepper serve hot over steamed rice.

1 carrot, peeled and diced

Kosher salt

6 stalks celery

2 pounds (910 g) medium to large shrimp

2 pounds (910 g) gluten-free smoked sausage, cut crosswise into ¼-inch (6-mm) slices

1 pound (455 g) gluten-free Creole-style hot sausage, cut crosswise into ¼-inch (6-mm) slices

1½ pounds (680 g) fresh or frozen okra, sliced crosswise into ¼-inch (6-mm) rounds

½ cup (120 ml) peanut oil

½ cup (57 g) Donut & Fritter Blend (page 47)

2 white onions, diced

1 green or red bell pepper, chopped

1 bunch scallions, green and white parts, chopped

6 cloves garlic, chopped

1 tablespoon minced fresh parsley

4 bay leaves

¼ cup (24 g) filé powder

2 tablespoons Creole seasoning, such as Tony Chachere's Original Creole Seasoning

½ teaspoon cayenne (optional)

1 pound (455 g) crabmeat, picked and cleaned

8 ounces (225 g) crab claw meat

Freshly ground black pepper

Steamed rice, for serving

CHURROS

FOR THE CHOUX PASTE:

2 large eggs

1 teaspoon baking powder

5 tablespoons (70 g) unsalted butter

2 tablespoons half-and-half

2 teaspoons sugar

¼ teaspoon kosher salt

½ cup plus 3 tablespoons (79 g) Donut & Fritter Blend (page 47)

1 teaspoon pure vanilla extract

4 cups (960 ml) peanut oil, for frying

1 cup (200 g) sugar, for dusting

2 teaspoons ground cinnamon, for dusting

The churro is Mexico's answer to the funnel cake . . . or maybe the funnel cake is the United States's answer to the churro. But which treat came first isn't important; what matters is how good it is.

The dry and wet ingredients here combine in a way that's out of the ordinary for this book, and it involves cooking the dough on the stove-top to a midway point. The result is so worth the extra couple of steps. This procedure, which makes a classic choux paste, also applies to the Jelly-Filled Donuts (page 74), Cream Puffs (page 76), and banana puffs in the Sundae Split (page 79). Whether there's some kind of etymological relationship between *churro* and *choux* is a riddle we can leave to linguistic-gastronomical scholars.

Roll the churros in enough of the coating so that when you bite into one, you get a cinnamon-sugar bib on your shirt.

MAKES 12 CHURROS

Make the choux paste: In a small bowl, crack the the eggs; do not whisk them. Pour the baking powder over the eggs and let it stand for at least 5 minutes, so the egg whites activate the baking powder.

In a heavy-bottomed medium saucepan, combine the butter, half-and-half, 2 teaspoons of the sugar, the salt, and 5 tablespoons (75 ml) water over medium heat and heat until the butter has melted and the mixture comes to a gentle boil. Add the Donut & Fritter Blend and stir vigorously with a wooden spoon, scraping the bottom of the pot for about 1 minute. Once the dough pulls easily from the sides of the pan and leaves a thin veil of butterfat on the bottom, it's ready to come off the heat.

Transfer the dough to a food processor fitted with the S-blade. Pulse the dough for 20 seconds to cool it slightly. Pour in the eggs and baking powder (still unwhisked) and process it all to a thick, sticky paste, about 90 seconds more. Add the vanilla and mix just until incorporated. Transfer the dough to a pastry bag fitted with a ½-inch (12-mm) star tip. At this point, the dough can be refrigerated: Wrap the pastry tip in plastic and then place a rubber band over the top of the tip so it's snug and keeps the plastic tight. Using a second rubber band, twist the top of the bag shut and fold the excess pastry bag over, pulling the rubber band over the excess flap. This will keep the dough fresh for up to 3 days before frying.

Make the churros: In a large skillet (or alternatively, in a deep-fryer), heat the oil over medium heat until it registers 350°F (175°C) on a deep-fry thermometer. Line a platter with paper towels, or line a baking sheet with a brown paper bag.

In a shallow dish or pan, mix the sugar and cinnamon together.

Pipe the dough directly into the hot oil in 4- to 6-inch (10- to 15-cm) strips (use a knife or kitchen scissors to separate the strips from the pastry bag tip, if necessary). Cook them for about 2 minutes on one side and then flip them and cook for up to 2 minutes more, until they are golden brown. Using tongs, transfer the churros to the lined plate to drain any excess oil. Roll the hot churros in the cinnamon-sugar to coat them well.

The churros are best served warm, but are still very good at room temperature.

VARIATION: French Crullers

Heat the oil as directed above. Spray small pieces of parchment paper (about 3 inches / 7.5 cm square) with nonstick cooking spray. Pipe the dough in 2½-inch (6-cm) rings onto the parchment paper. Carefully turn the uncooked crullers out into the hot oil and fry until they are pale golden, about 2 minutes per side. Using a large slotted spoon, transfer the fried crullers to a lined plate and serve them dusted with confectioners' sugar.

JELLY-FILLED DONUTS

2 recipes Choux Paste (page 51)

2 cups (480 ml) jam (such as strawberry, raspberry, blueberry, cherry, or a variety) or filling of your choice

4 cups (960 ml) peanut oil, for frying

1 cup (200 g) sugar, for coating

Echoing chef Fergus Henderson's sentiments about how to fill a donut in his incredible cookbook *Beyond Nose to Tail*, I too like to fill my fried dough so abundantly that the result "explodes on my glasses." I've gone with the simplest filling for a donut here, but these are extra-yummy stuffed with pastry cream (see Banana Cream Pie, page 105), store-bought lemon curd, or Nutella. Whatever you shoot inside your donuts, keep a thick stack of napkins close at hand for those glasses. I like my donuts best when the filling's at room temperature and the donut's still just a bit warm.

MAKES 24 PLUMP DONUTS

Scoop the prepared choux paste into a lidded container and refrigerate it for 2 to 3 hours.

Meanwhile, in a medium saucepan, melt the jam over medium heat until it is liquid. Strain the jam through a fine-mesh strainer into a bowl; discard any solids left in the strainer. Set the jam aside to cool completely.

To cook the donuts, in a large skillet (or alternatively, in a deep-fryer), heat the oil over medium heat until it registers 375°F (190°C) on a deep-fry thermometer. Line a platter with paper towels, or line a baking sheet with a brown paper bag.

Pour the sugar into a shallow dish. Shake the dish slightly to spread the sugar out into an even layer.

Working in batches of three or four donuts at a time, spoon tablespoon-size dollops of dough directly into the hot oil. Be sure not to overcrowd the pan or the oil will get cool. Fry until the donuts are golden brown on both sides, about 1 minute on the first side and a bit less than a minute on the second side. Using a slotted spoon or spider, transfer the fried donuts to the lined plate to drain any excess oil. Repeat with the remaining dough.

When the donuts are cool enough to handle, roll them in the sugar.

Transfer the cooled strained jam to a pastry bag fitted with a plain round tip. Pierce a donut with the pastry bag tip and pipe about 1 tablespoon of filling into the donut. Repeat to fill the remaining donuts.

Ideally, eat the donuts right away, before the sugar can absorb any of the residual frying oil.

If you have any leftovers, store the donuts in a brown paper bag or in a loosely covered container on the counter for a day or two.

BASIC CREAM PUFFS

FOR THE PUFFS:

1 recipe Choux Paste (page 51)

FOR THE FILLING:

1 cup (240 ml) heavy cream

2 tablespoons confectioners' sugar

1½ teaspoons pure vanilla extract

Like the Jelly-Filled Donuts (page 74), these cream puffs will accommodate any filling you like. I've listed a couple of variations below. You can even fill them with crab, lobster, or chicken salad, if you like, for a savory appetizer or luncheon sandwich. As the puffs are baked, rather than fried, they're a bit more delicate—like little puffs of air—which makes them both magical and sturdy enough to build French delicacies like the famed Ste. Honoré Cake and the Croquembouche.

MAKES 6 LARGE CREAM PUFFS

Make the puffs: Preheat the oven to 425°F (220°C).

Transfer the choux paste to a pastry bag fitted with a large (at least 1-inch or 24-mm) plain tip. Pipe the dough onto a baking sheet in 2-inch (5-cm) rounds, leaving 2 inches (5 cm) between each round. Using the back of a spoon and a little water, gently smooth the top of the cream puff so it has a smooth dome.

Bake the puffs for 20 minutes, without opening the oven door, until they are risen and golden. Transfer them to a wire rack and let them cool completely.

Make the filling: Meanwhile, in a stand mixer fitted with the whisk attachment, or in a bowl using a hand mixer, combine the cream, sugar, and vanilla and whip until the cream holds firm peaks. Refrigerate it for 10 minutes to set the cream. Transfer the whipped cream to a pastry bag fitted with a ½-inch (12-mm) star tip.

Cut the baked puffs in half, like a hamburger bun. Pipe a generous amount of whipped cream onto the base of each cream puff and cap it with the top half. If you have any leftover filling, it's fabulous in hot cocoa, or served with a slice of pie.

The puffs will keep in an airtight container in the refrigerator for up to 2 days. The choux will soften over time, especially with the filling inside, so keep this in mind as you plan that holiday party or baby shower.

VARIATION: Mocha Cream Puff Filling

You can swap out the instant espresso powder for regular instant coffee (as in, the less-caffeinated variety) in this filling—the Starbucks type isn't bad, but freeze-dried instant coffee gives a smoother consistency. Use less than the amount of corn syrup called for if you'd like a less-sweet filling.

In a small saucepan over medium heat, heat ¼ cup (60 ml) of the cream just to a simmer. Reserve the remaining cream in the refrigerator.

Place the chocolate chips in a medium bowl. Sprinkle the espresso powder over them. Pour the hot cream over the chocolate and let it stand for 5 minutes to melt the chocolate. Add the corn syrup and whisk until the chocolate is smooth and well combined, then set aside for 15 minutes; you want the chocolate mixture to cool, but not set.

In a stand mixer fitted with the whisk attachment, or in a bowl using a hand mixer, combine the remaining 1¼ cups (300 ml) cream, the sugar, and the vanilla and whip until the cream holds soft peaks. Fold in the cooled chocolate mixture. (It's beautiful if you don't get this completely homogenous; the white cream streaked with chocolate has a great look.) Transfer the filling to a pastry bag fitted with a star tip, seal the bag then refrigerate it so the filling can set a bit. Fill the puffs as directed on page 76.

1½ cups (360 ml) heavy cream

¼ cup (42 g) semisweet chocolate chips

1 tablespoon instant espresso powder

1 tablespoon light corn syrup

3 tablespoons confectioners' sugar

2 teaspoons pure vanilla extract

VARIATION: Chantilly–Apricot Cream Puff Filling

In a medium saucepan, melt the preserves over medium heat until they are liquid. Strain the preserves through a fine-mesh strainer into a bowl; discard any solids left in the strainer. Set the preserves aside to cool completely.

In a stand mixer fitted with the whisk attachment, or in a bowl using a hand mixer, whip together the cream, sugar, and vanilla. When the cream is just getting thick, add the strained preserves and whisk to combine them to firm peaks. The fruit pectin in the preserves will cause the cream to stiffen up beautifully.

Transfer the filling to a pastry bag fitted with a large (1-inch or 24-mm) star tip, seal the bag then refrigerate it so the fruit pectin will set and tighten up the cream. Fill the puffs as directed on page 76.

1 cup (320 g) apricot preserves

1 cup (240 ml) heavy cream

2 tablespoons confectioners' sugar

2 teaspoons pure vanilla extract

NOTE: Chantilly-Apricot Cream is traditionally the go-to filling for cream puffs used to assemble croquembouche. Any other filling is too heavy and would cause the tower to collapse.

SOPHISTICATED SUNDAE SPLIT

I always felt the classic banana split was missing something texturally, so I reworked it into a combo of split, sundae, and profiterole, which is a cream puff filled with ice cream. An American classic—all grown up.

Thankfully, all of the classic sundae toppings, even the Hershey's Chocolate Syrup, are gluten-free, so don't hold back! If you do use another brand, be wary and consult the label or the manufacturer's website, in case they've snuck gluten in somehow.

SERVES 4, HEARTILY

Preheat the oven to 425°F (220°C). Line a baking sheet with parchment paper or a Silpat mat.

Transfer the choux paste to a pastry bag fitted with a plain 1-inch (2.5-cm) tip.

Pipe 6 rounds of the dough, each about the diameter of a silver dollar, onto the prepared baking sheet, leaving at least 2 inches (5 cm) between each round.

Peel one of the bananas and cut it crosswise into six ¼-inch- (6-mm-) thick slices and press one slice into each round of dough, making the banana slices lie flush with the dough. Sprinkle the bananas with a little brown sugar. Pipe another round of dough over the banana slices, being sure that the slices are covered completely. Repeat until all of your banana slices are used up. Dip a spoon in lukewarm water and smooth the top of each puff.

Bake them for 15 to 20 minutes, without opening the oven, until the puffs are golden and risen. Transfer them to a wire rack to cool.

Meanwhile, in a stand mixer fitted with the whisk attachment, or in a bowl using a hand mixer, combine the cream, confectioners' sugar, and vanilla and whip them until the cream holds firm peaks. Transfer the whipped cream to a pastry bag fitted with a ½-inch (12-mm) star tip, seal the bag, then refrigerate it until you're ready to use it.

Slice the cooled puffs in half horizontally like a hamburger bun. Arrange the halved puffs on a rimmed baking sheet, cut-sides up. Fill two bottom halves with a scoop of vanilla ice cream each, two with a scoop of chocolate ice cream each, and two with a scoop of strawberry ice cream each. Set the tops of the puffs on top of the ice cream. Transfer the baking sheet to the freezer to re-firm the ice cream.

To serve, line each of two long, skinny dishes (ideally, banana split dishes) with one of each flavor of ice cream–filled profiterole. Peel the two remaining bananas and halve them lengthwise. Lay half on each side of the ice cream–filled puffs. Drizzle them with chocolate syrup, then pipe whipped cream on top. Crown each sundae with the cherries and peanuts.

1 recipe Choux Paste (page 51)

3 ripe bananas (with yellow and brown speckles)

2 tablespoons brown sugar

½ cup (120 ml) heavy cream

1½ teaspoons confectioners' sugar

¼ teaspoon pure vanilla extract

12 scoops ice cream (chocolate, strawberry, and vanilla are traditional, but let your conscience be your guide)

Hershey's Chocolate Syrup

6 maraschino cherries

½ cup (72 g) chopped roasted and salted peanuts (optional)

APRIL BLOOMFIELD'S CHEESE BEIGNETS

4 large eggs

1 teaspoon baking powder

4 tablespoons (½ stick / 56 g) unsalted butter

1 teaspoon sugar

½ teaspoon kosher salt

1½ cups (169 g) Donut & Fritter Blend (page 47)

1 cup (100 g) packed finely grated Parmigiano-Reggiano

½ cup (57 g) packed finely grated Gruyère

⅓ teaspoon freshly ground black pepper, plus more for garnish

4 cups (960 ml) peanut oil, for frying

Sea salt

NOTE: All beignets are best enjoyed immediately after they are prepared. They tend to lose that exterior crunch over time.

April Bloomfield, chef and co-owner of the John Dory Oyster Bar, The Breslin, and the Spotted Pig, all in New York City, is a chef I admire for many reasons. Not least among them is her take on the cheese beignet. Just the aroma convinced me I had to try for a gluten-free version, to express my gratitude for her coming up with this in the first place.

The beignet is a savory choux paste–based goodie, a cousin of the sweet applications of choux (like Churros, page 72, and the Sophisticated Sundae's banana puffs, page 79). It's essentially a fried *gougère*; both are to die for, and both are examples of how versatile choux paste really is.

MAKES 12 TO 18 BEIGNETS

In a small bowl, crack the eggs; do not whisk them. Pour the baking powder over the eggs and let it stand for at least 5 minutes, so the egg whites activate the baking powder.

In a heavy-bottomed medium saucepan, combine the butter, sugar, salt, and ¾ cup plus 2 tablespoons (210 ml) water over medium heat and heat until the butter has melted and the mixture comes to a gentle boil. Add the Donut & Fritter Blend and stir it vigorously with a wooden spoon, scraping the bottom of the pot, for about 1 minute. Once the dough pulls easily from the sides of the pot and leaves a thin veil of butterfat on the bottom, it's ready to come off the heat.

Transfer the dough to a food processor fitted with the S-blade. Pulse the dough for 20 seconds to cool it slightly. Pour in the eggs and baking powder (still unwhisked) and process it all to combine, about 30 seconds more. Add the cheeses and pepper and process the dough to a sticky, thick paste. Season it with additional salt and pepper as desired.

In a medium saucepan (or alternatively, in a deep-fryer), heat the oil over medium heat until it registers 350°F (175°C) on a deep-fry thermometer. Line a platter with paper towels, or line a baking sheet with a brown paper bag.

Using a 1½-inch (4-cm) retractable ice cream scoop (about 3 tablespoons), portion the dough into the hot oil in batches of three. (If you're watching the thermometer, the oil will drop about 20 degrees, which is perfect; if you add too many beignets to the oil, the temperature will drop too far.) Fry the beignets until they are golden-brown on both sides, 1 to 2 minutes on the first side and 1 minute on the second. Using a slotted spoon or spider, transfer the beignets to the lined plate to drain any excess oil.

Serve the beignets hot, sprinkled with sea salt and a bit more pepper.

PIE & PASTA BLEND

The Pie & Pasta Blend, second only to the Bread & Pizza blend, took me the longest to perfect—years, in fact! It was such slow going because the blend had to achieve two seemingly opposite results. How could I possibly create a blend that simultaneously produced a flaky shortcrust dough (page 88), a crumbly sweet crust (page 91), *and* a homemade pasta (page 114) as good as my grandma used to make? It's all about the science, my dear Watson.

THE RECIPE

1¼ cups plus 3 tablespoons (160 g) tapioca starch

1 cup plus ½ teaspoon (124 g) cornstarch

¾ cup plus 1½ tablespoons (96 g) glutinous rice flour

½ cup (52 g) sorghum flour

¼ cup plus 1½ teaspoons (48 g) potato starch

¼ cup (48 g) granulated sugar

1 tablespoon (9 g) guar gum

½ teaspoon (3 g) kosher salt

The approximate weight of the blend, by volume (for use in doing your own adaptations):

EACH	OF BLEND WEIGHS APPROXIMATELY
1 tablespoon	8 g
¼ cup	16 g
⅓ cup	42 g
½ cup	61 g
⅔ cup	80 g
¾ cup	91 g
1 cup	121 g

Here's the science behind the Pie & Pasta Blend: It's all about the individual traits of the constituent flours and starches, and in their implemented ratios.

Complete-protein grains provide structural integrity to your dough so your finished products will look the way they should. They also impart an incredible flavor profile that our tastebuds identify as "delicious" and are mutable enough to create a variety of different crumbs. Sorghum is one of the complete-protein grains I use most often and happens to be the starting point for creating any good gluten-free flour blend. It contains the ideal ratio of amino acids, carbohydrates, and proteins for the building blocks of life. Traditional unbleached flours contain these same building blocks, and when it comes to baking, these building blocks have both a figurative and literal meaning. I tell my students to imagine these biological characteristics as actual interlocking bricks. They're the foundation of the gluten-free house you are building.

Once the foundation of your blend is laid, the remaining flours and starches you add contribute to the taste, texture, and appearance of the finished product as needed. You will notice that the Pie & Pasta Blend has a high ratio of starches. Each of the starches reacts differently in water, and therefore, each one adds a different textural quality to the finished product. Potato starch becomes viscous and never gels, while cornstarch does the opposite. Tapioca starch is the middle sister to potato starch and cornstarch. Her characteristics are half of both, so when all three starches are combined, they create an elaborate web of cohesion that enables the at-home gluten-free baker to achieve magical, flaky results. This is why the amount of guar gum in this blend is relatively low. Any more guar gum and the finished goods would be rubbery rather than flaky (pie crusts) or dense rather than tender (pasta).

For more information on the individual flours, starches, and other ingredients in the blend, see the Pantry section on page 215.

MAKES 4¼ CUPS (540 G), ENOUGH FOR 2 BATCHES OF SHORT CRUST OR HOMEMADE PASTA

Using the spoon-and-sweep method, measure each ingredient into a large bowl. Whisk together and then sift the mixture into a separate large bowl. Repeat several times. Since you are working with so many different starches, you really need to sift and whisk the blend several times to ensure an even distribution of all the ingredients.

Kept in an airtight container, the Pie & Pasta Blend will keep for up to 1 year in your pantry.

THE DOUGH

PAY ATTENTION TO KNEADING, FOLDING, AND ROLLING

The handling of the various doughs made with the Pie & Pasta blend will dictate the texture of the finished product. Little differences in how you knead, fold, and roll the doughs make exponential differences in the finished product, whether it be a pie crust or a nest of pasta strands, so keep this in mind as you work. Unlike many of the gluten-free pie crust recipes out there, I always tell my students that this dough isn't Play-Doh, where you have to press it into a pie pan. This is *real* dough—you can roll it, cut it, and shape it in any way you please.

PIE AND TART CRUSTS

Now, aside from the blend itself, there are only two ingredients that are added to the short crust recipe to make it sing, so the quality of these two ingredients should be high. For the flakiest pie and tart crusts, always use the best butter you can get your hands on, especially high-fat, European-style butters. "European-style" denotes the fat content of the butter—regular ol' Land o' Lakes–type butter contains at least 80 percent butterfat but usually less than 82 percent, while European-style butters contain between 82 and 85 percent butterfat. Making them extra-delicious, obviously, and elevating your baked goods accordingly; the higher the ratio of butterfat, the flakier your pie crusts. The butter's fat content also has an effect on the texture and workability of the dough: the less the butterfat, the more elbow grease it's gonna take to get the dough just right; the more butterfat, the easier it is to roll out the dough. Keep in mind, however, that if you do use a butter with a higher butterfat ratio, it means you need to work quickly and efficiently so the dough doesn't get too soft. At Blackbird Bakery, we roll out our dough in the walk-in cooler so the dough stays below 60°F (15°C), even when our hands are on it. When I'm at

home, however, I typically chill a marble slab before I roll out my dough, but if you don't have one, fear not, your dough will still roll out like a dream. Some bakers swear by using equal parts Crisco to butter, but I personally don't care for the lack of flavor in vegetable shortening. If you're going to use any kind of shortening, use real lard (rendered pork fat) for best results in recipes like my Empanadas (page 113) or chicken potpies (page 110).

Crusts made with the Pie & Pasta Blend also respond beautifully to a fun bit of culinary sleight of hand: try replacing a few tablespoons of butter for an equal quantity of cream cheese. This will give you a slightly more moist and tangy crust.

The freshness and size of your eggs also plays a pivotal role in the quality of your tart crusts. If you are using enormous eggs, be prepared for a softer dough; if you are using little bitty eggs, your dough will be more firm. If you have an egg allergy and need to use egg replacer, remember to make sure the egg replacer foams before adding it to the dough. This indicates that all of the ingredients are active and will perform as expected. If the replacer does not foam, it will not work as efficaciously, so proceed with caution.

For pastas, use only the very best pure olive oil and the freshest possible eggs. It was ground into me at a young age that extra-virgin olive oil is used only on fish and in dressings or dipping sauces. For everything else, pure olive oil all the way. This doesn't mean I don't blur the lines from time to time, but then I see my grandmother shaking her wooden spoon at me, even though she is no longer with us. When it comes to homemade egg pasta, I personally prefer the custardy flavor of the eggs over the intense floral bouquets that make good extra-virgin olive oils so precious, but if your palate is different than mine, by all means, use extra-virgin olive oil. I'll send my grandmother after you when you go to sleep. Plus, conventional pastas get most of their flavor from these two ingredients, so it's no surprise that the same thing goes for their gluten-free cousins.

The addition of vodka, wine, or vinegar is a wonderful way to achieve that flakes-of-crust-all-over-your-shirt result. This method, common in the Deep South, is one I use with tremendous pleasure throughout the book (pages 94 and 165). The alcohol burns off during cooking, creating visible layers of flaky crust. I also use vodka in conjunction with my Donut & Fritter Blend (page 47) if I want to achieve a light-as-air crunch for the tempura on page 58.

Need to make a sweet shortcrust? Simply add 1 cup (100 g) confectioners' sugar to the Pie & Pasta blend before combining the blend with the other crust ingredients, and you're all set.

BASIC KNEADING

First and foremost, always let the dough rest in the coldest part of your fridge (not the freezer!) for the prescribed time; in many cases, you leave it to chill overnight. Then, when it's time to work with the dough, let it sit on the counter for at least 5 minutes so it can warm up a tad, but will still be cool when you begin to work with it. *Always* use glutinous rice flour to roll out any kind of dough, be it for a pie crust or a loaf of bread, as this flour will not ruin the texture of the finished product. (Cornstarch, for example, creates a rubbery coating that will destroy a crust.) Dust the counter with glutinous rice flour then, rather than barely touching the dough as with a traditional short crust, you want to knead the dough until it's very pliable. When you initially begin to handle the dough, it might be a little crumbly, which is normal, so don't fret. Using the heel of your

hand, press down firmly and gather all the pieces of dough into a ball. Pull the dough from bottom to top and fold it over in a clockwise direction. Repeat this kneading until there are no fissures in the dough and it looks like a smooth leather ball.

ROLLING

As described on page 17, rolling out your dough should be done on a very clean work surface with both the counter and the rolling pin lightly floured with glutinous rice flour. I prefer an un-tapered French rod-style pin, especially when I'm making pie and tart crusts. This type of pin allows for an intimate connection between myself and the dough, so I know instantly if I'm applying even pressure and getting that perfectly flat, ripple-free surface.

As I touched on before, if you do not have glutinous rice flour on hand to begin rolling out your dough, the next best options would be to flour your pin and work surface with tapioca starch or a bit more of the Pie & Pasta blend as a last resort. After you have kneaded your dough and reformed it into a smooth disk, using the rolling pin, gently roll the dough from the center toward the edge of the dough disk, always rolling outward. Turn the dough 45 degrees after each pass of the rolling pin. This helps keep the rolling even and lets you ensure the dough is not sticking to your work surface. If it *does* stick a little, use a bench scraper to gently lift the stuck-on portion and then dust your work surface with a bit

more glutinous rice flour or blend. Flip the dough to make sure both sides are level. Repeat the rolling and turning until the dough is the thickness and/or size indicated by the recipe.

FOLDING

This is a different kind of folding than what we discussed on page 15. In this case, *folding* refers to turning, or letter-folding, dough. This is a technique often used for puff pastry in which layers of butter alternate with thin layers of dough. Using a folding technique in recipes like my Pop-Tarts (page 88) or quiche (page 96) happens to replicate those incredibly thin layers of crust without the tedious layering of the butter.

To letter-fold short crust, roll out the dough into a rectangle about a third as wide as it is long. Fold one of the shorter edges to the center, leaving a third of the dough unfolded. Repeat with the other short side, laying the dough on top of the folded portion. The dough should look like a letter just before you place it in an envelope. Gently pound the dough with your

rolling pin to stretch the dough while compressing the layers. Finally, roll the dough back into a rectangle. This is called one turn of the dough. Repeat this process—folding the dough in thirds, pounding the dough, and rolling it out into a rectangle—as many times, or "turns," as indicated in the recipe. And no matter what, don't stress—if your dough gets too soft to handle, simply place it back in the fridge for 30 minutes before proceeding as directed in the recipe.

LE POP-TART

FOR THE SHORT CRUST:

2¼ cups (272 g) Pie & Pasta Blend (page 83)

1 cup (2 sticks / 226 g) unsalted butter, diced and kept cold

2 large eggs

Glutinous rice flour (or additional Pie & Pasta blend, page 83), for dusting

FOR THE BUTTERCREAM ICING:

1 cup (200 g) granulated sugar

1 vanilla bean, split

1 cup (2 sticks / 226 g) unsalted butter, softened

4 cups (400 g) confectioners' sugar

1½ cups (360 ml) jam or preserves of your choice (classics are strawberry, blueberry, and cherry)

Dried or dehydrated fruit to match the preserves

NOTE: Try baking your pop tarts on convection (400°F / 205°C) for an even flakier finish.

My only beef with the original of this ingenious little treat is that the icing never seemed to make it all the way to the edge of the pastry. After enduring a full decade without this cornerstone of my youth, I finally engineered a gluten-free pop tart. The fancy version, with lemon-cardamom icing (see Variation on page 90), is likened by employees and patrons of Juan Pelota Café and Jo's Coffee, both located in Austin, to "edible crack." That is pretty much the best compliment I could imagine.

These tarts are incredibly versatile, so have fun and play around with different simple syrups to customize your buttercream. And by all means, don't limit yourself to sweet preparations. In the fall, I make *le pop tart de cochon*, a buttery short crust filled with bacon, goat cheese, and chives.

The unsweetened short crust, or *pâte brisée*, used here can also be used for any quiche, tart, pie, or turnover, and is particularly good for liquidy and custard-based fillings. You'll see it's my go-to for all kinds of recipes made with this blend.

MAKES 12 TARTS

Make the short crust: In the bowl of a stand mixer fitted with the paddle attachment, or in a food processor fitted with the S-blade, combine the Pie & Pasta Blend with the butter and beat or pulse them on the lowest setting until the mixture resembles damp cornmeal. Add the eggs and keep mixing until the dough pulls together and starts to ball up, about 1 minute with the mixer on high speed. The dough is done when it is sticking to the sides of the bowl and the paddle.

Dust your work surface with glutinous rice flour. Turn the dough out and lightly dust it with more rice flour. Knead the dough with the heel of your hand just until it is smooth. Form the dough into a ball, cut it in half, and shape each half into a 6- to 7-inch (15- to 17-cm) disk. Wrap each disk in plastic wrap and refrigerate for at least 2 hours, or overnight for best results.

Make the buttercream: In a small saucepan, combine the granulated sugar and ½ cup (120 ml) water and bring to a boil, stirring to dissolve the sugar. Add the vanilla bean. Reduce the heat to low and simmer the syrup for 5 minutes, swirling to be sure all the sugar has dissolved. Remove it from the heat and let the syrup infuse for 30 minutes. Remove the vanilla bean and discard it or rinse and reserve it for another use. Let the syrup cool.

CONTINUED

In the bowl of a stand mixer fitted with the paddle attachment, beat the butter until it is smooth and free of lumps. Add in the confectioners' sugar and 3 tablespoons of the cooled vanilla syrup and beat the mixture on high speed until it is very smooth. Set it aside in a cool place (not refrigerated), covered so the icing won't harden, until you're ready to use it.

Assemble the tarts: Preheat the oven to 425°F (220°C). Arrange the oven racks in the middle and lower positions. Let the dough sit at room temperature for 5 minutes.

Lightly dust your work surface with glutinous rice flour and knead the dough until it is very uniform and smooth, about 8 turns. Shape the dough into two 4-by-6-inch (10-by-15-cm) rectangles. Roll them out to ⅛ inch (3 mm) thick, maintaining their rectangular shape. Trim each rectangle to 8 by 14 inches (20 by 35.5 cm), then cut each into four 4-by-7-inch (10-by-17-cm) rectangles.

Spread 1 generous tablespoon of preserves onto four of the rectangles, being sure to keep a border of at least ½ inch (12 mm) on all sides. Using the tip of your finger or a pastry brush, lightly dampen the dough border with cool water. Top each filled rectangle with an unfilled rectangle and seal the edges by applying smooth even pressure with your fingers or with the tines of a fork. Transfer the tarts to two unlined baking sheets, leaving at least 1 inch (2.5 cm) between each tart.

Bake for 10 minutes, then switch the pans on the racks and bake for about 10 minutes more, until the tarts are browned on the edges.

Let cool on the baking sheets for 5 minutes, then transfer to a wire rack to cool completely.

Using an offset spatula, ice each tart with 1 to 2 tablespoons of the buttercream. If desired, dip your fingers in water and run them over the icing to smooth it out for that trademark sleek finish. Garnish each with a dried or dehydrated fruit reflective of the filling. The buttercream will keep for up to 2 weeks in an airtight container in the fridge for that next batch of pop tarts! Simply allow the icing to come to room temperature 1 hour before you plan on using it.

VARIATION: Lemon-Cardamom Pop-Tarts (aka Edible Crack)

Proceed as for the basic tart, but when it's time to make the buttercream, add 4 whole cardamom pods and 3 whole cloves to the simple syrup mix as it is simmering. Proceed as directed. As you beat the syrup into the buttercream, add the zest of 1 lemon. Fill the tarts with raspberry jam (my favorite brand is Bonne Maman), bake as above, cool, and ice with the lemon-cardamom buttercream.

FREE-FORM BERRY GALETTE

This gorgeous, rustic-looking galette is a nice change from its perfectly round, fluted-edged relatives. It's a great option if you've got a baking sheet but no tart pan. Galettes aren't supposed to look flawless, so when you're folding the border, don't worry too much about making it perfectly symmetrical; this dessert is prized for its physical imperfections.

And by the way—cut the amount of butter for the crust in half, substitute an equal amount of cream cheese, and you have the short crust needed to make everything from rugelach to pinwheels.

SERVES 6

Make the sweet short crust: In the bowl of a stand mixer fitted with the paddle attachment, or in a food processor fitted with the S-blade, combine the Pie & Pasta blend, confectioners' sugar, and butter and beat or pulse them on the lowest setting until the mixture resembles damp cornmeal. Add the eggs and keep mixing until the dough pulls together and starts to ball up, about 1 minute with the mixer on high speed. The dough is done when it is sticking to the sides of the bowl and the paddle.

Dust your work surface with glutinous rice flour. Turn the dough out and lightly dust it with more rice flour. Knead the dough with the heel of your hand until it feels like a smooth leather ball, about four turns. Form the dough into a ball and wrap it in plastic wrap. Refrigerate it for at least 2 hours, or overnight for best results.

Make the filling: In a large bowl, toss the berries with the sugar, almond flour, and nutmeg. Set them aside.

Assemble the tart: Preheat the oven to 375°F (190°C). Let the dough rest at room temperature for 5 minutes.

Lightly dust your work surface with glutinous rice flour and knead the dough until it is very uniform and smooth, six to seven turns. Roll the dough into a 14-inch (35.5-cm) round with a thickness of 1/8 inch (3 mm). Gently fold the dough in half and then in half again, then transfer it to a baking sheet and unfold it. Brush the surface of the dough with the vodka.

Scatter the butter over the dough, leaving a 2-inch (5-cm) border of dough. Pour the berry mixture over the butter. Fold the border of the dough up over the fruit, overlapping it in places, so the dough has soft pleats. Brush the folded edge with additional vodka and sprinkle it with sugar.

Bake the galette for 20 to 30 minutes, until the crust is golden.

CONTINUED

FOR THE SWEET SHORT CRUST:

2¼ cups (272 g) Pie & Pasta Blend (page 83)

1 cup (100 g) confectioners' sugar

1 cup (2 sticks / 226 g) unsalted butter, diced

2 large eggs

Glutinous rice flour (or additional Pie & Pasta Blend, page 83), for dusting

FOR THE FILLING:

2 cups (250 g) mixed fresh berries

2 tablespoons granulated sugar

1 tablespoon almond flour

⅛ teaspoon freshly grated nutmeg

2 tablespoons gluten-free vodka (I like Tito's Handmade Vodka)

1 tablespoon unsalted butter, cubed

Granulated sugar, for dusting

Clotted cream, whipped cream, crème fraîche, or ice cream, for serving

Serve slices with clotted cream, whipped cream, crème fraîche, or ice cream. The galette will keep, covered, in the refrigerator or at room temperature for up to 3 days.

VARIATION: Nectarine-Thyme Galette

This alternative filling has a nice bright note from the thyme leaves. Pit and slice (but do not peel) enough nectarines to make 2 cups (240 g). Toss them with 1 tablespoon granulated sugar, 1 tablespoon light brown sugar, the leaves from 2 sprigs of thyme (lemon thyme is fabulous, too!), and the scraped seeds from ½ vanilla bean. Cut the 1 tablespoon butter into pieces, scatter it over the nectarines in a pan, and roast at 350°F (175°C) for 15 minutes, until the top is golden. Let it cool, then fill the dough and bake as directed above.

BLUEBERRY CREAM HAND PIES

FOR THE SHORT CRUST:

2¼ cups (272 g) Pie & Pasta Blend (page 83)

1 cup (2 sticks / 226 g) unsalted butter, preferably cultured

2 large eggs

1 tablespoon gluten-free vodka, such as Tito's Handmade Vodka (optional)

Glutinous rice flour (or additional Pie & Pasta Blend, page 83), for dusting

FOR THE FILLING:

1 cup (200 g) granulated sugar, plus more for dusting

¼ cup (55 g) packed light brown sugar

¼ cup (35 g) cornstarch

¾ teaspoon ground cinnamon (or more if you like the kick)

36 ounces (1 kg) fresh blueberries

2 tablespoons unsalted butter

Juice of 1 lemon, strained of pulp

6 ounces (170 g) cream cheese, cut into 24 pats

¼ cup (60 ml) whole milk

Splash of pure vanilla extract

I never outgrew this tactile and tasty treat, put in my hand as I was shooed out the door so I wouldn't disrupt the clockwork precision of my mother's kitchen. The recipe makes a traditional—and killer—blueberry pie (see the variation). Just soften the cream cheese and spread it on the bottom of the pie crust before you pour in the filling.

What's with the booze, you say? As I touched on in the introduction, in the Deep South, the addition of either vinegar or vodka to pie dough is hugely popular. My preference is vodka, but as with all spirits, make sure it's gluten-free. The alcohol evaporates during the baking process, making the crust extremely flaky (and the final dessert kid-safe).

MAKES 24 HAND PIES

Make the short crust: In the bowl of a stand mixer fitted with the paddle attachment, or in a food processor fitted with the S-blade, combine the Pie & Pasta Blend with the butter and beat or pulse them on the lowest setting until the mixture resembles damp cornmeal. Add the eggs and vodka and keep mixing until the dough pulls together and starts to ball up, about 1 minute with the mixer on high speed. The dough is done when it is sticking to the sides of the bowl and the paddle.

Dust your work surface with glutinous rice flour. Turn the dough out and lightly dust it with more rice flour. Knead the dough with the heel of your hand until it feels like a smooth leather ball, four to eight turns. Form the dough into a disk and wrap it in plastic wrap. Refrigerate it for at least 2 hours, or overnight for best results.

Make the filling: In a large bowl, combine the granulated sugar, brown sugar, cornstarch, and cinnamon and whisk them with a fork until there are no lumps and the cornstarch is uniformly incorporated. Toss half the blueberries in the sugar mixture; reserve the remaining blueberries.

In a heavy-bottomed saucepan, melt the butter over medium-low heat. When the butter foams, add the cornstarch-blueberry mixture and the lemon juice and cook, stirring occasionally, until the berries begin to burst and bubble and thicken, 5 to 7 minutes. Fold in the reserved blueberries and remove the mixture from the heat. Set it aside to cool slightly.

Assemble the hand pies: Preheat the oven to 425°F (220°C). Line two baking sheets with Silpat mats or parchment paper. Let the dough rest at room temperature for 5 minutes.

Lightly dust your work surface with glutinous rice flour and knead the dough until it is very uniform and smooth, eight turns. Roll the dough to a thickness of ⅛ inch (3 mm). Using a 4½-inch (11-cm) round biscuit cutter, cut out circles of dough. Form any scraps of dough into a disk and roll it out again. Continue to cut out rounds until all the dough has been used. You should have 24 rounds.

Place a slice of cream cheese on one half of each round and top it with a heaping tablespoon of the blueberry filling, making sure to leave a border of dough around the filling. Wet the dough border and fold over the unfilled side to form a half-moon. Using the tines of a fork, seal the open edge. Repeat until all of the turnovers are filled and sealed. Place them on the prepared sheets 1 inch (2.5 cm) apart.

In a small bowl, whisk together the milk and vanilla. Using a pastry brush, glaze the top of each turnover with the milk mixture and sprinkle it with a bit of granulated or sanding sugar.

Bake the turnovers for 15 to 20 minutes, until they are golden and the sugar is sparkling. Let cool for 20 minutes before serving so the filling doesn't burn your tongue.

They will keep in an airtight container at room temperature for 3 to 4 days.

VARIATION: Blueberry Pie

Prepare the dough and filling as directed above. Divide the chilled dough in half and roll each piece out to circle ⅛ inch (3 mm) thick and 14 inches (35.5 cm) in diameter. Fit one round of dough into a 9 inch (23 cm) pie plate, trimming any excess to 1 inch (2.5 cm). Freeze the unbaked bottom crust for 10 minutes. Meanwhile, allow the cream cheese to soften and then mash it up with a spoon, so it's creamy. Spread the cream cheese over the bottom of the frozen dough, then pour the blueberry filling over the cream cheese. Wet the edge of the dough and set the remaining round of dough on top. Decoratively crimp the edges or seal them with the tines of a fork. Brush the top crust with the milk mixture, then dust it with either granulated or sanding sugar. Cut decorative slits in the top to let steam escape. Bake the pie for 20 to 25 minutes, until the crust is golden and the filling has started to bubble through the vents in the crust. Let it cool for at least 1 hour so the filling can set before serving it.

CELERY, CHICKEN & LEEK QUICHE WITH SUN-DRIED TOMATO SAUCE

FOR THE CRUST:

1 recipe Short Crust (page 86)

Glutinous rice flour (or additional Pie & Pasta Blend, page 83), for dusting

1 large egg

1 teaspoon kosher salt

FOR THE FILLING:

2 tablespoons unsalted butter

1 cup (155 g) ground chicken

½ teaspoon kosher salt

¼ teaspoon freshly ground black pepper

¼ teaspoon ground allspice

1 large leek, cleaned and cut into very thin 1½-inch (4-cm) strips

2 stalks celery, strings pulled, quartered, and thinly sliced

½ cup (80 g) coarsely chopped white onion

1 cup (240 ml) whole milk

4 large eggs

Heaping ¼ teaspoon freshly grated nutmeg

1 cup (120 g) grated Swiss cheese

½ cup (50 g) finely grated Parmesan

The quiche of my youth is ready for a comeback—or maybe more like a graduation day. This savory custard is what I like to call the perfect "seasonal transition dish," and it's known as my fall quiche. I adore how the sun-dried tomatoes echo the flavors of summer, while the leeks announce that it's already October. Emmental and Gruyère are both great, but good old American Swiss-type cheese does the job, too, and when served with a farm-fresh salad or roasted root vegetables, you have a very fine meal on your hands.

You can, of course, fill the quiche with anything you like. Remember, if you slip some bacon in with the onion and green vegetables, then voilà—you've pretty much made the grande dame of the quiche world, la Quiche Lorraine.

SERVES 6

Make the crust: Preheat the oven to 425°F (220°C). Place a 9-inch (36-mm) scalloped tart pan, with a removable bottom and 2-inch sides, on a jelly-roll sheet pan and set aside. Let the dough rest at room temperature for 5 minutes.

Lightly dust your work surface with glutinous rice flour and knead the dough until it is very uniform and smooth, about eight turns. Shape the dough into a disk and roll it out into a roughly 12-inch (30-cm) round, no thinner than ⅛ inch (3 mm).

Gently fold the round in half and transfer it to the tart pan. Unfold it into the tart pan, gently pressing the dough into the crease and then into the sides; you should have at least a ½-inch (12-mm) overhang of dough. Roll your rolling pin over the top of the pan to trim off the excess dough. With a knife, lightly score the top edge of the dough. Line the dough with parchment paper and fill it with pie weights (see note).

Bake the crust for 15 minutes. While the crust is still warm, remove the pie weights and parchment paper. Set the crust aside to cool; leave the oven on.

In a small bowl, beat the egg and salt with 1 teaspoon water. Using a pastry brush, coat the bottom and sides of the cooled crust with this egg wash. Return it to the oven and bake for 10 minutes more. (This seals the crust, so it doesn't get soggy when you add the filling.) Allow the sealed crust to cool. Reduce the oven heat to 350°F (175°C).

Make the filling: In a skillet, melt 1 tablespoon of the butter over medium heat. When it foams, add the chicken and season it with the salt, pepper, and allspice. Cook until the chicken is browned, then, using a slotted spoon, remove it from the pan and set it aside. Leave any juices in the pan and simmer them until they have reduced to no more than 1 tablespoon.

Add the remaining 1 tablespoon butter; when it foams, add the leeks, celery, and onion. Cook until the vegetables are tender, 10 to 15 minutes.

In a medium bowl, whisk together the milk, eggs, and nutmeg. Stir in the Swiss cheese.

Set the blind-baked quiche shell back on the baking sheet. Line the bottom of the shell with the browned chicken. Top it with the celery, leek, and onion. Pour the egg mixture over top and dust the surface with the Parmesan cheese.

Bake the quiche for 35 to 45 minutes, until the filling puffs slightly in the middle, the Parmesan has gotten a tan, and the crust has contracted away from the tart pan.

As the quiche bakes, make the sauce: In a skillet, melt the butter. When it foams, whisk in the sun-dried tomato paste. Set it aside.

Place the cornstarch in a small bowl and whisk in 2 tablespoons of the stock. Place the remaining chicken stock in a small saucepan and bring it to a simmer over medium-low heat. As it starts to simmer, turn off the heat and stir in the cornstarch slurry. While whisking, pour the hot stock mixture into the tomato paste. Whisk it vigorously to combine, then return it to the pan. Simmer the sauce over medium-low heat, stirring occasionally, until it has thickened, about 7 minutes. Taste and season with salt and pepper as needed.

Serve the quiche warm, with a generous dollop of the sauce on or beside each slice.

The quiche and sauce will both keep, stored in separate airtight containers, in the refrigerator for up to 1 week.

FOR THE SAUCE:

1 tablespoon unsalted butter

3 tablespoons sun-dried tomato paste

1 tablespoon cornstarch

⅓ cup (75 ml) chicken stock

Kosher salt and freshly ground black pepper

NOTE: For the most uniform tart or pie crust, one that isn't scarred with unsightly pockmarks and dimples, I recommend using a combination of rice, lentils, and quinoa or millet as your pie weights.

CREAMY ALMOND DANISH

Glutinous rice flour (or additional Pie & Pasta Blend, page 83), for dusting

1 recipe Short Crust (page 86), chilled overnight

1 recipe Choux Paste (page 51), with 2 teaspoons almond extract added to the eggs, chilled overnight

FOR THE QUICK VANILLA GLAZE:

1½ cups (150 g) confectioners' sugar, preferably Imperial brand

2 tablespoons unsalted butter, at room temperature

2 to 3 tablespoons whole milk

1½ teaspoons pure vanilla extract

1 cup (240 ml) sliced almonds, toasted (see Note)

NOTE: I've found that for perfectly toasted nuts, it's best to just follow your nose. They are done the moment you can smell them.

Not even the Danes make Danish like the French do. One of their secrets, which I snagged while I was cooking at A l'Ombre du Château, was a double-dough approach to this breakfast classic—a short crust on the bottom to support a cream puff–type pastry on top. This layering proved the key to the gluten-free rescue of a lost breakfast treat of my childhood, complete with a sweet vanilla glaze. My mom's Danish lives!

SERVE 4 TO 6

Preheat the oven to 425°F (220°C). Set an oven rack in the middle position. Let the dough rest at room temperature for 5 minutes.

Lightly dust your work surface with glutinous rice flour. Knead the dough with the heel of your hand until it is very uniform and smooth, eight turns. Shape the dough into rectangles. Roll out the dough to ⅛ inch (3 mm) thick, maintaining the rectangular shape. Trim each piece to a 4-by-12-inch (10-by-30-cm) rectangle. Transfer the pieces to an unlined baking sheet.

Spread the choux paste evenly over the rectangles. Bake them for 20 to 25 minutes, until the layered doughs are puffed and golden. Transfer them to a wire rack to cool.

Meanwhile, make the glaze: Sift the confectioners' sugar into the bowl of a stand mixer fitted with the paddle attachment. With the mixer on high speed, work the butter into the sugar until it resembles damp talcum powder and you can no longer see any yellow clumps of butter. Add the milk and vanilla and beat them on high until they are smooth. I've noticed that there are many different kinds of confectioners' sugar with varying ratios of cornstarch, so you may need to add a bit more milk depending on the brand. The glaze is ready when a thick, fluid ribbon falls off the end of the paddle.

Assemble the Danishes: Drizzle half the glaze over each rectangle (this is easiest to do with a fork, or a squeeze bottle, if you have one) and scatter the toasted almonds over the glaze.

Serve the Danishes warm, sliced into rectangles or triangles, as you prefer.

The Danishes keep beautifully in an airtight container at room temperature for up to 2 days.

CHESS PIE

Glutinous rice flour (or additional Pie & Pasta Blend, page 83), for dusting

1 recipe Short Crust (page 86), chilled overnight

½ cup (1 stick / 113 g) butter, melted and cooled

2 cups (400 g) sugar

4 large eggs

2 tablespoons Pie & Pasta Blend (page 83)

2 teaspoons pure vanilla extract

¼ teaspoon freshly grated nutmeg

Food historians haven't been able to agree on why exactly chess pie is called "chess" pie. Is it a Southern slurring of the word *chest*, for the pie chests in which pastries were often stored? Or is it an archaic spelling of cheese? The origins of this simple dessert's name may be unclear, but the pie itself is easy to puzzle out—just a single crust with a sweet, rich filling of butter, sugar, and eggs.

MAKES ONE 9-INCH (23-CM) PIE

Preheat the oven to at 350°F (175°C). Let the dough rest at room temperature for 5 minutes.

Dust your work surface with glutinous rice flour and knead the dough with the heel of your hand until it is very uniform and smooth, eight turns. Roll out the dough into a roughly 12-inch (30-cm) round large enough to fit a 9-inch (23-cm) pie pan. Gently fold the dough in half and transfer it to the pie pan, then unfold and gently press the dough into the pan. Trim and crimp or decorate the edges as desired.

In a large bowl, whisk together the butter, sugar, eggs, Pie & Pasta Blend, vanilla, and nutmeg. Whisk until the mixture is good and smooth.

Pour the filling into the pie crust and bake it for 35 to 40 minutes. The pie is done when the filling is golden and firm to the touch.

SWEET POTATO PIE

The ancient Greeks were really the first to layer flaky pastry dough with spicy meats, as they quickly discovered that the pastry helped preserve the meats baked inside. But the advent of sweet pies is still a bit of a hazy memory in the American consciousness. All the records can tell us with absolute certainty is that sweet pies are a (relatively) recent obsession. According to Lettice Bryan's book *The Kentucky Housewife*, published in 1839, the sweet potato pie is one of the first sweet pies to capture the fancy of Americans, but no one really knows for certain. There just isn't enough documentation to prove it.

No matter where this pie came from, I know I'm grateful for its creation, and intuition tells me that the sweetness of the potatoes led a particular chef to assume that it would be delicious when folded together with eggs, cinnamon, and allspice and poured into a flaky pie crust. My take mixes ancient culinary tradition with gluten-free modernity, with a marshmallow-y meringue on top.

MAKES ONE 9-INCH (23-CM) PIE

Preheat the oven to 350°F (175°C). Let the dough rest at room temperature for 5 minutes.

Dust your work surface with glutinous rice flour and knead the dough with the heel of your hand until it is very uniform and smooth, eight turns. Roll out the dough into a roughly 12-inch (30-cm) round large enough to fit a 9-inch (23-cm) pie pan. Gently fold the dough in half and transfer it to the pie pan, then unfold and gently press the dough into the pan. Trim and crimp or decorate the edges as desired.

Make the filling: In a large bowl, combine the sweet potato, milk, sugar, eggs, butter, Pie & Pasta Blend, cinnamon, allspice, and salt. Whisk until they are well combined and very smooth, then pour the filling into the prepared pie crust. Bake the pie for 40 to 45 minutes, until the filling is firm to the touch but still jiggles slightly in the center. Remove it to a wire rack to cool slightly.

Meanwhile, make the meringue: In a saucepan, combine the sugar and ¼ cup (60 ml) water. Clip a candy thermometer to the side of the pan and warm it over medium heat until the sugar has dissolved. Use a wet pastry brush to remove any sugar from the sides of the pan. Cook until the syrup reaches soft-ball stage, or 239°F (115°C). Remove the pan from the heat.

CONTINUED

1 recipe Short Crust (page 86), chilled overnight

Glutinous rice flour (or additional Pie & Pasta Blend, page 83), for dusting

FOR THE FILLING:

1½ cups (340 g) canned organic or mashed cooked sweet potato

1 cup (240 ml) whole milk

¾ cup (150 g) sugar

4 large eggs

2 tablespoons unsalted butter, melted

2 tablespoons Pie & Pasta Blend (page 83)

1 teaspoon ground cinnamon

1 teaspoon ground allspice

½ teaspoon kosher salt

FOR THE MERINGUE:

½ cup (100 g) sugar

2 large egg whites, room temperature

Pinch of cream of tartar

In the bowl of a stand mixer fitted with the whisk attachment, combine the egg whites and cream of tartar and whisk them on high speed until soft peaks form. With the mixer running, slowly pour the hot syrup into the egg whites in a thin steady stream, doing your best to keep the stream between the beater and the edge of the bowl to prevent the hot sugar from skipping out of the bowl. Continue whisking nonstop until the meringue is very thick and the bowl is cool to the touch, 7 to 10 minutes.

Assemble the pie: Preheat the broiler on high or preheat the oven to its highest setting.

Pile the meringue onto the pie. Place the pie under the broiler or in the super-hot oven just long enough for the meringue to brown, literally just a few seconds. If you have a kitchen torch, lightly toast the crests of the meringue waves for the same effect.

FARMSTEAD APPLE SLAB PIE

Spanning the full surface of a baking sheet, slab pies are a great way to feed a hungry crowd. The first time I ate this pie was in Dallas, Texas, at the state fair in the mid-eighties. It was so homey and delicious; the memory of eating it never left me, so I re-created it here, in gluten-free form. After studying baking for the last decade, however, it actually reminds me of a rustic French apple tart, Americanized by replacing the flower-petal apples on top with another layer of tart crust and finishing with a simple apple-infused glaze.

MAKES ONE 18-BY-13½-INCH (46-BY-34-CM) PIE; SERVES 18 FARMHANDS

Make the filling: In a large bowl, whisk together the granulated sugar, brown sugar, cornstarch, cinnamon, and salt. Add the apples and toss to coat them in the mixture.

In a large saucepan, heat 4 tablespoons of the butter. When it foams, add the apple mixture and 2 tablespoons of the lemon juice. Cook until the apples are tender, about 15 minutes. Set aside to cool.

Assemble the pie: Preheat the oven to 350°F (175°C). Let the dough rest at room temperature for 5 minutes.

Divide the dough in half. Rewrap one half of the dough and return it to the fridge. Lightly dust your work surface with glutinous rice flour and knead the dough with the heel of your hand until it is very uniform and smooth, ten turns. Roll out the dough into a 20-by-16-inch (50-by-40.5-cm) rectangle. Gently fold the dough into thirds and transfer it to an 18-by-13.5-inch (46-by-34-cm) jelly-roll pan or a large, shallow baking dish. Unfold the dough and fit it into the pan, then brush it with 2 tablespoons of the remaining melted butter. Place the pan in the freezer. Roll out the remaining dough as you did the first section.

Remove the pan from the freezer and fill it with the apple mixture. Drape the second piece of dough over the apples. Trim the overhanging edge of the dough and tuck it between the apples and the pan, pressing the edge with a fork to crimp them. Cut slits in the top to vent steam.

Bake the pie for 1 hour, or until the crust is golden brown. Allow it to cool completely, at least 1 hour.

Meanwhile, cook the apple juice in a small saucepan over medium heat until it has reduced to ¼ cup (60 ml). Add the remaining 2 tablespoons melted butter, a few pinches of salt, and the last tablespoon of lemon juice. Whisk until it is smooth. Sift the confectioners' sugar and then whisk it into the warm apple juice mixture. Pour the glaze over the cooled pie and smooth it with a spoon or spatula, so it covers the pie evenly.

Let the glaze set and then slice and serve the pie.

FOR THE FILLING:

1 cup (200 g) granulated sugar

½ cup (110 g) packed light brown sugar

¼ cup (28 g) cornstarch

2¼ teaspoons ground cinnamon

¼ teaspoon kosher salt, plus more as needed

8 Granny Smith apples, peeled and diced

8 Golden Delicious apples, peeled and diced

½ cup (1 stick / 113 g) salted butter, melted

3 tablespoons (45 ml) fresh lemon juice

¾ cup (180 ml) apple juice

1½ cups (150 g) confectioners' sugar

2 recipes Short Crust (page 86), chilled overnight

Glutinous rice flour (or additional Pie & Pasta Blend, page 83), for dusting

NOTE: The pie keeps beautifully, covered, in the refrigerator for up to 1 week, or lightly wrapped and stored in a cool part of the kitchen or in a pie safe for up to 3 days.

BANANA CREAM PIE

Not only is banana cream pie delicious, the pastry cream filling is perfect for piping into cream puffs (page 76) and donuts (page 74) and for serving with vanilla wafers (page 144) for another American classic, banana pudding. My dad was a coconut cream pie fanatic, so I included the variation for that here, too. Can you tell I'm all about killing two (or three!) birds with one stone?

MAKES ONE 9-INCH (23-CM) PIE

Preheat the oven to 425°F (220°C). Let the dough rest at room temperature for 5 minutes.

Dust your work surface with glutinous rice flour and knead the dough with the heel of your hand until it is very uniform and smooth, eight turns. Roll out the dough into a roughly 12-inch (30-cm) round large enough to fit a 9-inch (23-cm) pie pan. Gently fold the dough in half and transfer it to the pie pan, then unfold and gently press the dough into the pan. Trim and crimp or decorate the edges as desired.

Line the dough with parchment paper and fill it with pie weights (see page 97). Blind bake the crust for 15 minutes. While the crust is still warm, remove the pie weights and parchment paper. Bake the crust for 7 to 8 minutes more, until it is a pale golden brown. Remove it to a wire rack to cool slightly.

Make the pastry cream: In a large bowl, whisk together the granulated sugar and cornstarch until they are smooth and free of lumps. Add the eggs and egg yolks and whisk until an unbroken ribbon falls from the whisk.

In a saucepan, heat the heavy cream and half-and-half over low heat until it steams. While whisking, very slowly and gradually pour the hot milk into the egg mixture. Pour the milk-egg mixture back into the pot. Set the pan over medium heat and cook, whisking nonstop, until you have a very thick custard. (Be careful not to let the custard boil, as you'll wind up with milky, sweet scrambled eggs.) Whisk in the butter and vanilla.

Assemble the pie: Peel and slice the bananas into rounds. Spread one-third of the custard on the bottom of the pie crust. Follow with a layer of bananas. Add another one-third of the custard, another layer of bananas, and top with a final layer of custard. Refrigerate the pie, covered, for at least 4 hours so the custard can set.

CONTINUED

Glutinous rice flour (or additional Pie & Pasta Blend, page 83), for dusting

1 recipe Short Crust (page 86), chilled overnight

FOR THE PASTRY CREAM:

1 cup (200 g) granulated sugar

¼ cup (35 g) cornstarch

3 large eggs

6 large egg yolks

2 cups (480 ml) heavy cream

1 cup (240 ml) half-and-half

3 tablespoons unsalted butter, at room temperature

1¼ teaspoons pure vanilla extract

3 ripe bananas

1 cup (240 ml) heavy cream

3 tablespoons confectioners' sugar, sifted

In the bowl of a stand mixer fitted with the whisk attachment, or in a bowl using a hand mixer, whip the cream with the confectioners' sugar until it holds firm peaks. Mound the whipped cream on top of the pie or transfer the whipped cream to a piping bag fitted with a 1-inch (3-cm) star tip and pipe it into florets on top of the pie. Slice the pie into wedges and serve.

The pie will keep, covered, in the refrigerator for up to 3 days.

VARIATION: Coconut Cream Pie

Forget the bananas—add ¼ teaspoon almond extract when you add the vanilla and then fold ¾ cup (125 g) shredded sweetened coconut into the custard. Fill the pie with the coconut custard, refrigerate it, and top it with the whipped cream. Optional décor: Reserve a bit of the coconut, toast it in a hot oven for just 5 minutes, and strew it over the whipped cream.

BREAD CRUMB SOUP

My grandmother grew up very poor during the Great Depression. This is a soup she and her family survived on many a cold winter by drying out the heels of their leftover bread on their wood-burning stoves. Don't let the provenance scare you off, though, because this soup is incredibly delicious, and even though our economic health is slightly more robust, I still applaud a chef who has little to no waste. I recommend using homemade stock and bread for the best results.

SERVES 6

In a food processor fitted with the S-blade, pulse the bread crumbs with the Parmesan until a very fine powder forms. Transfer the ingredients to the bowl of a stand mixer fitted with the paddle attachment. Add the Pie & Pasta Blend, shortening, pepper, guar gum, and salt and mix them on the lowest speed until you can no longer see the shortening. Add the eggs and lemon juice. Mix them on high until the dough folds in on itself and is clinging to the paddle.

Cover the bottom of a roasting pan with a few tablespoons of glutinous rice flour.

Attach the meat grinder attachment to your stand mixer. Place the roasting pan beneath the grinder. Force the dough, ½ cup (70 g) at a time, through the meat grinder. Cut the dough every 1 inch (2.5 cm) into your prepared pan. Toss the noodles to coat them in the glutinous rice flour. Repeat until all the dough has been used. You can also press the dough through the holes of an aluminum colander if you don't have a meat grinder.

In a large saucepan, bring the stock to a rolling boil. Toss in the noodles and cook them until they float, then boil them for 2 minutes more.

Ladle the soup into individual bowls and serve it with additional Parmesan and fresh parsley.

The soup will keep in an airtight container in the fridge for up to 3 days. Reheat it in a small saucepan over low heat. The noodles can be made the day before and refrigerated, or can be frozen, double wrapped, for up to 1 month.

2 cups (200 g) gluten-free bread crumbs, dried out on a warm stove (from about 1 loaf; see sidebar, page 197)

1 cup (100 g) finely grated Parmesan, plus more for serving

¼ cup (16 g) Pie & Pasta Blend (page 83)

¼ cup (56 g) vegetable shortening

½ teaspoon freshly ground black pepper

¼ teaspoon guar gum

¼ teaspoon fine sea salt

3 large eggs

Juice of 1 lemon

Glutinous rice flour, for dusting

6 cups (1.4 L) chicken stock

Chopped fresh parsley, for serving

SPECIAL EQUIPMENT:

Stand mixer with meat grinder attachment

CHICKEN & DUMPLINGS

FOR THE SOUP:

1 tablespoon pure olive oil

1 white onion, diced

3 stalks celery, diced

2 carrots, sliced into ¼-inch (6-mm) rounds

Pinch of kosher salt

4 cups (960 ml) chicken stock, preferably homemade

2 cups (280 g) shredded cooked chicken

8 sprigs fresh dill

FOR THE DOUGH:

2 cups (272 g) Pie & Pasta Blend (page 83)

1 tablespoon millet flour

1½ teaspoons baking powder

1 teaspoon kosher salt

¼ teaspoon freshly ground black pepper

½ teaspoon dried parsley (optional)

½ teaspoon dried dill (optional)

2 large eggs

¼ cup (60 ml) milk

¼ cup (60 ml) plain seltzer water, at room temperature

Glutinous rice flour (or additional Pie & Pasta Blend, page 83), for dusting

Made in vast quantities, my mom's stick-to-your-ribs chicken and dumplings fed our large family well. Too bad what that carb-load was actually doing was fueling the internal combustion phase of celiac inflammation for me. Light as air, these gluten-free dumplings are just as satisfying—and do double-duty as matzo balls. You will notice that I've added a smidge of millet flour here for enhanced flavor and texture.

MAKES TWENTY-FOUR 2-INCH (5-CM) DUMPLINGS

Make the soup: In a heavy stockpot, heat the oil over medium heat. Add the onion, celery, carrots, and salt and sauté until the onions are translucent and the carrots are tender. Add the stock and dill and bring everything to a simmer.

Meanwhile, make the dough: In a large bowl, whisk together the Pie & Pasta Blend, millet flour, baking powder, salt, pepper, and parsley and dill (if using).

In a separate bowl, whisk together the milk and eggs.

Add the egg mixture to the dry mixture, stirring vigorously with a wooden spoon to combine them. Fold in the seltzer. The dough should be thick enough that it sits up on a spoon, holding its shape.

Lightly dust your work surface and the dough with glutinous rice flour. Working by hand, form the dough into two ropes, about 24 inches (61 cm) long and ½ inch (12 mm) thick. Cut the ropes into 1-inch (2.5-cm) pieces. Set the pieces atop the simmering chicken-vegetable stew, leaving about ½ inch (12 mm) between each. Keep the stew at a low simmer and cover it loosely, with the lid on at an angle to trap heat but let most of the steam escape, until the dumplings double to triple in size. Season the stew with salt and pepper as needed. Stir in the shredded chicken.

Serve it hot, as a hearty one-dish meal. The chicken and dumplings will keep, in the same container, in the fridge for up to 3 days.

VARIATION: Hearty Chicken Noodle Soup
Increase the broth in the soup to 6 cups (1.4 L). Forget the dumplings and cook up 8 ounces (225 g) gluten-free pasta (in your preferred shape) and add that instead.

VARIATION: Matzo Ball Soup
Increase the millet flour in the dumpling ingredients to 3 tablespoons. This gives the dough a heavier consistency and makes a firmer dumpling. Add more broth if you want a less stewy soup.

CHILI-PORK EMPANADAS

Empanadas are a savory hand pie made, in various iterations, in many Latin American countries, as well as Texas. (Texas really is a whole other country!) These gluten-free hand pies function perfectly as a casual entrée, a quick lunch, or made in a smaller size, the perfect party food.

MAKES 12 SNACK-SIZE EMPANADAS

Make the filling: In a large bowl, knead the meat, chiles, paprika, salt, cumin, oregano, cayenne, and pepper together until they are well combined.

Heat the oil in a large skillet over medium heat. Sauté the onions with a pinch of salt, until they are translucent. Add the pork mixture and cook it for 10 to 12 minutes, stirring occasionally, until the juices run clear. Remove it from the heat and stir in the olives, raisins, tomato paste, and hard-boiled egg (if using).

Assemble the empanadas: Preheat the oven to 425°F (220°C). Line two baking sheets with parchment paper or Silpat mats. Let the dough rest at room temperature for 5 minutes.

Dust your work surface with glutinous rice flour. Knead the dough with the heel of your hand until it is very uniform and smooth, six to eight turns. Roll out the dough into a 24-inch (61-cm) square. Cut the sheet of dough into 5-inch (12-cm) rounds. Gather up the scraps into a ball, roll out the dough, and cut out more rounds. Repeat until you have cut out as many rounds as you can.

Place the dough rounds on the lined baking sheets. Fill each round with the pork mixture, keeping the filling on one half of the round. Wet the edges of the dough and then fold the unfilled side over into a half-moon. Crimp the edges with a fork to seal. Whisk the egg with 1 teaspoon water to form an egg wash. Brush the tops of the empanadas with the egg wash.

Bake the empanadas for 20 to 25 minutes, until they are golden brown and shiny.

The empanadas will keep in an airtight container in the refrigerator for up to 3 days, or in sealed zip-top bags in the freezer for a few weeks. Reheat the empanadas, wrapped in foil, in a 350°F (175°C) oven for 10 to 15 minutes.

FOR THE FILLING:

1 pound (455 g) ground pork or beef

1 (4.5-oz / 130-g) can diced green chiles

1½ teaspoons paprika

1 teaspoon kosher salt, plus more as needed

½ teaspoon ground cumin

½ teaspoon dried oregano

½ teaspoon cayenne

½ teaspoon freshly ground black pepper

1 tablespoon peanut oil

½ medium white onion, minced

1 (4.5-oz / 130-g) can black olives, drained and minced

¼ cup (35 g) seedless golden or black raisins

¼ cup (60 g) tomato paste

1 hard-boiled egg, minced (optional)

1 recipe Short Crust (page 86), chilled overnight

Glutinous rice flour (or additional Pie & Pasta Blend, page 83), for dusting

1 large egg

THREE-CHEESE RAVIOLI WITH OVEN-ROASTED GRAPE-TOMATO SAUCE

FOR THE OVEN-ROASTED GRAPE-TOMATO SAUCE:

1 large white onion, diced

3 cups (450 g) grape tomatoes or cherry tomatoes, halved

2 cups (300 g) seedless red grapes

2 tablespoons olive oil

1 teaspoon kosher salt, plus more as needed

Freshly cracked black pepper

2 cloves garlic, crushed

1 (28-oz / 785-g) can diced tomatoes with basil

1 bay leaf

FOR THE RAVIOLI FILLING:

1 pound (455 g) whole-milk ricotta

1¼ cups (150 g) grated mozzarella

1 cup (100 g) grated Asiago or Parmesan

2 tablespoons chopped fresh curly parsley (optional)

1 large egg, whisked

¼ teaspoon kosher salt

¼ teaspoon freshly ground black pepper

FOR THE PASTA:

2 cups plus 2 tablespoons (258 g) Pie & Pasta Blend (page 83)

¾ teaspoon kosher salt, plus extra for cooking

2 large eggs

2 tablespoons pure olive oil

Glutinous rice flour (or additional Pie & Pasta Blend, page 83), for dusting

This is an heirloom recipe from my grandmother, whose ravioli were just *the* best, hands down. This egg pasta figures in all the homemade pastas in this book, so it's your go-to for homemade gluten-free linguini, spaghetti, pierogies, ciccatelli, or whatever pasta is your favorite. (Grandma used this same cheese filling in her lasagna when she didn't feel like making a béchamel sauce.)

You can sub in Parmesan for the Asiago in the filling, but Asiago's a bit tangier. The recipe yields 6 to 7 cups (1.4 to 1.7 L) Grape-Tomato Sauce. This sauce is all my own, and it beguiles all who try it. Most red sauces have processed sugar added to balance out the acids from the onions and tomatoes, but in this case, I went all natural and used the sweetness of red seedless grapes, slow roasted to carmelized perfection with the tomatoes and onions.

MAKES 48 RAVIOLI; SERVES 6

Make the sauce: Preheat the oven to 350°F (175°C).

In a large Dutch oven or roasting pan, combine the onion, tomatoes, and grapes and toss them with the oil, salt, and pepper. Roast them for 30 minutes. Add the diced tomatoes, 1 cup (240 ml) water (or vinho verde), and the bay leaf and roast them until everything has caramelized, the tomatoes have deflated, and the grapes have burst, about 2 hours more.

Remove the bay leaf and season the mixture with salt and pepper to taste.

For a chunky sauce, use an immersion blender to coarsely puree the sauce. If you want a smooth sauce, pass the sauce through a food mill with the fine screen attached, or puree the sauce in a blender and pass the puree through a sieve into a bowl. Transfer the sauce to a saucepan and keep it warm.

Make the filling: In a large bowl, combine the ricotta, mozzarella, Asiago, parsley (if using), egg, salt, and pepper. Stir them well with a wooden spoon to combine. The filling should be thick, like a lumpy pudding. Set it aside.

Make the pasta: In the bowl of a stand mixer fitted with the paddle attachment, or in a food processor fitted with the S-blade, combine the Pie & Pasta Blend and salt. Mix or pulse just to combine them.

In a medium bowl, whisk together the eggs, oil, and ⅓ cup (75 ml) water. Add the egg mixture to the dry ingredients and beat them on low for 30 seconds, then beat them on medium-high until the dough is thick and folds into a smooth ball. (In a food processor, just pulse at first, and then process steadily until the dough forms a ball.) If the dough is sticky,

CONTINUED

add additional Pie & Pasta Blend or glutinous rice flour, in tablespoon increments, until the dough folds in on itself and is no longer sticky. Knead the dough with your hands a few times in the bowl.

Lightly dust your work surface with glutinous rice flour. Turn out the dough and shape it into a rectangle. Cut the rectangle into quarters. Working with one piece of dough at a time (keep the other pieces covered until ready to use, so they don't dry out), roll the dough into ½-inch- (12-mm-) thick sheets. If you have a pasta machine, pass each sheet of dough through on the widest setting, then pass it through again on progressively thinner settings until you reach the desired thickness. I usually stop at 4 or 5. If you don't have a pasta machine, just roll the dough out to just under 1/16 inch (2 mm) thick.

Assemble the ravioli: Bring a pot of heavily salted water (use at least a couple of tablespoons of salt) to a boil.

Place one sheet of dough flat on your work surface. At even intervals, dot the dough with 1½-teaspoon-size dollops of the filling. You should get 12 ravioli per sheet. Wet the edge of the dough with water and then top it with a second sheet of dough. Press gently around the filling to seal the ravioli, then, using a pizza cutter, ravioli cutter, or a knife, cut out the raviolis. Repeat until you run out of pasta or filling; they should come out close to even. At this point, the uncooked ravioli can be stored in the refrigerator for up to 3 days until they are ready to use. Alternatively, they can be frozen in a single layer on a baking sheet and then transferred to a flat, airtight container and frozen for up to 3 months.

To cook them, working in batches, gently drop the ravioli into the boiling water. They will float to the surface after a minute or two; cook them for 2 minutes more after this point. Remove the ravioli with a slotted spoon to serving bowls or a platter. Repeat until all the ravioli are cooked.

Serve them with the grape-tomato sauce or another sauce of your choice.

VARIATION: Nonna's Ciccatelli

This hand-rolled pasta was my grandmother's favorite, and she would make it by the truckload.

Start with the dough for the ravioli, skipping the filling. Knead the dough until it is feels like the soft skin of your cheek. Pinch off ½-teaspoon-size pieces with your fingertips and press them into your kneading surface, drawing your fingers toward yourself as you press. The scalloped, flattened pieces of dough will look like a wrinkly mess, but these wrinkles hold all your favorite sauces beautifully.

Boil the ciccatelli as you would the ravioli, but allow the pasta to boil for just 1 minute once it floats in the water. Toss the ciccatelli with butter or olive oil and eat them with any pasta sauce, or just with a grating of cheese. My Nonna would spoon some of the pasta water onto the counter with a pinch of kosher salt and then drag the pasta through it so I could taste the pasta for doneness. This is a ritual I still fondly practice with my son.

PASTA & MEATBALLS

Once you've gone gluten-free, this standby, at first, might seem totally out of reach. The double-dose of gluten-laden pasta and bread crumb–bound meatballs usually spells trouble. Luckily, you can use the Pie & Pasta blend to make delicious gluten-free noodles, while my Bread & Pizza blend provides the fresh bread crumbs from one of my Pullman loaves (page 195) or French Boule (page 206) for the meatballs, so there's no reason to fear this classic.

MAKES 18 MEATBALLS; SERVES 6

Make the meatballs: In a large bowl, combine the pork, veal, bread crumbs, egg, Parmesan, parsley, thyme, kosher salt, garlic salt, onion powder, and pepper and mix them well. Use your hands to combine them, but do not overwork the mixture, or the meatballs will be tough. Scoop out 1 tablespoon-size portions of the meat mixture and roll them into balls.

In a large heavy-bottomed skillet, heat 2 tablespoons of the oil over medium-high heat. Fry the meatballs until they are crispy and browned on all sides, 2 to 3 minutes per side. Remove the pan from the heat.

Meanwhile, place half of the tomato sauce in a large saucepan and bring it to a boil, then reduce the heat to maintain a simmer and add the meatballs. Cook them for 10 minutes more. Season the sauce with salt and pepper. Place the remaining sauce in a separate pan and gently reheat it.

Bring a large pot of heavily salted water to a boil. Add the pasta and cook until it is al dente, 5 to 7 minutes for fresh pasta (follow the directions on the package for cooking dry pasta). Drain it immediately if you're using fresh pasta; if you're using dry pasta, keep it in the water it was cooked in, off the heat, for 5 minutes.

Toss the pasta with the plain tomato sauce. Plate the pasta in individual shallow bowls or pasta plates. Spoon a few meatballs over each portion and dust the tops with grated Parmesan and parsley.

The meatballs, in the sauce, will keep in a sealed container in the refrigerator for up to 1 week.

FOR THE MEATBALLS:

8 ounces (227 g) ground pork

8 ounces (227 g) ground veal

½ cup (50 g) fresh finely ground gluten-free bread crumbs, from a Pullman loaf (page 195) or French Boule (page 206), or store-bought

1 large egg

⅓ cup (35 g) finely grated Parmesan, plus more for serving

1 tablespoon minced fresh parsley, plus more for serving

1 teaspoon chopped fresh thyme

½ teaspoon kosher salt

½ teaspoon garlic salt

½ teaspoon onion powder

½ teaspoon freshly cracked black pepper

¼ cup (60 ml) olive oil

1 recipe fresh pasta (page 86) or 1 pound (455 g) store-bought gluten-free pasta

1 recipe Oven-Roasted Grape-Tomato Sauce (page 114)

GNOCCHI

Oh, the gluten-free gnocchi. Seemingly easy to adapt—but not so much. That is, of course, until I got the Pie & Pasta Blend *just* right. The addition of the millet gives the gnocchi their trademark creamy flavor, but getting the gnocchi's texture nice and light absolutely requires the use of a potato ricer or food mill. If you don't have one and your gnocchi aren't as light as you'd hoped, you will know why. This technique adds a tremendous amount of air to the potatoes, whereas mashing the potatoes over-activates the starches, resulting in far denser gnocchi.

MAKES 150 GNOCCHI; SERVES 6 TO 8 AS AN ENTRÉE

Place the potatoes in a saucepan and add enough water to cover them. Bring them to a boil and cook until the potatoes are fork-tender, about 15 minutes. Drain them and then pass the potatoes through a food mill, ricer, or the holes of a coarse strainer into a bowl. Add the butter and mix until it is completely melted. Season the potatoes with salt. Pass through a ricer a second time.

In a medium bowl, whisk together the Pie & Pasta Blend, millet flour, ½ teaspoon salt, and the white pepper.

On a 9-by-13-inch (23-by-33-cm) baking sheet, scatter the mashed potatoes with a fork, spreading them out evenly. Mash in the milk, egg, and egg yolks. In tablespoon increments, sprinkle the dry ingredients over the potatoes and work them in with the fork. By the third addition, start kneading the dough by hand.

Dust your work surface with glutinous rice flour. Turn the dough out and knead it until it's smooth and not sticky. Divide the dough into 8 sections and then roll each section into ropes 24 inches (61 cm) long and ½ inch (12 mm) thick. Cut each rope into equal ½-inch (12-mm) segments, and then roll each segment into an oval. Roll each oval down your heirloom gnocchi roller, if you've got one, or down the back of the tines of a fork to give the surface a striated texture. (This will give the cooked gnocchi just the right consistency and trap the sauce.) Set the formed gnocchi on a tray or plate and refrigerate them, covered, for 2 hours.

Bring a large pot of heavily salted water to a boil. Using a slotted spoon or spider, carefully lower the chilled gnocchi into the water, working in batches, if necessary. Boil until the gnocchi float to the surface, then cook for 2 minutes more; they should be puffed up and tender.

Using a slotted spoon, transfer the cooked gnocchi to individual serving bowls and top them with the sauce of your choice. Here, I tossed them in butter to brown them and sprinkle a chiffonade of basil over the top for garnish.

2½ cups (300 g) diced peeled russet potatoes

3 tablespoons unsalted butter

Kosher salt

½ cup plus 1 tablespoon (70 g) Pie & Pasta Blend (page 83)

2 tablespoons millet flour

¼ teaspoon freshly ground white pepper

¼ cup (60 ml) whole milk

1 large egg

2 egg yolks

Glutinous rice flour (or additional Pie & Pasta Blend, page 83), for dusting

Pasta sauce of your choice, for serving

NOTE: You can make the gnocchi a day in advance, and store it in a covered container in the fridge until you're ready to cook. Freeze any uncooked gnocchi in an airtight container for up to three weeks.

COOKIE JAR BLEND

The Cookie Jar Blend was born and bred to celebrate our national fixation with cookies. I've experimented with literally thousands of variations of cookie recipes over the years to get this blend to where you can use it to make a mountain of cookies that have a multitude of textures. To keep the chapter accessible and light, rather than daunting, I made a point to create an arsenal of recipes that show you how to make any kind of cookie *perfect* and bundled them into their constituent groups. The chapter begins with drop cookies, with nearly all of the recipes in that group essentially a variation on the Ultimate Chocolate Chip Cookie (because let's face it, most drop cookies are a variation on a the same ingredients). In doing this, I will show you how to make minute adjustments to a flawless recipe so you can then take these suggestions and come up with or make adaptations of your own. The rolled-and-cut grouping of recipes is different because rolled-and-cut cookies vary more widely, so you will notice a change of pace in that batch. From there, we transition into hand-formed cookies and finish with bars. So wade right in, make a batch, and see the method to the madness.

THE RECIPE

2 cups plus 1 tablespoon plus 1 teaspoon (240 g) glutinous rice flour

1½ cups plus 1 tablespoon plus 1 teaspoon (174 g) tapioca starch

1 ¼ cups plus 2 teaspoons (156 g) cornstarch

1⅓ cups plus 1 teaspoon (150 g) sorghum flour

¼ cup plus 3 tablespoons (60 g) freshly ground gluten-free quick oats

4½ teaspoons (13.5 g) guar gum

The approximate weight of the blend, by volume (for use in doing your own adaptations):

EACH	OF BLEND WEIGHS APPROXIMATELY
1 tablespoon	6 g
¼ cup	27 g
⅓ cup	32 g
½ cup	54 g
⅔ cup	71 g
¾ cup	82 g
1 cup	108 g

The real trick of the Cookie Jar Blend was, again, getting the size of the foundation figured out so the amount of starches could be decided on. The addition of gluten-free oats here is primarily for flavor and texture, but their high level of protein helps provide structure, too. You will notice that the amount of fat used in gluten-free cookies is only one-quarter to one-third of the amount of fats used in traditional cookies. Egg yolks are used in place of butter, as is whole milk, for texture and flavor, but the main reason for this dramatic difference comes down to how starches and fats marry one another. In the absence of plant fibers, amino acids, and minerals, fats have a tendency to bleed through starches very easily because there is nothing for the butterfat to be absorbed into. Starches change the viscosity of liquids, but they do not create a tight covalent bond with butterfat. Thus, less fat is required in gluten-free baking and especially in gluten-free cookies.

After perfecting the Cookie Jar Blend, I found this low ratio of butter was essential to consistently manifesting both a tender, bendy cookie, and a crisp and crunchy one. I can't tell you how many sheets of cookies I pulled out of the oven where all of the ingredients melted all over the pan rather than emerging as perfectly round morsels of joy. So keep this in mind as you read and make the recipes.

You will also notice that the amount of extracts used in this chapter is double or triple that of traditional cookie recipes. This is necessary to balance the flavors of all the various flours. Each flour and starch imparts a specific flavor, so the more flours you use, the more extract you will need.

For more information on the individual flours, starches, and other ingredients in the blend, see the Pantry section on page 215.

MAKES 7½ CUPS (793.5 G), ENOUGH FOR 3 BATCHES OF COOKIES OR 108 COOKIES

Using the spoon-and-sweep method, measure each ingredient into a large bowl. Whisk together and then sift the mixture into a separate large bowl. Repeat several times.

THE DOUGH

COAT THE DRY INGREDIENTS WITH BUTTER

In traditional baking, most cookie recipes begin by having you creaming the butter and the sugars together. Next, the eggs are added, and finally, the flours go into the bowl. I've found that for the very best texture, you've got to evenly coat all of the ingredients with the butter before the liquids are added. Therefore, all of the dry ingredients are added to the bowl with the butter, and you mix this on low until the mixture resembles damp cornmeal. Next, the wet ingredients are added, and finally, the add-ins. It's counter to what you've always under-stood about making cookies, but I assure you, if you follow my instructions, you cannot fail.

After this reverse-engineered step, the basic rules for this blend are easy. Rest the dough, handle it lightly, and bake it uniformly. Do that, and you're all set. And more than any other blend in the book, the key to getting fabulous, melt-in-your-mouth results with the Cookie Jar Blend is patience—it might take 24 hours of dough chilling and 15 minutes in the oven to get to that perfect cookie, but the waiting will be worth it.

CHILL THIS BLEND OUT

Chilling cookie dough solidifies the fat in the dough and gives the flours and sugars in the dough time to uniformly absorb liquids. The solidified fat makes it easier to work with the dough, helps it keep its shape, and lessens the spread of the cookie as it bakes. For some Cookie Jar Blend doughs, refrigeration before forming and baking the cookies is essential. Scientists of traditional baking have proven that chilling is key so the sugars in the dough can absorb the mois-ture of the eggs for the ideal texture; in gluten-free baking, it goes double. Texture is all-important, and it's the refrigeration and rest that make the crucial

difference between a soft and supple cookie and a hard and dry one.

For drop cookies (such as Ultimate Chocolate Chip Cookie, page 126) or rolled-and-cut cookies (like the Gingerbread Persons, page 146), I recommend chilling the dough in a glass or ceramic bowl tightly covered with plastic wrap. The individual recipe will guide you on how long to chill the dough (for 3 hours, or 24 hours, or overnight, for example).

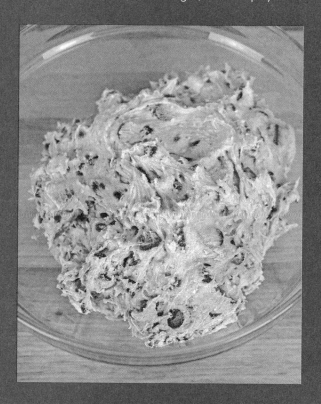

ROLLING

When rolling out Cookie Jar Blend dough, move quickly and avoid overworking the dough. Dough made with this blend tends to soften quickly (espe-cially the dough for the Sugar Cookies on page 129), so you don't want to handle or knead the dough

too much or work in too much flour as you roll it out. This will result in a denser, drier cookie (the kind that has given gluten-free cookies such an undeservedly bad rep).

To roll out Cookie Jar Blend dough, dust your work surface with some glutinous rice flour. (Dusting with any other flour or starch will form a rubbery coating on the dough.) Lightly roll the dough in the flour to coat it evenly and re-dust the counter if needed. Form the dough into a disk or rectangle as directed by the recipe. Gently roll the dough from the center toward the edge of the disk or rectangle, always rolling outward. Turn the dough 45 degrees after each pass of the rolling pin. This helps keep the rolling even and lets you ensure the dough is not sticking to your work surface. If it *does* stick a little, use a bench scraper to gently lift the stuck-on portion and then dust your work surface with a bit more flour or blend. Repeat the rolling and turning. The recipe will indicate how thin the dough should be rolled.

For rolled-and-cut cookies, such as Gingerbread Persons (page 146), make sure the dough is rolled to an even thickness before you cut out the cookie shapes. This will ensure that they bake evenly and you don't end up with one crispy-armed gingerbread person. If the dough feels very soft after you have rolled it out, slide the dough onto a cookie sheet and freeze it for a few minutes before you cut out your shapes, so you get good clean cuts, for a nice even bake.

FOR DROP COOKIES

Measure out single-cookie portions of the dough with a teaspoon, tablespoon, or a retractable ice cream scoop (the recipe will suggest a measuring utensil) and weigh each portion. You want each one to have the same weight so the cookies not only look the same, but bake the same (and if you're cooking for kids, this can save you some pointless her-cookie-is-bigger-than-mine fights). Then dust your hands with glutinous rice flour and roll the portion of dough between your hands into a smooth ball. The flour will keep the dough from sticking to your hands as it warms and will maintain the perfectly round shape. Repeat with the remaining dough. Place the cookie portions evenly spaced on prepared sheet pans, with enough room between them so they won't touch as they spread during baking, and so they all have the same texture.

You can also form any of the drop cookie doughs into logs, wrap them in plastic wrap, and freeze them to use later as slice-and-bake cookies.

ULTIMATE CHOCOLATE CHIP COOKIE

2½ cups minus 2 teaspoons (258 g) Cookie Jar Blend (page 121)

¾ cup (165 g) packed light brown sugar

⅓ cup (65 g) granulated sugar

1¼ teaspoons baking powder

1 teaspoon baking soda

½ teaspoon kosher salt

7 tablespoons (98 g) unsalted butter, cold and diced

1 large egg

2 egg yolks

¼ cup (60 ml) half-and-half

1 tablespoon pure vanilla extract

1½ cups (264 g) milk chocolate chips

1 cup (168 g) semisweet chocolate chips

Minus the chocolate chips, this dough works for just about any kind of drop cookie, with a variety of flavors and add-ins. Variations on this dough include the Trash Can Cookies, the Triple Chocolate Macadamia Nut Cookies, and the Maple Oatmeal Raisin Cookies. For slice-and-bake cookies, roll any of the drop doughs—except the Trash Can Cookie, as the pretzels soften too much upon freezing—into a log, wrap them in plastic wrap, and freeze until you're ready to bake.

The key to getting the absolute *perfect* flavor and texture out of this versatile dough is to refrigerate for at least 24 hours—48 hours for the best results. This is a case when the maxim "Good things come to those who wait" holds true.

MAKES 36 COOKIES

In the bowl of a stand mixer fitted with the paddle attachment, combine the Cookie Jar Blend, sugars, baking powder, baking soda, and salt and beat them briefly to combine. With the mixer still running, add the butter and beat it on the lowest speed until the mixture resembles damp corn-meal, about 5 minutes. Add the egg, egg yolks, half-and-half, and vanilla and beat the mixture on high until the dough coats the sides of the bowl.

Scrape down the sides of the bowl and add the chocolate chips. Mix just until they are combined.

Transfer the dough to a glass bowl, cover it with plastic wrap, and refrig-erate it for at least 24 and up to 48 hours, for the best results.

Preheat the oven to 350°F (175°C). Line two baking sheets with Silpat mats or parchment paper.

To make cookies of uniform size (and prevent fights and claims of favor-itism), spoon out 2-tablespoon portions of the dough and then weigh them. A weight of 65 g will bake into a 3-inch (7.5-cm) diameter cookie. Lightly dust your hands with glutinous rice flour (or water—seriously, try it!) and roll the balls of dough between your hands. Stagger the cookie portions on the lined baking sheets, leaving 2 inches (5 cm) between each. Place two in the first row, one in the second. You will get 5 cookies per sheet.

For a golden cookie that will bend when cool, bake them for 11 minutes exactly. If you prefer a crunchier cookie, bake them for a few minutes more. Repeat until all of your dough has been baked. Let cool on the pan for 10 minutes, then transfer to wire racks to cool completely.

CONTINUED

These cookies keep beautifully in an airtight container at room temperature for up to 4 days. The dough freezes exceptionally well, double-wrapped, and can be kept for up to 1 month.

VARIATION: Triple-Chocolate Macadamia Nut Cookies
Macadamia nuts and white chocolate have a special understanding, and this version of the Ultimate lets them bring out each other's alchemical best. Prepare the Ultimate Chocolate Chip Cookie dough up to the point when you'd add the chocolate chips, then fold in 1 cup (168 g) milk chocolate chips, 1 cup (168 g) white chocolate chips, 1 cup (168 g) semisweet chocolate chips, and ½ cup (77 g) roughly chopped macadamia nuts. Proceed as directed.

SOUR CREAM SUGAR COOKIES

This is a go-to cookie for those with a sweet tooth who inexplicably don't go for chocolate. I make these cookies for birthdays, baby showers, and especially the holidays. They hold their shape beautifully and look even better when decorated.

MAKES 30 COOKIES

In the bowl of a stand mixer fitted with the paddle attachment, or in a food processor fitted with the S-blade, combine the Cookie Jar Blend, sugar, salt, and baking powder and beat them briefly to combine. Add the butter and continue to mix on the lowest speed until the mixture resembles damp cornmeal. Add the eggs, egg yolks, sour cream, rum, vanilla, and almond extract and mix on high until the dough is clinging to the sides of the bowl. Scrape down the sides of the bowl and mix for 20 seconds more. The dough will be soft.

Transfer the dough to a glass bowl, cover it with plastic wrap, and refrigerate it overnight (8 to 12 hours).

Preheat the oven to 350°F (175°C). Line two baking sheets with parchment paper or Silpat mats.

Dust a cutting board that will fit in your freezer with glutinous rice flour. Turn out the dough and knead it with the heel of your hand until it is pliable, just a couple of turns. Roll out the dough to a thickness between ⅛ inch (3 mm) and ¼ inch (6 mm). Place the cutting board in the freezer for 20 minutes to set the dough. Using cookie cutters in shapes you like, cut cookies out of the dough. Place them on the lined baking sheets, leaving 1 inch (2.5 cm) between each. Gather up the scraps of remaining dough, reroll it, chill, and cut out cookies until all of your dough has been used.

Bake the cookies for 8 to 10 minutes, until there's a touch of color at the edges of the cookies. Let the cookies cool for 5 minutes on the baking sheets, then transfer them to a wire rack to cool completely.

If you'd like to use several different colors of icing, divide the icing among individual bowls and add a few drops of food coloring. Mix the food coloring into the icing until the color is uniform, then either spoon the icing onto the cookies or transfer it to a piping bag fitted with a small, plain tip and pipe designs onto the cookies. Decorate the icing with sanding sugar. Let the icing dry completely before stacking the cookies.

The cookies will keep in an airtight container at room temperature for up to 1 week. Freeze the dough, double-wrapped, for up to 1 month.

2 cups plus 2 tablespoons (230 g) Cookie Jar Blend (page 121)

1 cup plus 2 tablespoons (225 g) granulated sugar

½ teaspoon kosher salt

½ teaspoon baking powder

6 tablespoons (84 g) unsalted butter, cold and diced

1 large egg

2 egg yolks

2 tablespoons (30 ml) sour cream

2 tablespoons white rum or brandy

1 teaspoon pure vanilla extract

Glutinous rice flour, for dusting

½ teaspoon almond extract

1 recipe Royal Icing (page 146)

Assorted food colorings

Assorted colored sanding sugars

PEANUT BUTTER BOMBS

The name says it all. But even better? Try the variation—Nutter Butters.

MAKES 24 COOKIES

In the bowl of a stand mixer fitted with the paddle attachment, combine the Cookie Jar Blend, sugars, salt, and baking soda and beat them briefly to combine. With the mixer still running, add the butter and beat it on the lowest speed for 5 minutes, until the mixture resembles damp cornmeal. Add the eggs, egg yolk, and vanilla and beat the mixture on high until the dough coats the sides of the bowl. Add the peanut butter and mix just to combine it.

Transfer the dough to a glass bowl, cover it, and refrigerate it for at least 24 hours and up to 48 hours for the best results.

Preheat the oven to 350°F (175°C). Line two baking sheets with parchment paper or Silpat mats.

Spoon out a heaping tablespoon-size dollop of the dough (45 g) and roll it between your hands to form a ball. Pour ½ cup (100 g) granulated sugar on a plate and shake to level it. Roll the balls in the sugar and set them on the lined baking sheets. Stagger the cookie portions, leaving 2 inches (5 cm) between each. Press a peanut half into the top of each ball of dough.

Bake the cookies for 8 to 10 minutes, until they are golden. Let cool on the pan for 10 minutes, then transfer to wire racks to cool completely.

These cookies keep beautifully in an airtight container at room temperature for up to 3 days. The dough can be frozen, double-wrapped, for up to 1 month.

VARIATION: Nutter Butters

Prepare the dough as directed above but reduce the peanut butter to ½ cup (120 ml). Roll out the chilled dough to ⅛ inch (3 mm) thick and cut it into twenty-four 1-by-2-inch (2.5-by-5-cm) rectangles. Set the rectangles on parchment paper– or Silpat-lined baking sheets and press them flat with the tines of a fork. Squeeze the center of each rectangle, to give it a peanut-shell shape, and bake as directed above. Meanwhile, in a bowl, beat together 1 cup (240 ml) creamy or crunchy peanut butter, 2 cups (256 g) confectioners' sugar, 1½ tablespoons milk, and ½ teaspoon pure vanilla extract. After the cookies have cooled, smear a little filling onto the backs (the side without fork marks) of half of the cookies. Make a sandwich by topping with a second cookie, back-side down. The cookies will keep in an airtight container for up to a week. The dough can be frozen, double-wrapped, for up to 1 month.

1¼ cups (135 g) Cookie Jar Blend (page 121)

½ cup (110 g) packed light brown sugar

½ cup (100 g) granulated sugar, plus more for coating

1 teaspoon kosher salt

½ teaspoon baking soda

4 tablespoons (½ stick / 56 g) unsalted butter, cold and diced

2 large eggs

1 egg yolk

2 teaspoons pure vanilla extract

1 cup (240 ml) creamy peanut butter

24 roasted, salted peanut halves

TRASH CAN COOKIES

2⅕ cups (238 g) Cookie Jar Blend (page 121)

1 cup (220 g) packed light brown sugar

½ cup (100 g) granulated sugar

½ cup (40 g) gluten-free quick oats

2 teaspoons finely ground coffee, such as Vietnamese, or instant espresso

1¼ teaspoons baking powder

1 teaspoon baking soda

1 teaspoon kosher salt

½ cup (1 stick / 113 g) unsalted butter, cold and diced

1 large egg

2 egg yolks

3 tablespoons half-and-half or whole milk

1 tablespoon light corn syrup

1 tablespoon pure vanilla extract

1 cup (168 g) milk chocolate chips

1 cup (168 g) semisweet chocolate chips

⅔ cup (110 g) gluten-free butterscotch chips

½ cup (18 g) coarsely crushed sea salt potato chips

2 cups (70 g) gluten-free mini pretzels

These everything-but-the-kitchen-sink cookies are made in gluten-free homage to David Chang's Compost Cookie, sold at Momofuku Milk Bar in New York. Note that when it comes to the coffee, the stronger, the better. As the pretzels and potato chips will get soggy, it's not a good idea to store the completed dough in the refrigerator or freezer, but you can certainly make the dough, store it, and add the pretzels and chips when you're ready to bake.

MAKES 36 COOKIES

In the bowl of a stand mixer fitted with the paddle attachment, combine the Cookie Jar Blend, sugars, oats, coffee, baking powder, baking soda, and salt and beat them briefly to combine. Add the butter and beat on the lowest speed until the mixture resembles damp cornmeal, about 5 minutes. Add the egg, egg yolks, half-and-half, corn syrup, and vanilla and beat the mixture on high until the dough coats the sides of the bowl.

Scrape down the sides of the bowl and add the chocolate and butterscotch chips. Mix just until they are combined.

Transfer the dough to a glass bowl, cover it with plastic wrap, and refrigerate it for at least 24 and up to 48 hours for the best results.

Preheat the oven to 350°F (175°C). Line two baking sheets with parchment paper or Silpat mats. Let the chilled dough sit on the counter for 10 minutes.

Gently fold the potato chips and pretzels into the dough. The dough will be sticky, so try not to touch it too much. Place the dough in the freezer for 10 minutes to set it.

To make cookies of uniform size, spoon out 2-tablespoon portions of the dough and then weigh them. A weight of 70 g will bake into a 4.5-inch (11-cm) diameter cookie. Lightly dampen your hands with water and roll the dough between your hands. Stagger the cookie portions on the lined baking sheets, leaving 2½ inches (6 cm) between each. Place two in the first row, one in the second. You will get 5 cookies per sheet.

For a bendy-soft cookie, bake them for 12 to 14 minutes, until the cookies are just golden. If you prefer a crispier cookie, go for 15 to 16 minutes. Let cool on the pan for 10 minutes, then transfer to wire racks to cool completely. (Alternatively, line an 8-inch (20-cm) square pan with foil and spread the dough evenly over the bottom. Bake for 35 to 45 minutes, then let cool completely and cut into bars.)

The cookies will keep in an airtight container at room temperature for up to 1 week. You can freeze the dough for up to 1 month before adding the potato chips and pretzels. (Just let it thaw completely before you add them.)

BROWN BUTTER BLONDIES

These blondies have people asking, "What's the secret that makes them *soooo* good?" You can keep them coming back to try to figure it out, or let them in on the key ingredient: brown butter. As tempting as they are, be sure to let the brownies cool in the pan before slicing, as they are delicate right out of the oven.

MAKES 12 BLONDIES

Preheat the oven to 350°F (175°C). Line an 8-inch (23-cm) square baking dish or pan with enough foil to give it a 1-inch (2.5 cm) overhang and then lightly grease the foil with butter.

In a small saucepan, melt the butter over medium heat. Keep the melted butter over the heat, swirling the pan often, until the butter just begins to brown. You'll see the top layer of clear yellow butter take on a nut-brown shade and the milk solids caramelizing at the bottom. As soon as you see the milk solids taking on color, pull the butter off the heat and pour it into a cup or small bowl. This will keep the butter from over browning. Pop the butter into the freezer for at least 15 minutes to cool.

In the bowl of a stand mixer fitted with the paddle attachment, combine the Cookie Jar Blend, sugars, baking powder, and salt and beat them on low speed just to combine. With the mixer still going, add the chilled browned butter and beat it until the mixture resembles tan, damp cornmeal. Add the egg, egg yolks, half-and-half, and vanilla and mix them until the batter sticks to the sides of the bowl. Scrape down the sides of the bowl as necessary and mix for 30 seconds more.

Using a spatula, fold in the pecans and chocolate chips, if desired.

Spread the dough evenly over the bottom of the prepared baking dish and bake for 35 to 45 minutes, until the blondies are uniformly golden and pull away from the sides of the pan. (They'll pull the foil with them.) Let cool completely in the pan on a wire rack, then use the foil to pull the blondie block out of the pan and cut it into 12 pieces.

The blondies keep well in an airtight container at room temperature for up to 1 week, in the fridge for 10 days, or frozen, double-wrapped, for 2 months. (Try a not-quite-thawed blondie for a chewy, chilly treat.)

7 tablespoons (98 g) unsalted butter, plus more for the pan

2½ cups plus 2 teaspoons (274 g) Cookie Jar Blend (page 121)

¾ cup (165 g) packed light brown sugar

⅓ cup (65 g) granulated sugar

1¼ teaspoons baking powder

½ teaspoon kosher salt

1 large egg

2 egg yolks

5 tablespoons (75 ml) half-and-half

1 tablespoon pure vanilla extract

½ cup (70 g) coarsely chopped pecans (optional)

1 cup (168 g) semisweet chocolate chips (optional)

MARBLE CHOCOLATE-CHEESECAKE BROWNIES

FOR THE BROWNIE BATTER:

¾ cup (82 g) Cookie Jar Blend (page 121)

½ teaspoon plus a pinch of kosher salt

½ teaspoon baking powder

½ cup (84 g) semisweet chocolate chips

½ cup (1 stick / 113 g) unsalted butter, plus more for the pan

½ cup (110 g) packed light brown sugar

½ cup (100 g) granulated sugar

3 large eggs

2½ teaspoons pure vanilla extract

FOR THE CREAM CHEESE MARBLING:

1 pound (455 g) cream cheese, at room temperature

¼ cup (50 g) granulated sugar

2 egg yolks

2 teaspoons fresh lemon juice

⅛ teaspoon kosher salt

These brownies are a favorite among my clientele in Austin. The richness of the chocolate marries perfectly with the tangy cream cheese. For best results, I like to pipe the cream cheese over the chocolate for the perfect marbling effect, but using the back of a knife to swirl works just as well.

MAKES 16 BROWNIES

Preheat the oven to 350°F (175°C). Line an 8-inch (20-cm) square pan or a 9-by-13-inch (23-by-33-cm) jelly-roll pan with enough foil to give it a 1-inch (2.5 cm) overhang and then lightly grease the foil with butter or non-stick spray.

Make the brownie batter: In a large bowl, whisk together the Cookie Jar Blend, salt, and baking powder. Set aside.

Place the chocolate chips in a large bowl and set them aside. In a small saucepan, melt the butter over medium-low heat. Pour the butter over the chocolate and let stand for 5 minutes to melt the chocolate. Whisk until smooth and well combined.

Whisk in the sugars, then the eggs, one at a time, whisking until each egg is incorporated before adding the next. Whisk in the vanilla. Add the dry mixture and whisk until the batter reaches the consistency of thick pudding.

Pour the batter into the prepared pan and set it aside.

Make the cream cheese marbling: In the bowl of a stand mixer fitted with the paddle attachment, combine the cream cheese and sugar and whip on high speed until silky smooth, 1 to 2 minutes. Add the egg yolks, lemon juice, and salt and mix until smooth.

Transfer the cream cheese mixture to a pastry bag fitted with a round tip and pipe a scalloped pattern over the chocolate. Alternatively, simply drop the cream cheese mixture over the chocolate batter in tablespoon-size portions. Using the tip of a knife, swirl the cream cheese mixture through the brownie batter to give it a marbled look.

Bake the brownies for 25 to 30 minutes, until the edges have begun to pull away from the sides of the pan (bringing the foil with them). Allow the brownies to cool completely in the pan on a wire rack so they set. For best results, freeze the brownies for 30 minutes before slicing. I always get the cleanest cuts after my brownies are ice-cold. Use the foil to pull the brownie block out of the pan and cut into 16 pieces.

The brownies will keep in an airtight container in the fridge for up to 10 days, and in the freezer, double-wrapped, for up to 1 month.

GIOVANNA'S DREAM BARS

1 recipe Short Crust (page 86)

1⅓ cups (295 g) packed light brown sugar

3 large eggs

2 cups (200 g) shredded sweetened coconut

1 cup (128 g) coarsely chopped pecans

1 cup (77 g) coarsely chopped pitted Medjool dates

1 cup (200 g) granulated sugar

1 tablespoon Cookie Jar Blend (page 121)

Finely grated zest of 1 lemon

2 tablespoons fresh lemon juice

¼ teaspoon kosher salt

This is an heirloom recipe passed down from my grandmother to my mother, and from my mother to me. I now pass the gluten-free version on to you and yours. The collection of flavors and textures makes these bars pretty darn dreamy. They're best served warm.

MAKES 12 BARS

Preheat the oven to 350°F (175°C).

Divide the short crust dough in half; wrap one half in plastic wrap and place it in the freezer to chill for 15 minutes. Meanwhile, roll out the remaining half into a rectangle no thinner than ⅛ inch (3 mm). I like my crust a bit thicker so I always go with a ¼ inch (6 mm) base. Fit the sheet of dough into a 9-by-13-inch (23-by-33-cm) jelly-roll pan and put it in the freezer for 15 minutes.

Brush the chilled dough with water. Dock the dough with the tines of a fork so it will not expand while baking. Crumble on ⅓ cup (65 g) of the brown sugar and brush the sugar into the water, so it is uniformly distributed.

Bake the base for 20 minutes, or until the sugar is bubbly.

Meanwhile, in a large bowl, whisk the eggs and mix in the coconut, pecans, dates, granulated sugar, Cookie Jar Blend, lemon zest, juice, salt, and the remaining 1 cup (200 g) brown sugar. Spoon the filling over the hot sugar-topped crust and level it.

Bake for 15 to 20 minutes, until the topping is set and the coconut is golden.

Cut into 12 bars and serve them warm. The bars will keep for up to 1 week, covered, at room temperature.

THUMBPRINT COOKIES

Fully baked and multicolored, these cookies remind me of the glass ornaments that hang from Christmas trees; and when they are served on a tray, they embody the spirit of the holidays. These are ideal filled with strawberry, plum, raspberry, apricot, fig, currant, and blueberry preserves. Eat them in the brief interval when they're no longer hot but not yet quite cooled. I also like to put them in the fridge so the pectin in the preserves sets and becomes slightly chewy.

MAKES 36 COOKIES

Preheat the oven to 400°F (205°C). Line two baking sheets with parchment paper or Silpat mats.

In the bowl of a stand mixer fitted with the paddle attachment, combine the Cookie Jar Blend, confectioners' sugar, potato flour, brown sugar, and salt and beat them on the lowest speed to combine. Add the butter and continue to mix it on the lowest speed until the mixture resembles damp cornmeal. Add the egg yolks, almond extract, and vanilla and mix them on high until the dough wraps itself around the paddle. (At this point, you can freeze the dough, double-wrapped in plastic, for up to 1 month.)

Using a 1½-inch (4-cm) retractable ice cream scoop, form balls of dough and then weigh them. A weight of 35 g will bake into a 1½-inch (4-cm) diameter cookie. Lightly dust your hands with glutinous rice flour and roll the dough between your hands. Place the dough balls on the lined baking sheets, leaving 1 inch (2.5 cm) between them. With your index finger, press on each ball to leave an indentation at least half as deep as the cookie ball is tall. (If you use your thumb, the indentations are asymmetrical, which will cause the filling to bubble over.) Fill the indentations with preserves, to just below the top of the dough, so they don't bubble over while baking.

Bake the cookies for 7 to 10 minutes, until they have just a hint of color and the preserves are melted. Let cool on the pan for 10 minutes, then transfer to wire racks to cool completely.

Store the cookies in a metal tin in the cool part of your kitchen for up to 1 week.

1½ cups plus 1 teaspoon (164 g) Cookie Jar Blend (page 121)

1 cup (100 g) confectioners' sugar, sifted

¼ cup (44 g) potato flour

3 tablespoons packed light brown sugar

⅛ teaspoon kosher salt

11 tablespoons (154 g) unsalted butter, cold and diced

3 egg yolks

1¼ teaspoons almond extract

1 teaspoon pure vanilla extract

Preserves, for filling

PISTACHIO-CRANBERRY-ALMOND BISCOTTI

Forget those commercial biscotti—grace your morning cup of coffee with a couple of these delicate bites. They're a cinch to make and are excellent served with a demitasse of coffee, a glass of red wine, or a thimbleful of grappa.

MAKES 36 BISCOTTI

Preheat the oven to 375°F (190°C). Line two baking sheets with parchment paper or Silpat mats.

In a food processor fitted with the S-blade, pulse together the sorghum flour, Cookie Jar Blend, sugar, almond flour, baking soda, and salt to combine. Add the eggs, almond extract, and vanilla. Process until the dough is very thick, about 1 minute.

Dust your work surface with glutinous rice flour. Turn out the dough and knead it with the heels of your hands until it is smooth. Flatten the dough and pour the pistachios and cranberries into the middle. Letter-fold the dough over the nuts and berries (see page 87). Dust the counter with more flour, if needed, and knead the dough a few times to evenly distribute the nuts and berries.

Cut the dough into 4 pieces. Shape the pieces into ropes no more than 2 inches (5 cm) wide and 8 inches (20 cm) long. Place two ropes on each baking sheet, with 4 inches (10 cm) between them. Brush each rope with some of the egg white. Sprinkle them with sanding sugar.

Bake the ropes for 20 minutes. Remove the biscotti from the oven and reduce the oven temperature to 225°F (110°C). With a serrated knife, cut the biscotti into ½-inch (12-mm) pieces at a 45-degree angle. Lay the biscotti flat on the baking sheets and bake them for 30 minutes. The biscotti should dry completely. Transfer them to a wire rack to cool.

The biscotti will keep in an airtight container at room temperature for up to 1 month. The dough can be frozen, double-wrapped, for up to 1 month.

1½ cups (165 g) sorghum flour

1 cup (108 g) Cookie Jar Blend (page 121)

1 cup (200 g) granulated sugar

½ cup (44 g) almond flour

1 teaspoon baking soda

¼ teaspoon kosher salt

4 large eggs

2½ teaspoons almond extract

½ teaspoon pure vanilla extract

Glutinous rice flour (or additional Cookie Jar Blend, page 121), for dusting

½ cup (70 g) chopped salted pistachios, toasted

¼ cup (35 g) chopped dried cranberries

1 egg white, lightly beaten

Sanding sugar, for sprinkling

VANILLA WAFERS

1½ cups plus 3 tablespoons (181 g) Cookie Jar Blend (page 121)

¾ cup (75 g) confectioners' sugar

½ cup (100 g) granulated sugar

2 tablespoons potato flour

¾ teaspoon baking powder

½ teaspoon kosher salt

7 tablespoons (98 g) unsalted butter, cold and diced

1 large egg

3 egg yolks

1 tablespoon plus 2 teaspoons pure vanilla extract

1 tablespoon whole milk

Banana pudding wouldn't be pudding without 'em. And these work perfectly to crush and convert into a cookie-crumb crust for a cheesecake, chocolate mousse pie, or the like. Be sure to form the cookies with your palm, as the bottom of a glass flattens the dough too much, and a vanilla wafer should have that beautiful rounded surface.

MAKES 36 COOKIES

In the bowl of a stand mixer fitted with the paddle attachment, combine the Cookie Jar Blend, sugars, potato flour, baking powder, and salt and beat them on the lowest speed just to combine. Add the butter and continue to mix on the lowest speed until the mixture resembles damp cornmeal. Add the egg, egg yolks, vanilla, and milk and mix them on high until the dough is smooth and sticking to the sides of the bowl, 30 seconds to 1 minute at most.

Transfer the dough to a glass bowl, cover it with plastic wrap, and refrigerate it for at least 3 hours.

Preheat the oven to 350°F (175°C). Line two baking sheets with parchment paper or Silpat mats.

Scoop out tablespoon-size balls of the chilled dough and then weigh them. A weight of 25 g will bake into a 1½-inch (4-cm) diameter cookie. Lightly dust your hands with glutinous rice flour and roll the dough between your hands. Set them on the lined baking sheets, leaving 2 inches (5 cm) between each. Dust your hands with more glutinous rice flour or additional Cookie Jar Blend and press the dough balls with your palm to flatten them to the size and shape of a classic vanilla wafer.

Bake the cookies for 15 to 20 minutes, until the edges take on color. These babies stay light in the middle and get tanned just at their edges. Let them cool on wire racks completely before serving.

The cookies will keep in an airtight container at room temperature for up to 1 week.

SHOTGUN WEDDING COOKIES

Also known as Mexican Wedding Cookies, Russian Tea Cookies, and Scottish something-or-others, these traditional shortbreads are a global go-to baked sweet. No holiday cookie tin is truly filled without them. The addition of the dates is what really sets these apart from all the other tea cookies you've tried.

MAKES 48 COOKIES

In the bowl of a stand mixer fitted with the paddle attachment, combine the Cookie Jar Blend, almond flour, sugars, potato flour, and salt and beat them on the lowest speed just to combine. Add the butter and continue to mix on the lowest speed until the mixture resembles damp cornmeal. Add the pecans, dates, and vanilla and mix on high until the dough wraps itself around the paddle and coats the sides of the bowl.

Transfer the dough to a glass or ceramic bowl, cover it with plastic wrap, and refrigerate it for at least 2 hours.

Preheat the oven to 400°F (205°C). Line two baking sheets with parchment paper or Silpat mats.

Using a 1½-inch (4-cm) retractable ice cream scoop, form balls of dough. (Since the ice cream scooper keeps the balls of dough uniform, there is no need to weigh them.) Lightly dust your hands with glutinous rice flour and roll the dough between your hands. Place the dough balls on the lined baking sheets, leaving 1½ inches (4 cm) between them.

Bake the cookies for 7 to 10 minutes. The cookies should be golden around the base, which will flatten slightly, become just barely tinted on their surface, and have domed tops.

Remove them from the oven and while they're still warm, roll the cookies in confectioners' sugar. Allow them to cool completely, and then roll them in confectioners' sugar again.

The cookies will keep in an airtight container at room temperature for up to 10 days.

1¾ cups (190 g) Cookie Jar Blend (page 121)

½ cup (44 g) almond flour

½ cup (50 g) confectioners' sugar, plus more for dusting

2 tablespoons packed light brown sugar

1 tablespoon potato flour

¼ teaspoon kosher salt

1 cup (2 sticks / 226 g) unsalted butter, cold and diced

½ cup plus 2 tablespoons (80 g) finely chopped or ground pecans

2 pitted Medjool dates, finely chopped

2 teaspoons pure vanilla extract

GINGERBREAD PERSONS

FOR THE COOKIES:

3 cups (324 g) Cookie Jar Blend (page 121)

¾ cup plus 1 tablespoon (160 g) granulated sugar

½ teaspoon baking soda

½ teaspoon kosher salt

½ teaspoon ground allspice

4 tablespoons plus 2 teaspoons (64 g) unsalted butter, cold and diced

¼ cup (60 ml) molasses

¼ cup (60 ml) whole milk

2 large eggs

2 teaspoons pure vanilla extract

1½ teaspoons finely grated peeled fresh ginger

¼ cup (34 g) minced candied ginger

Glutinous rice flour (or additional Cookie Jar Blend, page 121), for dusting

FOR THE ROYAL ICING:

3 tablespoons unsalted butter, softened

2 cups (200 g) confectioners' sugar

1 teaspoon gluten-free meringue powder

3 to 4 tablespoons milk, lemon juice, or water

½ teaspoon pure vanilla extract

Here is Grandma's recipe, made gluten-free and with a little candied ginger thrown in so I can feel like I'm upgrading tradition.

MAKES TWENTY-FOUR 4-INCH GINGERBREAD PEOPLE

Make the cookies: In the bowl of a stand mixer fitted with the paddle attachment, or in a food processor fitted with the S-blade, combine the Cookie Jar Blend, sugar, baking soda, salt, and allspice and beat them briefly to combine. Add the butter and continue to mix on the lowest speed until the mixture resembles damp cornmeal. Add the molasses, milk, eggs, and vanilla and mix on high until the dough folds in on itself and clings to the paddle. Add the grated and candied gingers and mix just until combined.

Form the dough into a ball, wrap it tightly in plastic wrap, and refrigerate it for 2 to 3 hours.

Preheat the oven to 350°F (175°C). Line two baking sheets with parchment paper or Silpat mats.

Lightly dust a cutting board that will fit into your freezer with glutinous rice flour. Knead the dough briefly with the heel of your hand, giving it just 4 turns. Roll it out into a rectangle 12 inches by 14 inches (30 cm by 35 cm) and no thinner than ⅛ inch (3 mm). Place the dough in the freezer for 20 minutes. Remove the dough from the freezer and, using a gingerbread cookie cutter, cut out people and place them on the lined baking sheets, leaving about 1 inch (2.5 cm) between each. Gather the scraps and roll them out again, chill the dough, and cut out as many gingerbread people as you can from the dough.

Bake the cookies for 12 to 14 minutes, until they are firm to the touch. Allow the cookies to cool on the pan for 10 minutes, then cool completely on a wire rack before icing them.

Meanwhile, make the icing: In the bowl of a stand mixer fitted with the paddle attachment, beat the butter with the confectioners' sugar and meringue powder until the mixture resembles damp talcum powder. Add the milk and vanilla and beat until the icing is thick.

Ice the cookies with a spoon, or transfer the icing to a piping bag fitted with a small, plain tip and give the figures buttons, shoes, faces—whatever you'd like. Let the icing dry completely before storing the cookies.

The gingerbread cookies keep in an airtight container at room temperature for up to 1 week. You can refrigerate the dough for up to 3 days, or roll it into a log and freeze it, double-wrapped, for up to 1 month.

CAKE & MUFFIN BLEND

The Cake & Muffin Blend combines gluten-free whole-grain flours and starches to satisfy the required characteristics for all kinds of crumbs that define the full range of cakes: from light, airy sponge cakes to dense, oil-based Bundt cakes, and every torte and gâteau in between. Traditional bakers use cake flour, which is inherently low in gluten, so you would think coming up with the perfect gluten-free blend would be a cakewalk, right? Well, for you it is. The flours used in this blend work overtime to get the baker's ideal of perfection, or what I like to call the trifecta: taste, texture, and appearance.

THE RECIPE

2½ cups plus ⅓ cup plus 1 tablespoon (320 g) sorghum flour

2½ cups plus 2 tablespoons (304 g) glutinous rice flour

½ cup plus ⅓ cup (144 g) potato starch

⅔ cup plus ½ cup plus 1 teaspoon (120 g) extra-fine brown rice flour

¼ cup plus 1 teaspoon (44 g) potato flour

8 teaspoons (24 g) guar gum

Like the previous blends, the base of the cake blend is sorghum flour, ensuring that the finished baked goods taste delicious, while the starches step in to help create a tender crumb. The biggest difference you will notice about this blend is that a scant amount of potato flour is present. Potato flour helps provide excellent structure, but it also helps retain moisture, so your gluten-free cakes stay tender, longer. The density of any of the cakes you find here comes from the kinds of fats and the amount of eggs used. The lightest cakes will be held together only by egg whites and a scant amount of butter, for example, and the densest cakes will boast butter or oil, sour cream, buttermilk, and eggs, or a combination of all.

For more information on the flours, starches, and other ingredients used in the blend, see the Pantry section on page 215.

MAKES 7¾ CUPS (956 G), ENOUGH FOR 3 CAKES, OR 4 BATCHES OF MUFFINS OR CUPCAKES

Using the spoon-and-sweep method, measure each ingredient into a large bowl. Whisk together and then sift the mixture into a separate large bowl. Repeat several times.

The approximate weight of the blend, by volume (for use in doing your own adaptations):

EACH	OF BLEND WEIGHS APPROXIMATELY
1 tablespoon	8 g
¼ cup	30 g
⅓ cup	43 g
½ cup	59 g
⅔ cup	77 g
¾ cup	88 g
1 cup	117 g

THE DOUGH

YOU'LL NOTICE MORE EXTRACTS

Some of the flours used in this blend have strong flavors, such as the potato and extra-fine brown rice flours. To compensate for these intense aromas, the quantities of the extracts used in the recipes are sometimes doubled, or are higher than they would be in a conventional recipe with a milder-tasting all-purpose flour.

TRY ADDING CORNSTARCH

To make even lighter cakes, and to achieve an even lighter crumb, you can add a small amount (about ¼ cup / 30 g per 2 cups / 234 g of the blend) of cornstarch to your Cake & Muffin Blend for heavenly results. Professional bakers have used this trick for years, and it works perfectly in gluten-free baking as well. The cornstarch, especially in the case of oil-based cakes, helps create larger cake crumbs, resulting in a moist yet crumbly confection.

WANNA TURN A LOAF INTO A CUPCAKE?

Remember that any of the cakes in this chapter make wonderful cupcakes. The muffins can be made into breakfast loaves, too—in either case, just be mindful of your baking time. Adjust accordingly: less time for cupcakes and more time for loaves. Start testing the cupcake or loaf after 20 minutes by inserting a toothpick or skewer into the center—if it comes out without crumbs, the baked good is done. Loaves typically take a full 30 to 45 minutes to cook all the way through.

USE PROPER MEASURING TOOLS

Most important, I do not recommend measuring your liquids in a dry measure container or cup. You will not get the amount of liquid you really need, so keep a liquid measuring cup on standby at all times.

SIFTING

Sifting loosens dry ingredients that may have become compacted in their packaging and removes any lumps; this is especially important when it comes to starches. It also helps mix different dry ingredients together. Always sift your Cake & Muffin Blend—sometimes multiple times (as in the case of the Angel Food Cake on page 172). This ensures the components in the blend are evenly distributed and you don't have rogue pockets of potato starch or guar gum wreaking havoc on your cakes.

You can sift dry ingredients through a utensil made specifically for that purpose, such as crank or canister sifters, or use a drum sieve or another fine-mesh sieve. If you're using a sifter, measure the flour or starch into the cup of the sifter and either crank or compress the sifter handle to move the ingredient through the mesh of the sifter cup. If you're using a sieve, hold the sieve over a bowl, measure the ingredient into the sieve, and tap the side of the sieve to pass the ingredient through the holes of the sieve.

To sift your Cake & Muffin blend, first measure the individual ingredients into a large bowl using the spoon and sweep method. Next, whisk the flours and starches to combine them. Finally, sift the mixture into a separate large bowl to further combine and scatter any remaining pockets of individual components. You can sift once or twice more, if you prefer. (There's really no such thing as over-sifting, so sift away!)

MIXING

Recipes will often describe what the batter should look like before it gets poured into a pan rather than going solely on the amount of time you should mix a batter. If you happen to walk away from the kitchen to fold some laundry and accidentally left your butter on the counter and it became very soft, for example, it will take far less time to amalgamate your ingredients than if you used cold butter. So pay attention to the visual descriptions *more* than adhering to a strict mixing time.

I've noticed that my ingredients come together twice as fast in the summer as they do in the winter, and because my ovens are blazing most of the year,

I find this interesting enough to mention. I depend heavily on my senses to tell me when something is ready in their varying stages of preparation. Sight, smell, taste, texture—all of these are barometers telling me yes, this is ready, or no, keep mixing. Take for example my classic vanilla cake, pictured below. If I am mixing the batter and it looks lumpy rather than pudding smooth, the butter has not emulsified fully and the liquids were added too soon, not giving the butter enough time to break down. This means I need to whip that batter until the friction of the paddle warms the butter enough to smooth it into the mixture.

Luckily, since this is gluten-free baking, we don't need to worry about overmixing our cake and muffin batters because we don't need to worry about the overproduction of the gluten protein. There are a couple of factors that will give you a too-thick batter, however. If you use small eggs, this can result in a thicker batter, and if you use enormous eggs, you will have a thinner batter; the recipes in this chapter were designed around a standard-size large egg, which is the most widely available.

FOLDING

As explained earlier (see page 15), *folding* means combining ingredients while retaining the air in the mixture. For some recipes made with the Cake & Muffin blend, you'll be folding in fluffy beaten egg whites to lighten batters or folding dry ingredients into beaten egg whites.

I recommend using a wooden spoon instead of a rubber or plastic spatula to fold ingredients into one another. When used for folding, spatulas have a tendency to take the wind out of beaten egg whites. Mashed and flattened is not what you want—your goal is to keep the dough light. You've worked hard to get as much air as possible into that dough or those egg whites, and you want to keep it there.

Again, the key to folding is exaggeration. Get your spoon way down to the bottom of the bowl and gently lift and fold the batter over itself, rolling the spoon

as you incorporate the egg whites or dry ingredients. (Think back to that analogy of turning a crank—the spoon is the crank and the batter is the gear being spun by the crank.) Rotate the bowl and repeat until the ingredients are incorporated to the proper degree—for example, "fold the egg whites into the batter until no white streaks remain," or "fold in the dry ingredients until just incorporated." Remember to keep as much air in the batter as possible.

A TRICK OF THE TRADE

I picked up this trick years ago from Jacques Pepin, and I love it. Cut out parchment paper rounds to fit your pan, then generously grease the pan with butter. Press the parchment into the bottom of the pan, then, using the tip of a knife, flip the parchment so both sides of the paper are evenly coated with butter. Isn't he amazing?

CLASSIC VANILLA LAYER CAKE WITH DOUBLE-CHOCOLATE FROSTING

FOR THE VANILLA CAKE:

2⅔ cups plus ¼ cup (350 g) Cake & Muffin Blend (page 149), sifted, plus more for the pan

2 cups (400 g) granulated sugar

3½ teaspoons baking powder

½ teaspoon kosher salt

¾ cup (1½ sticks / 170 g) unsalted butter, preferably cultured, diced, plus more for the pan

6 large eggs

1¼ cups (300 ml) milk

¼ cup (60 ml) sour cream

¼ cup (60 ml) pure vanilla extract, preferably double strength

Seeds from 1 vanilla bean

FOR THE DOUBLE-CHOCOLATE FROSTING:

½ cup (120 ml) milk or heavy cream

6 ounces (170 g) semisweet chocolate chips

2½ cups (250 g) confectioners' sugar

1 cup (118 g) unsweetened cocoa powder

Pinch of kosher salt

1½ cups (3 sticks / 339 g) unsalted butter, at room temperature

2 teaspoons pure vanilla extract

Didn't life begin when you were served your first slice of vanilla cake with chocolate buttercream? You don't want to forget the obligatory glass of cold milk to complete the whole regression-to-childhood experience here.

MAKES TWO 8-INCH (20-CM) CAKES

Preheat the oven to 350°F (175°C). Set an oven rack in the middle position. Butter two 8-inch (20-cm) round cake pans and line the bottoms with parchment paper cut to fit. Press the paper into the butter, then flip the paper over to evenly coat both sides with butter.

Make the cake: In the bowl of a stand mixer fitted with the paddle attachment, combine the Cake & Muffin Blend, baking powder, and salt and beat them briefly to combine. Pour the ingredients into another bowl and sift twice. Add the butter and sugar and mix on high until you can no longer see clumps.

In a medium bowl, whisk together the milk, sour cream, vanilla extract, and vanilla seeds until very smooth. Add the dry ingredients, followed by the eggs, and mix on high until very smooth.

Evenly divide the batter between the pans and bake for 25 to 35 minutes, until the cakes are golden and a wooden skewer inserted into the middle comes out clean.

Let the cakes cool in the pans for 10 minutes, then invert them onto wire racks to cool completely. Peel off the parchment.

Make the frosting: Place the chocolate chips in a medium bowl. In a small pan, heat the milk until it steams, but do not let it boil. Pour it over the chocolate chips and let stand for 5 minutes to melt the chocolate, and then whisk until smooth.

In the bowl of a stand mixer fitted with the whisk attachment, combine the confectioners' sugar, cocoa powder, and salt. Add the butter and beat on high speed until the frosting is fluffy and a uniformly dark chocolate color. Scrape down the sides of the bowl. Set the mixer on low and add the chocolate mixture and the vanilla. Beat the frosting on low at first until the melted chocolate begins to incorporate uniformly, then beat on high speed just until it is fluffy and shiny.

CONTINUED

Assemble the cake: Level the domed tops of the cake layers, if necessary, using a long serrated knife. Place one cake layer on a cake stand or serving plate. Take one-third of the frosting and spread it over the top of the first cake round. Using an offset spatula, level the frosting. Top the frosting with the second cake layer. Using a plastic pastry scraper, coat the entire cake with a very thin, even layer of frosting (this is called a "crumb coat" and helps trap any stray cake crumbs so they don't mar the surface of the frosting). Place the cake in the freezer to set the frosting for 15 minutes. Remove it from the freezer and use the remaining frosting to completely cover the cake.

The cake will keep under a glass cloche (see sidebar) or cake dome at room temperature for up to 3 days, or in the refrigerator for up to 1 week. If you'll be wrapping the cake in plastic wrap before placing it in the refrigerator rather than storing it in a cake box, spray the wrap with nonstick baking spray before delicately placing it over the cake. This will flatten the frosting somewhat, but will keep the cake well and prevent the frosting from sticking.

CLOCHE

Cloche in French means "bell" and indeed, glass cloches have the shape of a bell. They are often used in Europe to keep pastries and cheese fresh (and you've probably noticed them on the counter at your favorite pastry shop or bakery). Cake stand covers in America are more cylindrical in shape, but they still serve the same function. They allow us to keep cakes on the counter while providing a beautiful way to display them.

CHOCOLATE MAYONNAISE CAKE

It may sound crazy to use mayonnaise in a sweet, chocolatey cake, but when you break mayo down into its component parts—eggs, oil, vinegar—they're all things you're likely to be throwing into the mixer anyway. Vinegar even adds moistness and enhances chocolate flavor.

Chocolate mayonnaise cakes have been popular during times when eggs and oil were scarce (which is why they're sometimes called Depression-era or World War II cakes), but they've never gone out of style in my house. You can use any icing you like; my pick is Double-Chocolate (page 154). But this cake is so devilishly good, you can even serve it with just a sprinkling of confectioners' sugar and fresh berries to rave reviews.

Many "traditional" (as in, not gluten-free) bakers add a touch of cornstarch to cakes for a more tender crumb, which I've done here. You'll see that this technique works well for us gluten-free bakers as well.

MAKES ONE 9-INCH (23-CM) DOUBLE-LAYER CAKE

Preheat the oven to 350°F (175°C). Set an oven rack in the middle position. Grease two 9-inch (23-cm) round (or two 8-inch / 20-cm square) cake pans with unsalted butter and line the bottoms with parchment paper cut to fit. Flip the paper so both sides are greased (see page 153).

In the bowl of a stand mixer fitted with the paddle attachment, combine the Cake & Muffin Blend, brown sugar, cocoa, cornstarch, baking soda, baking powder, and salt and beat briefly to combine. Add the milk, oil, and mayonnaise and beat on medium speed until the batter looks shiny. It will be thick enough that you have to scrape down the sides of the bowl. Add the eggs and vanilla and beat on high speed until the batter is very smooth, about 1 minute. The batter should look like thick chocolate pudding.

Divide the batter evenly between the prepared pans. Bake for 40 minutes, swapping the pans on the rack halfway through, until a toothpick inserted in the middle of each cake comes out clean.

Let the cakes cool in the pans for 10 minutes. Line two wire racks with parchment paper and dust the paper with granulated sugar so the cakes won't stick. Invert the pans onto the parchment, remove the pans, and then peel off the parchment paper from the bottom of the cakes. Flip the layers so they're top-side up. Allow them to cool completely before frosting.

CONTINUED

2¼ cups (264 g) Cake & Muffin Blend (page 149)

2 cups (440 g) packed dark brown sugar

¾ cup (83 g) unsweetened Dutch-process cocoa powder

5 tablespoons plus 1 teaspoon (40 g) cornstarch

1¼ teaspoons baking soda

1 teaspoon baking powder

½ teaspoon kosher salt

1½ cups (360 ml) milk

½ cup (120 ml) pure olive oil, grapeseed oil, or other neutral-flavored oil

½ cup (120 ml) gluten-free mayonnaise

3 large eggs

2 tablespoons pure vanilla extract

Granulated sugar, for dusting

1 recipe Double-Chocolate Frosting (page 154)

Level the domed tops of the cake layers, if necessary, using a long serrated knife. Set one cake layer on a cake stand or serving plate. Frost the top of the cake with one-third of the Double-Chocolate Frosting. Set the second layer on top of the frosting and then lightly frost the top and sides of the cake to de-crumb it. Place the cake in the freezer for 15 minutes to set the frosting. When the cake comes out of the freezer, using an offset spatula, frost the top and sides with the remaining frosting; I wasn't shy with the frosting on this one.

The cake will keep under a glass cloche (see sidebar, page 156) or cake dome at room temperature for 3 to 4 days, or 1 week in the fridge.

SANDY'S COCONUT-PISTACHIO GÂTEAU WITH MARZIPAN FILLING

FOR THE CAKE:

2½ cups (293 g) Cake & Muffin Blend (page 149)

2 cups (400 g) granulated sugar

Scant 1 cup (106 g) finely ground roasted salted pistachios

⅓ cup (40 g) cornstarch

2 teaspoons baking powder

1 cup (240 ml) milk

½ cup (120 ml) pure olive oil

6 large eggs, separated

¼ cup (60 ml) sour cream

2 teaspoons almond extract

1¼ teaspoons coconut extract

½ cup (50 g) sweetened shredded coconut, plus more for garnish

⅛ teaspoon cream of tartar

FOR THE SEVEN-MINUTE ICING:

1 cup (200 g) granulated sugar

4 egg whites

⅛ teaspoon cream of tartar

½ teaspoon pure vanilla extract

FOR THE MARZIPAN FILLING:

1 pound (455 g) gluten-free almond paste (I like Solo Pure)

1 tablespoon light corn syrup

Green food coloring (optional)

Confectioners' sugar, for dusting

2 cups (245 g) salted pistachios, chopped, for garnish

Toasted coconut, for garnish

Sandy Reinlie, a genius pastry chef here in Austin, has an almost supernatural knack for combining flavors. I once asked what she considered her greatest success in the cake arena and her answer inspired this recipe. Ideally, to stay true to Sandy's flavor alchemy, use vanilla extract from Mexico.

MAKES ONE 10-INCH (25-CM) DOUBLE-LAYER CAKE

Make the cake: Preheat the oven to 350°F (175°C). Grease a 10-inch (25-cm) springform pan with butter and line the bottom with parchment paper cut to fit. Flip the the paper so both sides are greased.

In the bowl of a stand mixer fitted with the paddle attachment, combine the Cake & Muffin Blend, sugar, pistachios, cornstarch, and baking powder and beat them briefly to combine.

In a separate bowl, whisk together the milk, oil, egg yolks, sour cream, almond extract, and coconut extract until very smooth. With the mixer running on medium-low speed, add the egg yolk mixture to the dry ingredients in a slow, steady stream. Beat the batter on high speed for 1 minute, or until it is thick and smooth. Add the shredded coconut and mix until it is just incorporated.

In the clean bowl of a stand mixer fitted with the whisk attachment, or in a bowl using a hand mixer, beat the egg whites with the cream of tartar until they form stiff, glossy peaks. Using a wooden spoon, gently fold the egg whites into the batter until you can no longer see clumps of white.

Pour the batter into the prepared pan. Bake the cake for 45 to 55 minutes, until the top cracks slightly and the edges have pulled away from the sides of the pan.

Let the cake cool in the pan on a wire rack for at least an hour.

Make the icing: In a small, heavy saucepan, combine the sugar and ½ cup (120 ml) water. Clip a candy thermometer to the side of the saucepan and set the pan over medium-high heat. Bring the syrup to a boil, whisking to make sure the sugar dissolves, and cook until the temperature registers 239°F (115°C; soft-ball stage) on the thermometer. (This will take several minutes.)

CONTINUED

Meanwhile, in the clean bowl of a stand mixer fitted with a clean whisk attachment, beat the egg whites until they are opaque and frothy. Add the cream of tartar and continue to beat on high until the egg whites are thick and foamy.

With the mixer on high speed, pour the hot sugar syrup into the whipping egg whites in a slow, steady stream, being careful to keep the hot syrup between the bowl and the whisk to prevent sprays of sugar on your skin. Beat the meringue for 7 minutes, or until the egg whites are very shiny and hold deep folds; the mixer bowl should be cool to the touch on the bottom. Beat in the vanilla, just to combine it.

Make the filling: In a food processor fitted with the S-blade, combine the almond paste with the corn syrup and one to two drops of the food coloring (if using). Mix them on high until the paste is very smooth. If the almond paste is crumbly, add a bit more corn syrup, a teaspoon at a time, until it folds in on itself.

Lightly dust your work surface with confectioners' sugar. Turn out the marzipan mixture and roll it into a circle ¼ inch (6 mm) thick and 11 inches (28 cm) in diameter.

Assemble the cake: Invert the cooled cake onto a wire rack and peel off the parchment. Wrap a thread or piece of unflavored dental floss around the circumference of the cake, halfway from top to bottom and draw the thread or floss tight, using it to cut the cake into two layers. (You can also do this with a long, very sharp or serrated knife.

Set one layer on a serving plate or cake stand. Place the marzipan disk on top. Dollop ⅔ cup (165 ml) of the icing onto the marzipan and spread it toward the edges. Top it with the second cake layer. Ice the cake with the remaining icing. Press crushed pistachios into the sides of the cake and sprinkle the top with toasted coconut for a showstopping finish.

The cake will keep, covered under a glass cloche (see sidebar, page 156) or cake dome, in the refrigerator for up to 1 week or at room temperature for a few days.

ORANGE–OLIVE OIL CAKE

Infusing the eggs with the orange zest is the trick that gets the citrusy, aromatic tang that permeates every bite of this Italian classic. "Light" olive oil and extra-virgin work equally well in this cake, so don't feel like you have to use your finest bottle. This cake is a go-to for serving just about any time of day.

MAKES ONE 9-INCH (23-CM) SINGLE-LAYER CAKE

Preheat the oven to 350°F (175°C). Spray a 9-inch (23-cm) springform pan with nonstick cooking spray and line the bottom with parchment paper cut to fit. Spray the paper with nonstick cooking spray as well.

In the bowl of the stand mixer fitted with the whisk attachment, combine the eggs and citrus zests. Set them aside to infuse for at least 15 minutes.

Beat the eggs and zests on high speed until they froth. With the mixer running, add the granulated sugar in a slow, steady stream. Whisk until the mixture is pale yellow and has doubled in volume. Add the oil in the same fashion, scraping down the sides of the bowl as necessary.

In a large bowl, sift together the Cake & Muffin Blend, baking powder, and salt. Using a wooden spoon or a silicone spatula, fold the dry ingredients into the egg mixture, alternating it with the milk. Mix just until combined.

Pour the batter into the prepared pan and bake for 30 to 40 minutes, until the cake is golden brown and the edges pull away from the sides of the pan. Let the cake cool in the pan for at least 15 minutes before inverting it onto a cutting board. Remove the parchment paper. Immediately turn the cake back over, so the top of the cake will remain flawless, and then transfer it to a wire rack to cool completely.

In a small bowl, stir the confectioners' sugar into the crème fraîche.

Dust the cooled cake with confectioners' sugar and serve slices garnished with a mint sprig and some of the sweetened crème fraîche spooned on the side.

2 large eggs

Zest of 1 large orange

Zest of 1 large tangelo

1 cup plus 2 tablespoons (225 g) granulated sugar

⅓ cup plus 1 tablespoon (105 ml) olive oil

1½ cups (176 g) Cake & Muffin Blend (page 149)

1½ teaspoons plus ⅛ teaspoon baking powder

¼ teaspoon kosher salt

¼ cup plus 2 tablespoons (90 ml) whole milk

1 cup (240 ml) crème fraîche or sour cream

1 tablespoon confectioners' sugar, plus more for dusting

Fresh mint leaves, for garnish

CUCKOO CARROT CAKE

The rum-soaked raisins in this cake make everyone go cuckoo, but I like to believe it's the awesome flavor complement with the carrot and spices, not the booze effect. (The alcohol surely all bakes out. But just in case, serve each slice of cake with a big old glass of milk.)

MAKES ONE 8-INCH (20-CM) SQUARE SINGLE-LAYER CAKE

Make the cake: Preheat the oven to 350°F (175°C). Set an oven rack in the middle position. Grease one 8-inch (20-cm) square cake pan with butter and line the bottoms with parchment paper cut to fit. Flip the paper so both sides are buttered.

Put the raisins in a small bowl and pour the rum over them. Let them soak for at least 15 minutes.

In the bowl of a stand mixer fitted with the paddle attachment, combine the Cake & Muffin Blend, sugars, cinnamon, baking powder, salt, cloves, and allspice and beat them briefly on low speed to combine. Add the eggs, oil, milk, and vanilla and beat on medium speed until the batter is well combined.

Drain the raisins, reserving ¼ cup (60 ml) of the rum. Pour the reserved rum into the batter and mix just to combine. Fold in the carrots and raisins.

Cover the batter with plastic wrap and refrigerate for 1 hour. After 1 hour, remove the batter from the fridge and pour the batter into the prepared pan. Bake the cake for 25 to 35 minutes, until a toothpick inserted into the middle comes out clean.

Let the cake cool in the pan for 10 minutes, so the cake is fully set, then invert the cake onto a wire rack to cool completely. Peel off the parchment paper from the bottom.

Meanwhile, make the icing: In a bowl of a stand mixer fitted with the paddle attachment, beat the butter until it is pale and smooth. If there are any lumps of butter remaining, your icing will be lumpy, so remember: Not enough o's in *smooth*. Add the cream cheese and keep mixing until you no longer see streaks of butter, about 1 minute. Turn the mixer off and add the confectioners' sugar and vanilla. Starting on low speed and slowly increasing to high, whip the icing for 3 minutes, or until it is so fluffy that it could not conceivably be fluffier. Stop to scrape down the sides of the bowl a couple of times.

CONTINUED

FOR THE CAKE:

1 cup (225 g) golden raisins

⅓ cup (75 ml) dark rum

2 cups (234 g) Cake & Muffin Blend (page 149)

1½ cups (300 g) granulated sugar

½ cup plus 2 tablespoons (135 g) packed light brown sugar

2 teaspoons ground cinnamon

1¾ teaspoons baking powder

1¼ teaspoons kosher salt

½ teaspoon ground cloves

1 teaspoon ground allspice

4 large eggs

½ cup (120 ml) grapeseed oil

1 cup (240 ml) milk

2 tablespoons pure vanilla extract

1½ cups (285 g) finely grated carrots

FOR THE CREAM CHEESE ICING:

½ cup (1 stick / 113 g) unsalted butter, softened

1½ pounds (680 g) cream cheese, at room temperature

2½ cups (250 g) sifted confectioners' sugar

1 teaspoon pure vanilla extract

Red, yellow, and green food coloring

½ cup (64 g) roughly chopped walnuts or pecans

Put a couple of tablespoons of the icing into each of two bowls. Add a drop of red and a drop of yellow food coloring to one of the bowls and a drop of green food coloring to the other. Mix until no streaks of color remain. You should have a bowl of pale orange and a bowl of pale green icing. Transfer each color of icing to a separate pastry bag, fitted with a leaf tip for the green and a plain small tip for the orange. (This part is totally optional, but darn if it doesn't look amazing!) Transfer another uncolored ½ cup (120 ml) icing to a pastry bag fitted with a small plain tip for piping the decorative edge.

Assemble the cake: Place the cake on a serving plate or cake stand and spread a layer of icing over the top. Using a plastic pastry scraper, spread ¾ cup (180 ml) of the icing all over the cake for the crumb coat. Place the cake in the freezer for at least 15 minutes to set the icing, then remove the cake and cover it with the rest of the icing. With an offset spatula, make the icing as level and as smooth as possible.

Make a stencil: Cut a strip of parchment paper the width of the side of the cake. From one end, cut out a quarter-circle shape. Align the stencil on the side of the cake so the corners of the cake can be pressed with chopped pecans. Remove and repeat until all of the corners of the cake have been covered with pecans.

Pipe a pearl bead edge around the top and bottom of the cake with the white icing, then pipe a carrot into each corner with the orange and green icing.

The cake will keep, covered with a glass cloche (see page 156) or cake dome, in the cool part of your kitchen for 3 days, or in a cake box in the refrigerator for up to 1 week.

VARIATION: Carrot Muffins

If you aren't in the mood for the icing, use the cake batter to make muffins, or ice them with just the cream cheese icing and make cupcakes if you need something to take to your next party.

RUM'S CUSTARDY BUNDT CAKE

The secret ingredients here are the enriched milk-and-egg combo that gives the cake a custard-like quality and the raisins, which *don't* go into the cake, but flavor the rum. Save the rum-laced raisins for Cuckoo Carrot Cake (page 165) or to swirl into vanilla ice cream. (Another nice use is to mix them up with a bowl of yogurt, granola, and fruit for an adults-only breakfast.)

MAKES ONE 10-INCH (25-CM) BUNDT CAKE

Preheat the oven to 325°F (165°C). Butter a 10-inch (25-cm) non-stick Bundt pan and dust it with additional Cake & Muffin Blend, tapping to remove any excess.

In a small bowl, soak the raisins in the rum overnight. Strain the raisins, reserving the rum (you should have at least ½ cup / 120 ml left). Save the raisins for another use.

In a large bowl, sift together the Cake & Muffin Blend, cornstarch, powdered milk, baking powder, and salt.

In the bowl of a stand mixer fitted with the paddle attachment, cream together the butter and the sugars. When you can no longer see any lumps of butter, add the eggs and the egg yolks. Beat on high for 2 minutes, then add the oil and vanilla and beat for 1 minute more. Add the rum, mixing just until it is combined, and then add the dry ingredients and beat on high until the batter is smooth.

Pour the batter into the prepared pan. Bake for 1 hour and 15 minutes, or until a toothpick inserted into the middle of the cake comes out clean. Let the cake cool for 10 minutes in the pan and then invert it onto a wire rack and let it cool completely.

Serve the cake with a dusting of confectioners' sugar and good strong coffee.

The cake will keep, covered, in the refrigerator for up to 1 week.

1 cup (240 ml) rum

¾ cup (200 g) raisins

2½ cups (293 g) Cake & Muffin Blend (page 149), plus more for the pan

¼ cup (30 g) cornstarch

¼ cup (30 g) powdered milk

1 tablespoon baking powder

1¼ teaspoons kosher salt

3 tablespoons unsalted butter, at room temperature, plus more for the pan

2 cups (400 g) granulated sugar

¾ cup (165 g) packed light brown sugar

4 large eggs

4 egg yolks

½ cup (120 ml) pure olive oil

2 tablespoons pure vanilla extract

½ cup (120 ml) whole milk

Confectioners' sugar, for dusting

BUBBLY CHERRY COFFEE CAKE

FOR THE CHERRY FILLING:

2 pounds (910 g) fresh sweet cherries, pitted

1 cup (200 g) granulated sugar

¼ teaspoon kosher salt

Juice of 1 lemon

3 tablespoons cornstarch

⅛ teaspoon freshly grated nutmeg

1 tablespoon unsalted butter, plus more for the pan

1½ teaspoons almond extract

FOR THE CAKE:

3 cups (351 g) Cake & Muffin Blend (page 149)

1½ cups (300 g) granulated sugar

1½ teaspoons baking powder

½ teaspoon kosher salt

1 cup (2 sticks / 226 g) unsalted butter, cold and diced

4 large eggs

2¼ teaspoons pure vanilla extract

2 teaspoons almond extract

FOR THE GLAZE:

1 cup (100 g) confectioners' sugar

2 tablespoons milk

Splash of almond extract

When I was growing up, my mom made this coffee cake Every. Single. Weekend. And even she agrees: It's better gluten-free. The original cake came from her *Century of Success Cookbook*, and I fondly remember helping her measure out all the ingredients. The cake is buttery and crumbly beyond compare and is best described as a warm shortcake with a finer finish. Since most store-bought pie fillings are not gluten-free, I've made a super-simple one from scratch and as a result the cherry flavor is far more intense. The bubbling cherry filling, coupled with this delicate cake, is to die for. Who says you can't have cake for breakfast? I highly recommend trying this one for your next brunch.

MAKES ONE 9-BY-13-INCH CAKE

Make the cherry filling: In a large bowl, combine the cherries with ½ cup (100 g) of the sugar and the salt and toss well to coat them. Pour the cherries into the prepared pan and roast them until they are just soft, about 10 minutes.

In a large bowl, whisk together the remaining ½ cup (100 g) sugar with the lemon juice, cornstarch, and nutmeg. Add the hot cherries and toss them to coat.

Melt the butter in a large skillet over medium heat. When it foams, add the roasted cherry mixture and stir until the cherries begin to release their juices. Add ¼ cup (60 ml) water and simmer, stirring, until the filling is thick. Remove the pan from the heat and stir in the almond extract. Set the filling aside to cool completely.

Make the cake: Preheat the oven to 350°F (175°C). Grease a 9-by-13-inch (23-by-33-cm) baking pan with butter.

In the bowl of a stand mixer fitted with the paddle attachment, combine the Cake & Muffin Blend, sugar, baking powder, and salt and beat them briefly to combine. Add the butter and beat on the lowest speed until the mixture resembles damp cornmeal, about 5 minutes.

In a bowl, whisk together the eggs, vanilla, and almond extract. Add the egg mixture to the dry ingredients and beat on high speed for 1 minute. Scrape down the sides of the bowl and beat the batter for 30 seconds more. The batter should be thick.

Spread two-thirds of the batter over the bottom of the prepared pan and level it with a spatula. Spread the cooled cherry filling evenly over the batter. Spoon the remaining batter over the pie filling, leaving gaps for the filling to bubble up.

Bake the cake until the crust is golden brown and the filling is bubbling, 30 to 40 minutes.

Meanwhile, make the glaze: In a small bowl, whisk together the confectioners' sugar and milk. Add the almond extract and keep whisking until the glaze is smooth.

Assemble the coffee cake: Using a fork, a whisk, or a squeeze bottle, drizzle the glaze over the warm cake. Cut the cake into 2½-inch (6-cm) squares. The cake will keep, covered, at room temperature for up to 3 days or in the fridge for up to 1 week.

BOSTON CREAM PIE

FOR THE CAKE:

1 cup (117 g) Cake & Muffin Blend (page 149)

½ cup plus 2 tablespoons (125 g) superfine sugar

⅛ teaspoon kosher salt, finely crushed (see Note)

4 large eggs, at room temperature

2 teaspoons pure vanilla extract

2 tablespoons unsalted butter, softened, plus extra for the pan

½ recipe Pastry Cream (page 105), chilled

FOR THE GLAZE:

8 ounces (225 g) semisweet chocolate chips

¼ cup (60 ml) heavy cream

3 tablespoons unsalted butter

1 tablespoon light corn syrup

1 teaspoon pure vanilla extract

NOTE: I use the bottom of a glass, on a cutting board, to crush the salt.

This "pie," which is really a cake, is founded on a classic of French baking, the génoise, an egg-leavened sponge cake. My three tricks for making a perfect sponge cake: Use room-temperature eggs; beat the melted butter first into just a bit of the egg mixture, so they combine smoothly; and fold in the dry ingredients slowly and gently, never fast.

MAKES ONE 8-INCH (20-CM) CAKE

Preheat the oven to 350°F (175°C). Lightly butter an 8-inch (20-cm) round cake pan and line the bottom with parchment paper cut to fit. Press the paper into the butter, then flip the paper over to evenly coat both sides with butter.

Make the cake: In a medium bowl, sift together the Cake & Muffin Blend, 1 tablespoon of the sugar, and the salt.

In the bowl of a stand mixer fitted with the whisk attachment, whisk the eggs with the remaining ½ cup plus 1 tablespoon (112 g) sugar until they have tripled in size, 5 to 7 minutes. Whisk in the vanilla.

Melt the butter either in the microwave or in a small saucepan.

Whisk the butter with 2 to 3 tablespoons of the egg mixture. Once they're smoothly combined, whisk the butter mixture back into the remaining egg mixture. Using a wooden spoon, gently fold in the dry ingredients in three batches.

Pour the batter into the prepared pan. Bake for 10 to 12 minutes, until the cake is copper colored. Let the cake cool for 5 minutes in the pan, then invert it onto a wire rack, peel off the parchment paper, and let the cake cool completely.

Level the domed top of the cake, if necessary, using a long serrated knife. Cut the cake in half horizontally with the serrated knife or unflavored dental floss (see page 162). Place one layer on a serving plate and top it with the pastry cream. Place the second cake layer on top, cover it very lightly with plastic wrap, and refrigerate it for 3 hours to set the pastry cream.

Meanwhile, make the glaze: Place the chocolate chips in a small bowl. In a small saucepan, heat the cream, butter, and corn syrup. When the mixture steams, but doesn't quite boil, pour it over the chocolate chips. Let stand for 5 minutes to melt the chocolate. Whisk until the mixture is well combined and smooth, then add the vanilla. Let cool for 10 minutes.

Starting in the middle of the cake top and moving outward in a spiral, pour the glaze over the cake and down the sides. Refrigerate it for 2 hours before serving to set the chocolate. Store in a cake box in the fridge until you are ready to serve.

ANGEL FOOD CAKE

¾ cup (88 g) Cake & Muffin Blend (page 149)

¼ cup (30 g) cornstarch

¼ teaspoon kosher salt, crushed

1½ cups plus 1 tablespoon (312 g) superfine sugar

Scant 1 teaspoon cream of tartar

11 egg whites (about 1½ cups / 360 ml), at room temperature

¼ teaspoon pure vanilla extract

1 teaspoon orange flower water

Repeated sifting of the dry ingredients is what gets you the light-as-air texture of a traditional angel food cake. If you skip that step, the angels might get cross. Fresh mascerated strawberries and sweetened whipped cream are ideal accompaniments.

MAKES ONE 9-INCH (23-CM) TUBE CAKE

Preheat the oven to 375°F (190°C).

Sift the Cake & Muffin Blend, cornstarch, and crushed salt into a large bowl. Sift again into a separate bowl. Add ¾ cup (150 g) of the sugar and sift the mixture twice more. Set aside.

Sift the remaining ¾ cup plus 1 tablespoon (162 g) sugar with the cream of tartar into a medium bowl and set them aside.

In the bowl of a stand mixer fitted with the whisk attachment, whisk the egg whites until they begin to froth and turn opaque, then add the vanilla and orange flower water. Whisk on high until the egg whites become a stark white, about 2 minutes. Add the sifted sugar and cream of tartar and whisk on high until the meringue is firm, glossy, and holds stiff peaks, 1 to 2 minutes more.

Using a wooden spoon, gently fold the meringue into the sifted dry ingredients in ¼-cup (60-ml) increments, mixing just until they are incorporated after each addition.

Pour the batter into a 9-by-4.5-inch (23-by-11-cm) tube pan with legs and a removable bottom. Place the pan on a rimmed baking sheet and bake the cake for 30 to 35 minutes. The cake is done when it's a golden copper color and springs back like a sponge at a gentle touch.

Run an offset spatula or flexible knife along the insides of the pan to free the cake, if necessary, and immediately invert the cake onto a wire rack—the sides of the pan should fall away so you can remove the bottom. Let the cake cool for 1 to 2 hours.

Serve the cake upside down and cut slices with a serrated knife.

The cake will keep, covered, at room temperature for up to 3 days or in the refrigerator for up to 1 week.

JEWISH STACKED APPLE CAKE

This rich-tasting but dairy-free cake is perfect for serving during the big holidays and is dedicated to my lovely friend, Rebecca Saltsman.

MAKES ONE 9-INCH (23-CM) TUBE CAKE

Preheat the oven to 350°F (175°C). Set an oven rack in the middle position. Liberally grease a 9-by-4.5-inch (23-by-11-cm) tube pan with legs and a removable bottom, with vegetable shortening, being careful to wedge extra shortening into any creases or joints. Line the bottom with parchment paper cut to fit and lightly grease the paper.

Make the apples: In a large bowl, combine the sugar, cinnamon, zest (if using), and salt. Add the apples and toss to coat them evenly. Set aside.

Make the cake: In a large bowl, sift together the Cake & Muffin Blend, sugar, baking powder, and salt.

In a separate bowl, combine the olive oil, orange juice, and vanilla and whisk to combine.

In the bowl of a stand mixer fitted with the whisk attachment, whisk the eggs on high speed until they begin to froth. In a steady stream, add the sugar and whisk until the mixture has doubled in volume. Reduce the speed and add the dry ingredients and the olive oil mixture in alternating batches, scraping down the sides of the bowl as necessary. Mix until the dry ingredients are completely incorporated, then whisk on high for 2 minutes, or until the batter is thick.

Pour a ½-inch (12-mm) layer of batter into the prepared pan. Arrange a layer of apples on top, leaving a ½-inch (12-mm) border between the apples and the sides of the pan. Pour in another ½-inch (12-mm) layer of batter, or whatever it takes to cover the apples. Repeat with another layer of apples and finish with the remaining batter.

Bake the cake for 30 to 35 minutes, then loosely tent it with foil and bake for 20 to 25 minutes more, until the top of the cake is golden brown and a toothpick inserted into the middle comes out clean.

Let the cake cool in the pan for 30 minutes, then invert it onto a wire rack. Run an offset spatula or flexible knife along the insides of the pan to free the cake, if necessary, and remove the bottom. Peel off the parchment. Serve the cake cooled or warm.

The cake will keep, covered with plastic wrap, at room temperature for a few days, or in the refrigerator for up to 1 week.

Vegetable shortening, for greasing the pan

FOR THE APPLES:

½ cup (100 g) sugar

2½ teaspoons ground cinnamon

1 teaspoon freshly grated orange zest (optional)

Pinch of kosher salt

4 medium Golden Delicious apples, peeled, cored, and sliced very thin

FOR THE CAKE:

3¼ cups (381 g) Cake & Muffin Blend (page 149)

2¾ cups (550 g) sugar

4 teaspoons baking powder

¾ teaspoon kosher salt

1 cup plus 3 tablespoons (285 ml) pure olive oil

¾ cup (180 ml) orange juice

2½ tablespoons pure vanilla extract

6 large eggs

TITO'S TEXAS SHEET CAKE

FOR THE CAKE:

1 cup (230 g) sliced pitted Medjool dates

1 teaspoon baking soda

2 tablespoons Tito's Texas Handmade Vodka

2 linden tea bags

4 prunes, pitted and halved

2 cups (235 g) Cake & Muffin Blend (page 149)

1½ cups plus 2 tablespoons (325 g) granulated sugar

¼ cup (28 g) almond meal

¼ cup (28 g) black onyx cocoa powder (see Note)

4 teaspoons baking powder

1 teaspoon kosher salt

¼ teaspoon cayenne

1 cup (2 sticks / 226 g) unsalted butter, cold and diced

3 large eggs

½ cup (120 ml) whole milk

4 teaspoons pure vanilla extract

Tito Beveridge (yes, that's his real name, and yes, I thought he was kidding) is the founder of Tito's Handmade Vodka. If it weren't for a life-changing conversation that he and I had one afternoon, I would have thrown up my hands and walked away from gluten-free cooking forever. To show my appreciation, I figured the least I could do was bake him a cake. Tito's a chocolate lover to the core, and I decided to add a little Texas heat (and a generous pour of Tito's famous vodka) for a cake that will curl your gluten-free eyelashes. Like your vodka, Tito, you are one in a million.

MAKES ONE 9-BY-13-INCH (23-BY-33-CM) SHEET CAKE; SERVES 16

Make the cake: In a medium saucepan, bring 1 cup (240 ml) water to a boil. Add the dates and boil them for 1 minute. Remove them from the heat and add the baking soda—the dates will bubble and fizz. Add the vodka and let the mixture cool; the dates will absorb most of the liquid. Drain them if they don't.

In a separate small saucepan, bring 2 cups (480 ml) water to a boil. Add the tea and prunes, reduce the heat to low, and simmer for at least 20 minutes, until the prunes are tender. Remove and discard the tea bags. Strain the prunes through a fine-mesh sieve, set over a bowl, and reserve the syrup.

Transfer the prunes and the vodka-soaked dates (with any residual liquid), to a food processor and puree until they are thick and foamy.

Preheat the oven to 350°F (175°C). Line a 9-by-13-inch (quarter sheet) jelly-roll or sheet cake pan with foil. Lightly grease the foil.

In a large bowl, whisk together the Cake & Muffin Blend, sugar, almond meal, cocoa powder, baking powder, salt, and cayenne.

In the bowl of a stand mixer fitted with the paddle attachment, combine the butter and the dry ingredients and beat them on the lowest speed until the mixture resembles damp cornmeal, about 5 minutes.

In a medium bowl, whisk together the eggs, milk, and vanilla. Add the egg mixture to the butter mixture and beat on medium-high speed until the batter begins to fluff up and fold in onto itself. Turn off the mixer, scrape down the sides of the bowl, and add the pureed prunes and dates. Mix just until combined and the batter looks like thick pudding.

Pour the batter into the prepared pan and bake for 30 to 40 minutes, until the cake begins to pull away from the sides of the pan (taking the foil with it) and feels like a delicate sponge to the touch. Let the cake cool in the pan for 5 minutes, then invert it onto a large serving platter while still warm. Remove and discard the foil.

Meanwhile, make the icing: In a medium bowl, sift together the confectioners' sugar and cocoa powders.

In a large saucepan, combine the butter, milk, and corn syrup and bring to a boil over low heat. When the mixture boils, whisk in the cocoa mixture. Keep whisking until the icing is smooth and a loose ribbon drips off the end of your whisk. Finish by stirring in the vanilla.

Pour the hot icing over the warm cake and smooth it with an offset spatula so the icing drips off and down the sides.

Toss the pecans in the oil and *sel gris* and scatter them over the iced cake. Allow the cake to cool completely.

Measure 2 cups (480 ml) of the reserved syrup from the linden tea and place it in a small saucepan with the caster sugar. Bring them to a boil over medium heat, then reduce the heat to low and simmer until the syrup has reduced to ½ cup.

To serve, drizzle a little of this linden nectar on a plate and top it with a slice of cake.

NOTE: Black onyx (sometimes just called black) cocoa powder is a highly alkalized, or "ultra-Dutch-processed" cocoa powder. When the cocoa's acidity has been neutralized, it becomes very smooth and not the least bit bitter. It lends a very dark color to whatever you're baking—but it can dry out your baked goods if not balanced with additional fat or a proportional ratio of Dutch-process (no ultra!) or standard cocoa. See page 227 for sources.

FOR THE ICING:

3 cups (300 g) confectioners' sugar

3 tablespoons black onyx cocoa powder (see Note)

¼ cup (28 g) unsweetened cocoa powder

6 tablespoons (84 g) butter

½ cup plus 3 tablespoons (120 ml) milk

1 tablespoon corn syrup

1 teaspoon pure vanilla extract

1 cup (128 g) pecan pieces, toasted

1 teaspoon olive oil

1 teaspoon *sel gris*

3 tablespoons caster sugar

HOSTESS-STYLE CUPCAKES

Those Hostess cupcakes were a big thing when I was a little thing. I rate these, and their cream filling, as write-it-in-my-epitaph gluten-free accomplishments.

MAKES 24 CUPCAKES

Make the cream filling: In the bowl of a stand mixer fitted with the whisk attachment, whip the cream with the confectioners' sugar and vanilla until thick.

Spoon 1 cup (240 ml) of the filling into a piping bag fitted with a small plain tip. Reserve the remainder in the bowl, covered. Set aside or refrigerate until you're ready to use.

Make the cupcakes: Preheat the oven to 350°F (175°C). Line the cups of two standard cupcake tins with paper liners.

Divide the cake batter among the cups, filling them three-quarters full. Bake for 15 to 20 minutes, until the cupcakes are springy to the touch.

Let the cupcakes cool in the pans for 5 minutes before transferring them to a wire rack to cool completely.

Meanwhile, make the icing: Place the chocolate chips in a bowl. In a small saucepan, melt the butter. Pour the hot butter over the chocolate and let stand for a few minutes to melt the chocolate. Whisk until smooth and well combined, then whisk in the corn syrup and espresso.

Assemble the cupcakes: Insert the point of a sharp paring knife into the top of a cupcake at a 45-degree angle. Cut a cone from the center of the cupcake. Cut the cone in half horizontally and set aside the top (unpointed) portion. Pipe about 1 tablespoon of the filling into the hole and then cover it with the reserved top portion of the cone. Repeat until all of your cupcakes have been filled.

Using a spatula or butter knife, ice the cupcakes with the chocolate icing and set them aside to let the icing set. Pipe the reserved filling on top in the trademark curlicue design.

The cupcakes will keep in an airtight container at room temperature for a few days or for up to 1 week in the fridge. These shouldn't be frozen.

FOR THE CREAM FILLING:

2 cups (480 ml) heavy cream

¼ cup (25 g) confectioners' sugar

Splash of pure vanilla extract

FOR THE CUPCAKES:

1 recipe Chocolate Mayonnaise Cake batter (page 157)

FOR THE ICING:

1½ cups (252 g) semisweet chocolate chips

½ cup (1 stick / 113 g) unsalted butter

2 tablespoons light corn syrup

1 teaspoon instant espresso

BIG RED VELVET CUPCAKES

Butter, for the pans

2¼ cups (264 g) Cake & Muffin Blend (page 149)

1½ cups (250 g) granulated sugar

½ cup (55 g) packed light brown sugar

⅓ cup plus 1½ teaspoons (50 g) cornstarch

5 tablespoons (34 g) unsweetened cocoa powder

1 tablespoon baking powder

1⅛ teaspoons kosher salt

½ cup (120 ml) vegetable oil

4 large eggs

1 tablespoon pure vanilla extract

¼ cup (60 ml) buttermilk

½ cup (120 ml) 2% milk

1 teaspoon apple cider vinegar

Red food coloring (optional)

1 recipe Cream Cheese Icing (page 165)

Life would be meaningless without a little red velvet cake. The tang of this one, with the pop of the icing, is truly a marvel. The food coloring is optional, but the cake is just plain velvet without. I get the best results with gel or powder food coloring, as some liquid red dyes will look pink. (If you do use food coloring, don't forget to pack a toothbrush and a tube of whitening toothpaste to get rid of the red devil-tongue effect that is part of the deal.) I make these in jumbo-size muffin cups for that extra-big effect.

MAKES 12 JUMBO CUPCAKES OR ONE 9-INCH (23-CM) DOUBLE-LAYER CAKE

Preheat the oven to 350°F (175°C). Line two 6-cup jumbo muffin tins with paper liners.

In the bowl of a stand mixer fitted with the paddle attachment, sift together the Cake & Muffin Blend, sugars, cornstarch, cocoa powder, baking powder, and salt.

In a separate bowl, whisk together the oil, eggs, and vanilla until they are uniform. Add the egg mixture to the dry mixture and mix on low speed until the combination is pudding-thick. Add the buttermilk, milk, and vinegar and mix on high until the batter is smooth.

If desired, whisk in 1 tablespoon (or more, if needed!) of the food coloring, until the batter is as red as you'd like it.

Evenly divide the batter among the muffin cups, filling them three-quarters full. Bake them for 25 to 30 minutes, or until a toothpick inserted in the center of the cupcakes comes out clean.

Cool the cupcakes in the pans on wire racks for 5 minutes. Transfer the cupcakes to the racks to cool completely.

Transfer the icing to a pastry bag fitted with a ½-inch (12-mm) star tip and pipe a generous portion onto each cupcake.

The cupcakes will keep, covered, at room temperature for 3 days or in the refrigerator for up to 1 week.

JELLY-FILLED CUPCAKES

1 cup (320 g) fruit preserves

1⅓ cups plus 2 tablespoons (176 g) Cake & Muffin Blend (page 149)

1½ teaspoons baking powder

¼ teaspoon kosher salt

6 tablespoons (84 g) unsalted butter, preferably cultured, cold and diced

1 cup (200 g) sugar

3 large eggs

1 cup (120 ml) milk

2 tablespoons sour cream

1 tablespoon pure vanilla extract

½ recipe Cream Cheese Icing (page 165)

VARIATION:
Get-Your-Goat Cupcakes

This is for a more *sophistiqué* version, or just to intimidate people with your culinary skill and incorporate a little chèvre into the filling. In the bowl of a stand mixer fitted with the paddle attachment, or in a bowl using a hand mixer, whip 1 cup (114 g) soft goat cheese until it is smooth and stir it into the strained, cooled preserves. Proceed as directed, then ice the cupcakes with a batch of French Buttercream Icing (page 88).

It was my vintage 1932 edition of the *Household Searchlight Recipe Book* of Topeka, Kansas, that made me aware there was such a thing as a jelly-filled cupcake. Jelly donuts, sure—but cupcakes? How such a delight fell out of culinary fashion is beyond me.

MAKES 12 CUPCAKES

Preheat the oven to 350°F (175°C). Set an oven rack in the middle position. Line the wells of a standard cupcake tin with paper liners.

In a small saucepan, heat the preserves over medium heat until they are liquid. Pour them through a fine-mesh strainer into a bowl; discard any solids in the strainer. Set the strained preserves aside to cool completely.

In the bowl of a stand mixer fitted with the paddle attachment, combine the Cake & Muffin Blend, baking powder, and salt and mix them briefly to combine. Transfer to another bowl and sift the dry ingredients 3 times. Return bowl to stand mixer.

Add the butter and sugar and beat on high speed until the mixture is pale and fluffy, about 5 minutes. Add the eggs, one at a time, and mix on high until very fluffy and smooth. In a separate bowl, combine the milk, sour cream, and vanilla and whisk until very smooth.

With the mixer running, add the dry ingredients to the egg mixture in two batches, beating the batter well after each addition, immediately followed by the remaining wet ingredients. Beat the batter on high speed until it is light and fluffy.

Pour the batter into the prepared muffin cups, filling each cup just two-thirds full. Spoon 1 tablespoon of cooled preserves into the center of each, then cover the preserves with additional batter, filling the cups so they are three-quarters full.

Bake the cupcakes for 15 minutes, or until the tops are just barely colored and are springy to the touch. Let cool for 5 minutes in the pan, then unmold the cupcakes onto wire racks, right-side up, and let them cool completely.

Using a spatula, ice the cupcakes with the Cream Cheese Icing. (Alternatively, transfer the icing to a piping bag fitted with a star tip and decoratively pipe icing onto the tops of the cupcakes.) The cupcakes will keep, covered, in the fridge for a few days or in an airtight container at room temperature for up to 2 days.

VARIATION: Caramel Nutty Cupcakes

Forget the preserves. Forget the icing. Fill the cupcakes with Nutella or hazelnut-chocolate spread. Ice the cupcakes with Caramel Buttercream (page 88).

CAKE-STYLE ICE CREAM SANDWICHES

When people in Texas hear the name Bluebell Ice Cream, they think of two things: their homemade vanilla ice cream and their ice cream sandwiches. The sandwiches are held together with a confection that exists somewhere between a cookie and a cake. Here is my gluten-free take on this childhood favorite—and the perfect thing to make on a hot summer day.

MAKES 6 SANDWICHES

Preheat oven to 350°F (175°C) and butter a 9-by-13-inch (23-by-33-cm) jelly-roll pan with butter. Line the pan with parchment paper, pressing it into the butter. Flip the paper so both sides are greased. Set aside.

In the bowl of a stand mixer fitted with the paddle attachment, combine the Cake & Muffin Blend, cocoa, sugars, and salt and mix on low until the mixture is uniform. Add the oil, egg, egg yolks, and vanilla and mix on high until the batter looks like thick melted chocolate.

Pour the batter into the prepared pan and level the batter with an offset spatula. Bake for 15 to 20 minutes, until the edges of the cake have pulled away from the sides of the pan.

Let the cake cool for 15 minutes in the pan. Dust a cutting board with granulated sugar. Invert the cake onto the dusted surface and then flip the cake back over so the top side is up. Cut the cake in half horizontally, then cut 6 rectangles from each side that are at least 2¼ inches (5.5 cm) wide. You should have 12 rectangles. Take one of the rectangles and scoop ice cream onto the back side. (Since these cakes are thin, you really want the ice cream to be soft enough to spread, so work quickly. I like to make these with a friend so they can help wrap the sandwiches right away and put them into the freezer.) Level it with a spatula, then top with another cake rectangle. Repeat to make a total of 6 sandwiches. Wrap in plastic and refrigerate for 1 hour to set. Serve whenever you please!

These sandwiches keep well in the freezer for up to 2 months.

½ cup (59 g) Cake & Muffin Blend (page 149)

¼ cup (30 g) Dutch processed-cocoa powder

¼ cup packed (55 g) light brown sugar

¼ cup (50 g) granulated sugar, plus more for dusting

¼ teaspoon kosher salt

⅓ cup (80 ml) vegetable oil

1 large egg

2 egg yolks

1 tablespoon pure vanilla extract

1 gallon Bluebell Homemade Vanilla Ice Cream or other vanilla ice cream, softened enough to spread like icing

ZUCCHINI WALNUT MUFFINS

The pomegranate seeds give these zucchini muffins distinction, but for fancy parties, I like to sub out the pomegranate seeds for 2 teaspoons freshly grated ginger and then make a ginger icing for really lovely tea-cakes (see the variation below). You can also bake this as a breakfast loaf.

MAKES 6 JUMBO OR 12 REGULAR-SIZE MUFFINS

Preheat the oven to 375°F (190°C). Grease a jumbo muffin tin well, or line a standard muffin tin with paper liners. (I used vintage ones here, which are wider than normal.)

In a large bowl, whisk together the Cake & Muffin Blend, cinnamon, baking powder, and salt. Set aside. After you grate the zucchini, gently squeeze it in a kitchen towel to remove any excess water.

In the bowl of a stand mixer fitted with the paddle attachment, beat together the sugars, olive oil, and walnut oil until they are well combined. Add the eggs and beat on medium-high until fully incorporated and fluffy, about 1 minute.

Add the dry ingredients to the sugar mixture, followed by the milk, and mix just until the dry ingredients are fully incorporated. Fold in the zucchini, walnuts, and pomegranate seeds (if using).

Divide the batter among the muffin cups, filling them three-quarters full.

Bake for 25 to 35 minutes (18 to 20 minutes if you're using a regular-size muffin tin), until the muffins are firm to the touch. Allow them to cool in the pan for 5 minutes before transferring them to a wire rack to cool completely. (But they're also excellent warm, so if you can't wait, dig in!)

The muffins will keep in an airtight container at room temperature for 2 to 3 days, or frozen, double-wrapped, for up to 1 month.

VARIATION: Ginger-Glaze Muffins

In a small saucepan, combine ½ cup (100 g) granulated sugar and ¼ cup (60 ml) water and bring to a boil. Add 2 ounces (55 g) peeled fresh ginger slices. Remove the syrup from the heat and let the ginger steep for 20 minutes. Strain the syrup through a fine-mesh sieve into a bowl and discard the solids. Dice 4 tablespoons (½ stick / 56 g) salted butter. In the bowl of a stand mixer fitted with the paddle attachment, cream the butter with 3 cups (300 g) confectioners' sugar. With the mixer running, add the ginger-infused simple syrup in a thin, steady stream and mix it on high until the mixture is fluffy. Add milk, 1 tablespoon at a time, until the glaze is liquid (you'll use about 2 tablespoons). Pour the glaze over the muffins and garnish them with pieces of candied ginger and a bay leaf.

2 cups (234 g) Cake & Muffin Blend (page 149)

2 teaspoons ground cinnamon

1¾ teaspoons baking powder

½ teaspoon kosher salt

¾ cup (150 g) granulated sugar

¾ cup (165 g) packed light brown sugar

3 tablespoons pure olive oil

2 tablespoons walnut oil

3 large eggs

¼ cup (60 ml) whole or 2% milk

2½ cups (375 g) coarsely grated unpeeled zucchini

½ cup (64 g) coarsely chopped walnuts

½ cup (115 g) pomegranate seeds (optional)

WILD BLUEBERRY MUFFINS

2 cups plus 2 teaspoons (252 g)
Cake & Muffin Blend (page 149)

1¾ teaspoons baking powder

¼ teaspoon plus ⅛ teaspoon kosher
salt

¼ teaspoon freshly grated nutmeg

¼ teaspoon ground cinnamon

5 tablespoons (70 g) unsalted butter

¾ cup (150 g) granulated sugar

½ cup (110 g) packed light brown
sugar

3 large eggs

⅓ cup plus 1 tablespoon (90 ml)
whole milk

1 tablespoon pure vanilla extract

2 cups (450 g) fresh or thawed and
strained frozen wild blueberries

For the best blueberry muffins, I always get the finest results when I use wild blueberries instead of their larger cousins. Most grocery stores stock frozen wild blueberries these days. Be sure to defrost them completely and strain out any liquid before you use them, though, unless you want Barney-the-Purple-Dinosaur Muffins.

To keep the muffins from drying out overnight, I throw in a little brown sugar. It holds moisture and helps the molasses work its magic on the crumb and consistency of the muffins.

MAKES 12 MUFFINS

Preheat the oven to 375°F (190°C). Line the cups of a standard muffin tin with paper liners.

In a large bowl, sift together the Cake & Muffin Blend, baking powder, salt, nutmeg, and cinnamon.

In the bowl of a stand mixer fitted with the paddle attachment, beat the butter and the sugars on high speed until light and fluffy. Add the eggs one at a time, waiting until each addition has been fully incorporated and scraping down the sides of the bowl before adding the next. Beat on high for 2 minutes, then add the dry ingredients alternately with the milk and vanilla, and mix until just combined.

Using a wooden spoon, fold in the blueberries. Scoop the batter into the prepared muffin tin, filling the wells three-quarters full. Bake for 20 to 25 minutes, until the muffins rise and show a touch of color at the edges. Serve immediately.

The muffins will keep in an airtight container at room temperature for up to 3 days. They can also be frozen, double-wrapped, for up to 1 month.

THE JUAN PELOTA POWER MUFFIN

This is a tribute to the good people of Austin's Juan Pelota Café and for all other believers in optimized health and fitness. Packed with protein and free of refined sugar, these muffins give you the crank without the crash. You can also bake the batter in a loaf pan for a slice-and-serve power bread—just butter and line a 9-by-5-inch (23-by-12-cm) loaf pan with parchment paper and proceed with the recipe as directed.

MAKES 6 JUMBO OR 12 REGULAR-SIZE MUFFINS

Preheat the oven to 375°F (190°C). Grease a jumbo muffin tin well, or line a standard muffin tin with paper liners.

In a stand mixer fitted with the paddle attachment, cream together the unsalted butter and the palm sugar. Mix until it is thick and you can no longer see clumps of butter, about 2 minutes.

Add the eggs, one at a time, mixing well after each addition, then mix on high until doubled in volume, 2 to 3 minutes.

Turn off the mixer, add the oats, almond meal flour, whey protein, maca powder, baking powder, salt, and cinnamon, and then turn the mixer to the lowest setting. Slowly add the almond milk and vanilla extract. When the milk is fully incorporated, turn the mixer to high and mix for 1 to 1½ minutes. Add the chia seeds last and mix just until combined.

Divide the batter among the muffin cups. Bake for 15 to 20 minutes until a skewer inserted into the middle comes out clean.

Like most muffins, these are best enjoyed the day they are made, but they will keep for up to 3 days in an airtight container.

5 tablespoons (70 g) unsalted butter, diced

1¾ cups (247 g) coconut palm sugar

3 large eggs

1½ cups (176 g) Cake & Muffin Blend (page 149)

¾ cup (113 g) gluten-free quick oats

¼ cup (22 g) almond meal flour

2 tablespoons (28 g) vanilla whey protein

2 tablespoons (22 g) maca powder

1¾ teaspoons baking powder

¾ teaspoon kosher salt

1 teaspoon ground cinnamon

1¾ cups (420 ml) almond milk

1 tablespoon pure vanilla extract

2 tablespoons chia seeds

BREAD & PIZZA BLEND

The Bread & Pizza Blend has a high ratio of complete protein grains to guar gum, with just a touch of starches to achieve the *strrreeetttc-cchhh* that makes bread "bready." It's customized specifically for hearty, yeast-risen breads, but also functions as the perfect blend for everyday white sandwich bread, pizzas, and the more delicate molded breads like my three-braid challah.

I think it's fair to say that one of the biggest problems in the gluten-free world is the dearth of good breads. Since bread is considered the source of all nourishment, I worked for years to come up with a blend that wasn't just a bag of starches. When it comes to gluten-free bread, the very best loaves have one thing in common: They are bubbling with complete-protein grains. Gluten-free breads that boast a laundry list of starches are, across the board, extremely dense and either turn to dust in your mouth or, as is the case with most gluten-free pizzas, taste and look raw in the middle. Sadly, most store-bought breads are flavorless. In the Bread & Pizza Blend, you'll notice that the ratio of complete grains to starches is almost the exact same. It is this delicate balance that gives breads made with this blend the elasticity needed for good volume and even better flavor.

THE RECIPE

2½ plus 1½ teaspoons (282 g) sorghum flour

1⅛ cups plus 1 teaspoon (156 g) glutinous rice flour

½ cup plus ⅓ cup plus 1 tablespoon plus 1 teaspoon (100 g) tapioca starch

⅔ cup (60 g) gluten-free oat flour

¼ cup plus 2 teaspoons (50 g) potato starch

8 teaspoon (24 g) guar gum

2 tablespoons (20 g) meringue powder

Guar gum is important here for two reasons: The first is because guar gum is almost pure fiber and rich in minerals like zinc, which most celiacs are severely deficient in, and the second is the incredible structure guar gum creates. The cellular structure of guar gum is that of an arbor and resembles the blooming top of a tree, so to say guar gum was genetically engineered by mother nature for volume couldn't be more accurate. Xanthan gum's cellular structure, on the other hand, looks like fixed crystalline bricks. This makes it particularly bad for bread baking since it does the opposite of adding volume. (I have staunchly avoided xanthan gum since 2002 for other reasons, too—see page 222.)

The addition you might find most curious here is that of meringue powder. All good gluten-free breads contain eggs, but as I was building this blend, the extra liquid from a full egg, yolk and all, often destroyed the doughs I worked so hard to master. Since the albumen in the egg whites was a necessity to enhance the structure of my breads, I reduced the number of whole eggs and added meringue powder, which is essentially powdered egg whites. When shopping for meringue powder, make sure it is gluten-free. For the best brands, see the Resources section (page 227).

For more information about the flours, starches, and other ingredients used in the blend, please see the Pantry section, page 215.

MAKES 6½ CUPS (692 G), ENOUGH FOR 2 LOAVES OF BREAD OR 4 PIZZAS

Using the spoon-and-sweep method, measure each ingredient into a large bowl. Whisk together and then sift the mixture into a separate large bowl. Repeat several times.

The approximate weight of the blend, by volume (for use in doing your own adaptations):

EACH	OF BLEND WEIGHS APPROXIMATELY
1 tablespoon	8 g
¼ cup	29 g
⅓ cup	43 g
½ cup	57 g
⅔ cup	75 g
¾ cup	85 g
1 cup	112 g

THE DOUGH

USING EGGS (OR NOT)

Many of my bread recipes include eggs, which assist the guar gum and meringue powder in the blend to create elasticity and volume. The eggs also impart their luscious flavor and richness. As I mentioned on page 86, if you can't, or don't, eat eggs, use an egg substitute like Egg Replacer. Just be sure the egg substitute foams after the water is added. (If it doesn't foam, it's not activated and will not do the job you need it to.) To check this, just give the egg replacer a quick whisk before adding it to the dough. Please note that the omission of the meringue powder will affect the blend pretty substantially, so if you attempt to make breads without using it and they don't turn out as well as you'd hope, this is the reason.

MAKING A SPONGE

A *sponge* is a mixture of flour (or in the case of this book, Bread & Pizza blend), yeast, water, and sometimes eggs and spices. The ingredients are mixed together and set aside to ferment for a period of time. After that initial fermentation, the remaining bread ingredients are then sprinkled on top of the sponge and are either left to rest for a second time, in which the sponge then bubbles up through the added ingredients, or are immediately mixed in to form the final dough.

A gluten-free sponge performs the same functions as sponges in traditional bread baking. It helps build a robust bread flavor, and in my humble opinion, it makes for a better cell structure (meaning the size of

the holes in the finished bread). Many of the breads in this book require a sponge. The pumpernickel on page 210 wouldn't be the same without it, and your sourdough (page 201) would be anything but sour if you didn't begin with a sponge.

To make a sponge, combine the sponge ingredients as called for in the recipe. Mix well—the sponge will be wet and won't look very appetizing. Cover the bowl and chill the sponge for the time indicated before adding the remaining dough ingredients as directed in the recipe.

COLD PROOFING AND RISING

Most bread doughs made with the Bread & Pizza Blend require a period of *cold proofing*, or rest and rising in the refrigerator. The cold proof is imperative to slow down the production of carbon dioxide in the dough. We need the CO_2 for the bread to rise, but it will dry out gluten-free breads about three times as quickly as traditional ones. Cold proofing also allows flavors to develop, so your bread will taste like, well, bread.

Gluten-free bread baking diverges from traditional bread baking in the number of rising cycles it requires. Traditional bread doughs have two and sometimes three rising cycles and are often "punched down" in between these risings. In gluten-free bread baking, there is a single rise and it takes place in the fridge. (Sometimes a short period of rising in a warm place is called for after the dough is placed in a bread pan, but this takes a maximum of 20 minutes, not a couple of hours.) You also won't need to punch down the dough. So as you read the bread recipes, don't be completely shocked that these steps are missing—it's just the law of the land.

To cold-proof your dough, begin by coating a bowl or other container with oil, shortening, or butter (usually the recipe will suggest which to use). *Beware of nonstick cooking spray*. I've noticed that it can cause unexplainable things to happen to gluten-free bread dough. Always use a pure oil (I favor olive oil) and organic shortening, like Spectrum, or butter to grease the container or bowl in which the dough will rise. Next, turn the dough into the greased container. Jostle the container a bit to coat the dough in the oil, shortening, or butter, then cover the container tightly with plastic wrap and set it in the fridge. Cold-proof the dough for the length of time indicated in the recipe.

After cold proofing, most doughs will be kneaded (see below) into their final shape—formed into loaves and set in loaf pans for Classic Sandwich Bread (page 197), for example, or pressed into a round for New York–Style Pizza (page 202). As mentioned above, some doughs are then covered lightly and set aside to rise at warm room temperature before being baked.

KNEADING

In traditional bread baking, *kneading* is done to activate the gluten protein in the dough. Since gluten-free baking is, obviously, free of gluten, you might wonder why kneading is necessary. When I first started experimenting with gluten-free breads, the dough crumbled apart like clumps of dirt when the proofing started. The expanding yeast was breaking the dough instead of pushing it outward like a balloon. I quickly realized that I didn't properly knead the dough in the bowl *before* proofing.

Doughs made with the Bread & Pizza Blend are kneaded as the dough is being made, and sometimes a second time after cold proofing.

When you initially assemble a dough made with this blend, the mixing of the ingredients acts as a first kneading. Please take note of how long to mix the dough in the bowl before proofing (usually a few minutes, but sometimes up to ten)—it's crucial to the end result. This first kneading helps activate the guar gum to increase elasticity in the dough. Increased elasticity ensures that when the dough is placed in the refrigerator to proof, it stretches rather than crumbles as the yeast expands.

When a recipe requires kneading *after* the proofing process, first dust the counter with a bit of glutinous rice flour or additional Bread & Pizza Blend. Lightly coat the dough with the glutinous rice flour or blend so it won't stick to your hands. Form the dough into a rough disk. Working on the dusted surface, fold the dough disk toward you and press down and forward, stretching the dough. Your goal should be to gently extend the dough outward without tearing it. Rotate the dough 90 degrees and repeat, folding and turning, maintaining a smooth disk. Recipes using the Bread & Pizza Blend will indicate for how long you should knead the dough—in most cases, an approximate number of turns.

CHEWY NEW YORK–STYLE BAGELS

FOR THE SPONGE:

3 cups (336 g) Bread & Pizza Blend (page 187)

2 large eggs

1 teaspoon gluten-free active dry yeast

FOR THE DOUGH:

2⅓ cups (270 g) Bread & Pizza Blend (page 187), plus more for dusting

2 tablespoons powdered milk

2 tablespoons sugar

1 tablespoon kosher salt

2½ teaspoons gluten-free active dry yeast

1 teaspoon freshly ground white pepper

4 tablespoons (½ stick / 56 g) unsalted butter, cold and diced

1 teaspoon baking soda

¼ cup (50 g) sugar

I like a bagel you can sink your teeth into and tear, and that's what I've gone for in this recipe.

MAKES 8 BAGELS

Make the sponge: In a large bowl, combine the Bread & Pizza Blend, eggs, yeast, and 2½ cups (600 ml) lukewarm water. Mix with a wooden spoon until well blended and thick. Cover and refrigerate the sponge, to let the yeast develop slowly, for at least 3 to 4 hours. I like to go 6 hours for the best flavor.

Make the dough: In a large bowl, whisk together the Bread & Pizza Blend, powdered milk, 2 tablespoons sugar, salt, yeast, and pepper until they are combined. Remove the sponge from the fridge and sprinkle this mixture over the top, being sure to cover as much of the sponge as possible. Cover the bowl with plastic and return it to the fridge to proof overnight (at least 8 hours).

Using a wooden spoon, stir the dry mixture into the sponge, continuing until the mixture is too thick to stir. Transfer the dough to a stand mixer fitted with the paddle attachment (or to a food processor fitted with the S-blade) and mix on high for 3 minutes. Add the butter and continue to mix on the lowest speed until you can no longer see lumps of butter, about 1 minute. The dough should be sticky.

Dust your work surface with Bread & Pizza Blend. Turn out the dough and knead it until it's smooth. Using a scale, divide the dough into eight equal sections. Roll each of these into an 8-inch (20-cm) rope, about 1 inch (2.5 cm) thick. Bring the ends of each rope together to form a circle (bagel shapes!), joining and sealing the ends with a bit of water.

Preheat the oven to 450°F (230°C). Line a baking sheet with parchment paper or a Silpat mat.

In a saucepan wide enough to accommodate two or three bagels, combine the baking soda, sugar, and 1 quart (960 ml) water. Bring the water to a moderate boil and use a wide, flat skimmer to lower the bagels into the water in groups of two or three. Boil the bagels for 3 to 4 minutes on each side. The bagels will puff up significantly and the dough will darken a bit on the underside.

Using the skimmer, transfer the boiled bagels to the prepared baking sheet. Bake them for about 20 minutes, until the bagels are raised, firm, and golden. Transfer them to a wire rack to cool.

The bagels will keep in an airtight container at room temperature for up to 3 days, or frozen in a sealed bag for up to 1 month.

ENGLISH MUFFINS

6 tablespoons (84 g) vegetable shortening

6 tablespoons (90 ml) honey

5 cups (560 g) Bread & Pizza Blend (page 187), plus more for dusting

4 teaspoons gluten-free instant yeast

4 large eggs

1 tablespoon kosher salt

3 tablespoons butter, plus more for greasing

Glutinous rice flour or additional Bread & Pizza Blend (page 187), for dusting

NOTE: The muffins will keep in an airtight container in the refrigerator for up to 3 days, or frozen, double-wrapped, for up to 1 month.

I worked up this gluten-free variant of the Thomas' classic as a tribute to my dad, who likes his egg poached and served on these English mainstays, to prevent yolk loss. The key to the genuine English muffin look and feel: You absolutely must first fry-bake the muffins on the stovetop, as the English do with their crumpets, and finish them in a hot oven.

MAKES 8 MUFFINS

In a small saucepan, melt the shortening with the honey over low heat. Set them aside to cool to the temperature of a cooled bath, about 100°F (38°C).

In the bowl of a stand mixer fitted with the paddle attachment, combine the Bread & Pizza Blend with the yeast and mix them at the lowest speed to combine. With the mixer running, add 2 cups (480 ml) lukewarm water, the eggs, and the shortening mixture. Beat vigorously on high speed for 1 minute. Scrape down the sides of the bowl and mix for 30 seconds more; add the salt and mix for 3 minutes more.

Liberally butter a large bowl. Set the dough in the bowl, cover with plastic wrap, and refrigerate for at least 4 hours, or overnight (at least 8 hours) for the best results.

Dust a baking sheet lightly with glutinous rice flour or additional Bread & Pizza Blend. Butter eight 3½-inch (9-cm) English muffin rings or crumpet rings and set them on the baking sheet, spacing them evenly.

Dust your work surface generously with Bread & Pizza Blend. Turn out the dough and knead until it is no longer sticky to the touch, at least 10 turns. Using a scale, divide it into eight pieces, each weighing about 155 g. Shape the pieces into little hockey pucks. Set a dough puck in the center of each ring. Swirl the rings around the pucks to shape the dough and to coat the edges with butter. Gently press the dough so it more or less fills the rings. Drape a kitchen towel over the baking sheet and allow the unbaked muffins to rise for 15 minutes.

Preheat the oven to 400°F (205°C).

In a large skillet, melt ½ to 1 tablespoon of the butter over medium heat until it foams. Working in batches, use a spatula to transfer the muffins, still in their rings, to the pan and fry them for 3 minutes per side (remember to keep them in the rings when you flip them!), or until they're puffed and golden. Add more butter to the skillet as needed between batches. Repeat until all the muffins have been fry-baked. Wipe the glutinous rice flour off the baking sheet and return the muffins to it as they finish fry-baking.

Bake for 20 to 25 minutes, until the muffins are fully raised and golden brown. Transfer to a wire rack, still in the rings, and let them cool. When cool enough to handle, remove the rings.

PULLMAN LOAF (AKA PAIN DE MIE)

Think French toast, grilled cheese, and every sandwich you've lusted after since going gluten-free. *Pain de mie* literally translates to "bread crumb" and is an everyday white bread that is typically used for making sandwiches or for drying out to make breadcrumbs. The closest thing we have to pain de mie in America is the Pullman Loaf, which refers to the kind of pan the bread is baked in—a long narrow pan that has a lid that must be slid on and pulled off.

MAKES ONE 10-BY-4-INCH (25-BY-10-CM) PULLMAN LOAF

Grease a 10-by-4-inch (25-by-10-cm) Pullman loaf pan. (If using a standard loaf pan, grease the pan and use a piece of heavy-duty aluminum foil as a lid.)

In the bowl of a stand mixer fitted with the paddle attachment, gently mix the Bread & Pizza Blend with the yeast and powdered milk on the lowest setting. Mix for a few seconds and then add the salt. Leave the mixer running so the salt does not come into direct contact with the yeast and kill it.

Combine the eggs, olive oil, honey, and 1¼ cups (300 ml) water in a separate bowl. With the mixer still running on low, slowly add the liquids to the dry ingredients and mix on high for 3 minutes. Return the mixer to low, add the apple cider vinegar, and mix on high for 2 more minutes. The dough should be quite sticky, sticking to the sides of the bowl and the paddle.

Turn the dough into your prepared pan, cover it with plastic wrap, and stretch a rubber band just under the lip of the pan to keep the plastic tight. Proof in the fridge for 2 hours, or until the dough is ½ inch (12 mm) from the top of the pan. If you let the dough rise any more, it will hit the plastic and ruin the loaf.

A full hour before baking, preheat the oven to 425°F (220°C). Set an oven rack in the lowest position. Butter the inside of the pan lid (or the side of the foil that will touch the bread).

Remove the pan from the fridge, remove the plastic and the rubber band, and slide on the lid.

Reduce the oven temperature to 350°F (220°C) and bake the bread for 1 hour and 15 minutes. Carefully remove the lid or foil and tap on the top—it should give a nice hollow thump. The bread should be dark brown and smell like heaven.

Let the loaf cool in the pan for 10 minutes, then invert it onto a wire rack to cool completely for at least 2 hours. (The bread will continue to bake internally as it cools, so resist the urge to slice it when it's piping hot.)

Butter, for the pan

3½ cups (390 g) Bread & Pizza Blend (page 187)

1 tablespoon gluten-free yeast

¼ cup (60 ml) low-fat powdered milk

2¼ teaspoons kosher salt

3 large eggs

3 tablespoons pure olive oil

2 tablespoons honey

2½ teaspoons apple cider vinegar

NOTE: The bread will keep in an airtight container at room temperature for up to 4 days or in the refrigerator for up to 2 weeks; it freezes exceptionally well in a freezer-safe bag, for up to 2 months.

CLASSIC SANDWICH BREAD

Followed with precision and made in the bowl of a stand mixer, this recipe will give you the perfect loaf of homemade bread. Bread crumbs made from this loaf (see sidebar) are ideal for Herb-Fried Mozzarella Sticks (page 55) and Pasta & Meatballs (page 117). The bread also makes exceptional French toast (see recipe page 200) and rock-star grilled cheese.

MAKES TWO 9-BY-5-INCH (23-BY-12-CM) LOAVES

In a large bowl, whisk together 2⅔ cups (630 ml) lukewarm water with the yeast and sugar. Let the mixture stand for 10 minutes and then whisk in the eggs.

Place the Bread & Pizza Blend in the bowl of a stand mixer fitted with the paddle attachment. With the mixer on low speed, add the egg mixture and beat on high speed for 2 minutes. Add the salt and mix to combine, then add the butter and beat until you can no longer see bits of butter and the dough sticks to the sides of the bowl. Scrape down the sides of the bowl and beat for 30 seconds more. The dough should be thick and slightly tacky.

Liberally butter a large bowl. Set the dough in the bowl and jostle the bowl, in a circular motion, to coat the dough with butter. Flip the dough and repeat. Cover the bowl with plastic wrap and refrigerate it for 3 hours. The dough should double in size.

Preheat the oven to 375°F (190°C). Butter two 9-by-5-inch (23-by-12-cm) loaf pans.

Dust your work surface with glutinous rice flour. Turn the dough out and divide it in half. Knead each piece until it's smooth, about ten turns. Shape the dough into two 8-by-16-inch (20-by-40.5-cm) rectangles. Starting at a narrower side, roll the dough onto itself to form a loaf 8 inches (20 cm) long. Crimp the loose end to form a seam. Pinch the ends and pull them up toward you. Flip the loaf so the seam side and turned ends are down. Set the formed loaves into the pans. Set the pans in a warm place, like on the warm stovetop or in a barely heated oven, cover them with a kitchen towel, and allow them to rise until the dough reaches the top of the pans, about 30 minutes.

Bake for 50 to 55 minutes, until the loaves are domed above the pans and their crusts are golden and firm to the touch. Turn the loaves out of the pans and let them cool completely on a wire rack. (The bread will continue to bake internally as it cools, so resist the urge to slice it when it's piping hot.)

These loaves bake beautifully in a convection oven, too, if you happen to have one. Just remember to lower the oven by 25 degrees and cut the baking time in half.

1½ tablespoons gluten-free active dry yeast

3 tablespoons granulated sugar

2 large eggs

7 cups (784 g) Bread & Pizza Blend (page 187)

4½ teaspoons kosher salt

4 tablespoons (½ stick / 56 g) unsalted butter, diced, at room temperature, plus more for greasing

Glutinous rice flour, for dusting

BREAD CRUMBS
For the best bread crumbs, preheat the oven to 325°F (165°C). Take the leftover heels and some middle slices of Classic Sandwich Bread and lay them on the stovetop for a few hours. This dries them out without toasting the bread. Process the dried bread in a food processor until it forms a coarse crumb.

NOTE: The bread will keep in a plastic bag in the refrigerator for up to 1 week, or frozen, double-wrapped, for up to 2 months.

CINNAMON-RAISIN BREAD

Butter, for the pans

Bread & Pizza Blend (page 187), for dusting

1 recipe Classic Sandwich Bread dough (page 197)

1½ cups (217 g) seedless black or golden raisins

1 large egg, beaten

½ cup (100 g) sugar

4 teaspoons ground cinnamon

⅛ teaspoon kosher salt

The smell of this simple, homey marvel while it's baking is so delicious that you may notice your neighbors' windows open and their noses poking out to catch another tantalizing whiff.

MAKES TWO 9-BY-5-INCH (23-BY-12-CM) LOAVES

Preheat the oven to 375°F (190°C). Liberally butter two 9-by-5-inch (23-by-12-cm) loaf pans.

Dust your work surface with Bread & Pizza Blend. Divide the dough in half and knead half the raisins into each piece. Roll the two halves into 8-by-16-inch (20-by-40.5-cm) rectangles. Brush the surface of each with some of the egg, leaving a ½-inch (12-mm) border around the edges.

In a small bowl, mix the sugar, cinnamon, and salt together and spread the mixture evenly over the rectangles, to cover the egg-brushed surfaces.

Starting at one of the narrower sides, roll each rectangle into a loaf 8 inches (20 cm) long. Crimp the loose end to form a seam. Pinch the ends and pull them up toward you. Flip the loaves, so the seam sides and crimped ends are down, and set them into the loaf pans. Drape a kitchen towel over the pans and set the pans in a warm place, like on the stovetop or in a barely heated oven. Let the dough rise just to the top of the pans, about 30 minutes.

Bake the bread for 50 to 55 minutes, until the loaves are domed above the pans and their crusts are golden and firm to the touch. Turn the loaves out of the pans and transfer them to a wire rack to cool. (The bread will continue to bake internally as it cools, so resist the urge to slice it when it's piping hot.)

The bread will keep in a plastic bag in the refrigerator for up to 1 week, or in the freezer, double-wrapped, for up to 2 months.

REHAB FRENCH TOAST

1 cup (240 ml) half-and-half

½ cup plus 2 tablespoons (125 g) caster sugar or superfine sugar

1 large egg

3 egg yolks

1½ teaspoons double-strength vanilla extract

1 teaspoon ground cinnamon, preferably Vietnamese

8 thick slices Classic Sandwich Bread (page 197) or Pullman Loaf (page 195)

2 tablespoons unsalted butter

The Classic Sandwich Bread (page 197) is perfect for this fabulous French toast recipe I learned from my friend Jim Hollingsworth. The name suggests a redo on an old classic; rather than just soak the bread for a few moments in the egg and cream mixture, we are "rehab-ing" it by soaking it for 30 minutes in the freezer. This creates a bread that is so moist and tender, you'll never make it any other way again. You can use any other gluten-free bread, too, but for most you'll want to cut the soaking time to 15 minutes. (Other gluten-free breads just don't hold together as well as mine!) This is good with the traditional toppings—maple syrup, confectioners' sugar and lemon, or preserves—but also wonderful just plain.

SERVES 4, TWO SLICES EACH

Lightly spray a jelly-roll pan with nonstick cooking spray. Make sure there is enough room for it to fit in your freezer.

In a blender, combine the half-and-half, sugar, egg, egg yolks, vanilla, and cinnamon. Mix until they are very smooth, about 30 seconds.

Lay the slices of bread on the prepared pan and then very slowly pour the egg mixture over them, covering each piece entirely. Continue until the bread is saturated and cannot absorb any more liquid. This will take 5 to 7 minutes. Pour any excess egg mixture into a measuring cup for additional slices, if you have anyone looking for seconds. Set the pan in the freezer for 30 minutes.

In a wide skillet, melt 1 tablespoon of the butter over medium heat. When the butter foams, use a spatula at least as wide as the slices of bread (they will be delicate) to transfer the slices to the skillet, working in batches as needed. Fry the bread for 2 to 3 minutes on each side, until they are golden. Add more butter as needed between batches in the skillet.

As the French toast just isn't the same when reheated, it's best to eat it all at once. Darn!

SOFT SOURDOUGH

This bread makes the best muffuletta sandwich this side of New Orleans! To try it for yourself, cut the loaf in half horizontally and top it with olive salad (a mixture of chopped olives, giardiniera, spices, garlic, and olive oil) and slices of salami, ham, mortadella, mozzarella, and provolone. (It's great for other deli sandwiches, too, of course. I also love to make bruschetta and garlic bread with it.)

MAKES ONE 12-INCH (30.5-CM) LOAF

Make the sponge: In a large bowl, stir together the Bread & Pizza Blend, eggs, honey, yeast, and ⅔ cup (165 ml) lukewarm water. The mixture should be runny. Cover the bowl with plastic wrap and refrigerate the sponge for 3 hours.

Make the dough: In a medium bowl, whisk together the Bread & Pizza Blend and the yeast, then whisk in the salt. Remove the sponge from the fridge and sprinkle this mixture over the top, being sure to cover as much of the sponge as possible. Cover the bowl with plastic and return it to the fridge to proof for 4 to 6 hours more.

Using a wooden spoon, stir together the sponge and dry ingredients. Transfer the sponge to the bowl of a stand mixer fitted with the paddle attachment and beat in the eggs, honey, oil, and vinegar. Beat them on high speed until you have a very soft, sticky dough.

Liberally butter a large bowl. Set the dough in the bowl, turn it to coat the surface with butter, cover it with plastic wrap, and refrigerate it overnight (at least 8 hours).

Preheat the oven to 425°F (220°C). Butter a 12-inch (30.5-cm) round baking pan with 1½- to 2-inch (4- to 5-cm) sides.

In a small bowl, whisk together the egg and cream.

Turn the chilled dough into the prepared pan and gently pull the dough to the edges. Brush the surface with the egg wash. Cover it with a kitchen towel and let it rise in a warm place just to the top of the pan, 20 to 30 minutes. Brush the top with additional egg wash and sprinkle it with sesame seeds, if desired.

Bake the bread for 35 to 40 minutes, until the loaf is domed and golden. Let it cool for 10 minutes in the pan before transferring it to a wire rack to cool completely. (The bread will continue to bake internally as it cools, so resist the urge to slice it when it's piping hot.)

The bread will keep in a plastic bag at room temperature for 2 to 3 days. It can be frozen, double-wrapped, for up to 1 month.

FOR THE SPONGE:

1 cup (112 g) Bread & Pizza Blend (page 187)

3 large eggs

2 tablespoons honey

1 teaspoon active dry yeast

FOR THE DOUGH:

2⅓ cups (268 g) Bread & Pizza Blend (page 187)

1¼ teaspoons gluten-free active dry yeast

3 teaspoons kosher salt

3 large eggs

¼ cup (60 ml) honey

¼ cup (60 ml) pure olive oil

1 tablespoon apple cider vinegar

Butter, for greasing

1 large egg

2 tablespoons heavy cream

Sesame seeds (optional)

NEW YORK–STYLE PIZZA

FOR THE DOUGH:

3½ cups (390 g) Bread & Pizza Blend (page 187), plus more for dusting

3 teaspoons gluten-free active dry yeast

2½ tablespoons olive oil

2 large eggs

2¼ teaspoons kosher salt

Butter, for greasing

Glutinous rice flour, for dusting

TOPPINGS:

2 cups (480 ml) Oven-Roasted Grape-Tomato Sauce (page 114)

Dried thyme

2 cups (200 g) freshly grated Parmesan

3 cups (360 g) grated or sliced mozzarella

This is thin-crust pizza, yo, with a fat, puffy edge that gets nice big fat bubbles that brown beautifully, especially in wood-burning stoves. Layering mozzarella on top of thyme-sprinkled Parmesan makes a significant contribution to the pizza's flavor and gives it that New York pizza *pop*. Luckily, with a few adjustments, you can also use this dough to make Neapolitan-style pies. See variations for more ideas.

MAKES TWO 12-INCH (30.5-CM) PIZZAS

Make the dough: In the bowl of a stand mixer fitted with the paddle attachment, combine the Bread & Pizza Blend and the yeast. With the mixer running, add 1 cup plus 3 tablespoons (285 ml) lukewarm water, the oil, and the eggs. Beat on medium-high speed for 1 minute. Scrape down the sides of the bowl. Add the salt and continue mixing the dough on medium-high speed for 3 minutes more, or until it is very thick.

Liberally butter a large bowl. Set the dough in the bowl, turn it to coat the surface with butter, cover it with plastic wrap, and refrigerate it overnight.

Preheat the oven to 500°F (260°C). Cut a piece of parchment paper to fit a pizza stone or baking sheet; set it aside. Set the pizza stone or baking sheet in the oven to heat.

Liberally dust your work surface with Bread & Pizza Blend. Divide the chilled dough in half. Roll half of the dough in the blend until it is no longer sticky and shape it into a ball.

Dust the prepared parchment paper with glutinous rice flour and gently press the dough into a 12-inch (30.5-cm) round on top of the parchment, making it as thin as you can but leaving a thicker edge. Carefully transfer the dough to the pizza stone (I like to slide the parchment onto the back of a baking sheet, then slide the pizza from the sheet to the pizza stone) or the preheated baking sheet. Bake it for 15 to 20 minutes, until it is browned around the edges and air bubbles are forming.

Remove the crust from the oven and top it with about ½ cup (120 ml) of the Grape-Tomato Sauce. Dust it with a few pinches of thyme. Sprinkle it evenly with 1 cup (100 g) of the Parmesan, followed by 1½ cups (180 g) of the mozzarella.

Bake it until the cheese has melted, 5 to 7 minutes. Cut and serve the pizza immediately. Repeat baking and topping the remaining dough round.

VARIATION: Neapolitan-Style

Rather than proof the dough in the refrigerator, let it rise on the warm stovetop, covered with a towel, for 15 to 20 minutes. Roll it out as instructed above for a thin crust. Be sure to pierce the dough with the tines of a fork a dozen times before baking. Top and bake as directed on the opposite page.

VARIATION: Calzones

Proof the dough in the refrigerator for 40 minutes. Roll it out as directed on the opposite page. Place fillings on one half of the dough round and fold over the unfilled half to form a half-moon. Roll the edges together to seal them. Make an egg wash by whisking together 1 large egg and 1 tablespoon heavy cream and brush this over the calzone. Place the calzone on the pizza stone and bake it for 20 to 30 minutes at 425°F (220°C), until golden brown.

VARIATION: Breadsticks

Omit the red sauce, mozzarella, and thyme. On a plate, toss together ½ teaspoon garlic powder, ½ teaspoon onion powder, ¼ teaspoon kosher salt, and freshly cracked black pepper. Divide the proofed dough into 12 sections. Roll each piece into a 12-inch (30.5-cm) rope and brush the ropes with a glaze of olive oil. Dust them with the seasonings, top them with a sprinkling of Parmesan, and bake them either on a pizza stone or a baking sheet for 15 minutes at 425°F (220°C), until golden brown.

FRENCH BOULE

3½ cups (395 g) Bread & Pizza Blend (page 187)

2½ teaspoons gluten-free active dry yeast

2⅛ teaspoons kosher salt

2½ tablespoons pure olive oil, plus more for greasing

2 large eggs

2 tablespoons clover honey

Butter, for greasing

Glutinous rice flour, for dusting

A French boule may be the odd man out in an all-American cookbook, but I'm sure the pioneers made bread similar to this one when they parked their Conestoga wagons. I love to use this bread to make pressed sandwiches or slice it thin to make crisp pieces of toast that are the hallmark of a good cheese plate.

MAKES ONE 10-INCH (25-CM) ROUND LOAF

In the bowl of a stand mixer fitted with the paddle attachment, combine the Bread & Pizza Blend and the yeast. With the mixer running, add the salt, followed by 1¼ cups (300 ml) lukewarm water, the oil, eggs, and honey. Beat vigorously on high speed for 3 minutes, or until the dough is very sticky.

Liberally butter a large bowl. Place the dough in the bowl, turn it to coat the surface with butter, cover it with plastic wrap, and refrigerate it for at least 3 hours, or overnight (at least 8 hours) for best results.

Preheat the oven to 425°F (220°C). Set an oven rack in the middle position and have a 6-quart (5.7-L) Dutch oven ready on the counter.

Dust your work surface with glutinous rice flour. Turn out the dough and knead it until it's very smooth and elastic, about ten turns. Using the heel of your hand, fold the dough over and over, rotating the dough clockwise as you work, until you form a nice tight ball. The top should be perfectly smooth. Coat the dough with a thin layer of glutinous rice flour and slash the top with a razor or sharp knife, cutting just ¼ inch (6 mm) in.

Set the dough into the Dutch oven (with the slash facing up), put on the lid, and bake for 25 to 30 minutes, until the loaf is domed and doubled in size. Remove the lid and continue baking until the crust is crisp and brown, 10 to 20 minutes more. Remove the bread from the Dutch oven and transfer it to a wire rack to cool. (The bread will continue to bake internally as it cools, so resist the urge to slice it when it's piping hot.)

The bread will keep in an airtight container at room temperature for up to 3 days. Double-wrapped, this bread freezes beautifully for up to 3 months.

VARIATION: Classic Dinner Rolls

For a classic dinner roll, follow the recipe above but divide the dough into 8 rounds, each weighing about 110 grams. In a small bowl, whisk together 1 large egg and 2 tablespoons heavy cream. Place the rounds on a rimmed baking sheet and bake them at 425°F (220°C) for 15 minutes. Brush them with the egg wash and bake them for 5 to 10 minutes more, until the rolls are golden brown. Serve warm or at room temperature. The rolls will keep in an airtight container at room temperature for up to 3 days, or frozen double-wrapped, for 3 months.

CHALLAH

This is the Jewish classic, in all its braided—and now gluten-free—glory and is dedicated to two of my favorite customers, Dan and Cheri Rozycki.

MAKES ONE 14-INCH (35.5-CM) LOAF

Make the dough: In a medium bowl, whisk together 2 cups (480 ml) lukewarm water, the yeast, and 1 teaspoon of the sugar. Let them stand for 15 minutes; the mixture will become milky.

Place the Bread & Pizza Blend in the bowl of a stand mixer fitted with the paddle attachment. With the mixer on low, slowly add the yeast mixture, followed by the honey, eggs, vinegar, and oil. Beat them on high speed for 1 to 2 minutes, or until the dough is tacky and sticks to the sides of the bowl. Scrape down the sides of the bowl and add the salt. Mix the dough for 7 minutes more, or until the dough is sticking to the sides of the bowl and the paddle.

Liberally butter a large bowl. Place the dough in the bowl. Melt the remaining 1 tablespoon butter and brush the top of the dough with it. Cover it with plastic wrap and refrigerate it for at least 4 hours, or overnight for the best results.

Preheat the oven to 375°F (190°C).

Dust your work surface with glutinous rice flour. Turn out the dough and knead it until it's very smooth and elastic, about 10 turns. Divide the dough into thirds. Keep the pieces you're not working with covered, so they don't dry out. Roll the pieces into ropes 18 inches (46 cm) long. Place the 3 ropes side by side on a baking sheet lined with parchment paper. Beginning in the middle of the ropes, braid the dough first to one end, tucking the ends under the loaf. Turn the pan and braid the other half, tucking the ends under.

Make the egg wash: In a small bowl, whisk together the egg, egg yolk, cream, and salt and brush this mixture over the braid. Cover the braid with an inverted roasting pan or other deep pot and let it rise for 15 minutes in a warm part of the kitchen.

Brush the braid with additional egg wash and bake it for 20 minutes. Brush it again with egg wash, making sure to cover any dough that is newly exposed from the expansion that occurs during baking. Bake the challah for 20 minutes more, or until dark brown.

Allow it to cool completely on a wire rack. (The bread will continue to bake internally as it cools, so resist the urge to slice it when it's piping hot.)

The challah will keep in an airtight container at room temperature for up to 3 days. It can be frozen, double-wrapped, for up to 1 month.

FOR THE DOUGH:

1 tablespoon gluten-free active dry yeast

¼ cup (50 g) sugar

5½ cups (616 g) Bread & Pizza Blend (page 187)

½ cup (120 ml) honey

5 large eggs

2 teaspoons apple cider vinegar

¼ cup (60 ml) vegetable oil

4½ teaspoons kosher salt

1 tablespoon unsalted butter, diced, plus more for the bowl

Glutinous rice flour, for dusting

FOR THE EGG WASH:

1 large egg

1 egg yolk

1 tablespoon heavy cream or water

⅛ teaspoon kosher salt

PUMPERNICKEL

FOR THE SPONGE:

¾ cup (85 g) Bread & Pizza Blend (page 187)

¾ cup (100 g) teff flour

2 large eggs

2 tablespoons sugar

1 tablespoon brown rice syrup

2 teaspoons gluten-free active dry yeast

FOR THE DOUGH:

2¼ cups (253 g) Bread & Pizza Blend (page 187), plus more for dusting

2 tablespoons caraway seeds

2¼ teaspoons kosher salt

2 teaspoons sugar

2 tablespoons vegetable oil

¼ teaspoon plus ⅛ teaspoon gluten-free active dry yeast

Glutinous rice flour, for dusting

Rye, of course, is not gluten-free, but teff flour is, and it gives this bread a convincing rye flavor. The dark color completes the illusion. And for a perfect sourdough, replace the teff flour called for in this recipe with additional Bread & Pizza Blend, eliminate the caraway seeds, increase the amount of yeast to 1 tablespoon, and replace the brown rice syrup with honey.

MAKES ONE 10-INCH (25-CM) LOAF

Make the sponge: In a large bowl, whisk together the Bread & Pizza Blend, teff flour, eggs, sugar, rice syrup, yeast, and 1½ cup (360 ml) lukewarm water to make a wet batter.

Make the dough: In a large bowl, whisk together the Bread & Pizza Blend, caraway, salt, sugar, oil, and yeast and sprinkle the mixture over the sponge. Cover it with plastic wrap and refrigerate it for 3 to 4 hours; for a more full-bodied flavor, refrigerate it even longer, up to 24 hours.

Preheat the oven to 450°F (230°C). Set a baking stone or baking sheet on the lowest rack.

Using a wooden spoon, stir the sponge and the dough ingredients together, until they are thick and well combined. Dust your work surface with Bread & Pizza Blend. Turn out the dough and knead it with the heel of your hand until it's smooth, about ten turns. Fold the dough over and over, rotating it clockwise as you work, until you form a nice tight ball. When you flip the dough over, the top should be perfectly smooth. Coat the dough with a thin layer of glutinous rice flour and slash the top a few times with a razor or sharp knife, cutting just ¼ inch (6 mm) in.

Set the loaf directly on the baking stone or preheated baking sheet, with the slashes facing up. Bake the loaf for 10 minutes, then reduce the oven temperature to 400°F (205°C) and bake it for 30 minutes more, until the bread has risen and is dark brown. Let it cool on a wire rack. (The bread will continue to bake internally as it cools, so resist the urge to slice it when it's piping hot.)

The pumpernickel will keep in an airtight container at room temperature for up to 3 days, or frozen, double-wrapped, for up to 1 month.

HONEYED PULL-APART DINNER ROLLS

These soft buns are perfect for game-day sliders, luncheon sandwiches, or little people's lunch boxes. Freezing the butter before grating it makes it less likely to melt in your hot little hands!

MAKES 12 ROLLS

Coarsely grate the frozen butter and store it in the freezer in an airtight container until needed.

In the bowl of a stand mixer fitted with the paddle attachment, combine the Bread & Pizza Blend, oat flour, and yeast.

In a separate bowl, whisk together the milk, eggs, and 6 tablespoons (90 ml) of the honey until smooth. With the mixer on low speed, add the milk mixture to the dry ingredients in a slow, steady stream and mix them until you can no longer see any dry ingredients. Add 5 tablespoons of the frozen grated butter and mix it on high speed, effectively kneading the dough, for 3 minutes. The dough should be nice and tacky, sticking to the sides of the bowl. Add the salt and mix for another 3 minutes.

Lightly grease a bowl with softened butter. Place the dough in the bowl, turn it to coat the surface with butter, cover it with plastic wrap, and refrigerate it overnight (at least 8 hours).

Preheat the oven to 200°F (90°C). Butter an 8-inch (20-cm) square pan.

Dust a work surface with glutinous rice flour. Turn out the dough and knead it until it's smooth, about seven turns, then form it into a smooth ball. Cut the dough into 9 equal sections. Form each section into a tight, smooth ball. Place the balls into the prepared pan, nestled in so they are just touching. Cover them with foil and put them in the oven to rise for 15 minutes.

Meanwhile, in a small saucepan, melt the remaining 1 tablespoon frozen butter with the remaining 1 tablespoon honey.

Pull the rolls from the oven and raise the oven temperature to 375°F (190°C). Brush the rolls with the honey-butter mixture and return them to the oven, loosely covered with an aluminum foil tent. Bake them for 25 minutes, or until the buns are puffed up, then remove the foil and bake them for 10 minutes more, or until the rolls are golden.

Cool the rolls in the pan, set on a wire rack, for 15 minutes, and then turn the rolls out onto the rack to cool completely.

The rolls will keep in an airtight container at room temperature for up to 4 days, and frozen, double-wrapped, for up to 1 month.

6 tablespoons (84 g) unsalted butter, frozen, plus softened butter for greasing

2¾ cups (310 g) Bread & Pizza Blend (page 187)

1½ cups (130 g) gluten-free oat flour

1 tablespoon gluten-free highly active yeast (bread machine yeast)

1¾ cups (420 ml) lukewarm whole milk (about 90°F / 32°C)

2 large eggs

7 tablespoons (105 ml) honey

2¼ teaspoons kosher salt

Glutinous rice flour, for dusting

black pepper corns

grey sea salt

sea salt

millet flour

oat flour

tapioca flour

glutinous rice flour

extra fine brown rice flour

sliced almonds

cinnamon

shredded coconut

THE GLUTEN-FREE PANTRY

Among the first things students ask me is: "What are the *essential* ingredients every gluten-free cook should have in the pantry?"

The question is important and deserves an in-depth answer.

There are three basic grains that contain gluten—wheat, rye, and barley. We're leaving those behind, but we've got a whole realm of options—dozens of grains, roots, seeds, nuts, and tubers, along with the flours, meals, and starches they provide. They come with a wealth of flavors and textures, and the only thing they don't bring to the mix is gluten. They're a whole parallel universe of culinary creativity. The key is thinking of these not as "alternatives" to the three standards, but as ingredients in their own right.

So now that we're looking into the pantry, streamline what you already have stocked. Pull items you're no longer using and get some instant karma by giving them away. As you experiment and expand your range, add the ingredients your preferred recipes call for, and what is most to your taste. Keep components for the six blends on hand and stock any components for blends you work out on your own.

In the list of pantry items that follows, you won't find many instances of "organic," "non-GMO," or "local" designations, but that's not at all because I don't shop and cook with those qualifications in mind. To the contrary—I'm such a staunch supporter of the farm-to-table movement and non-genetically modified foods that those adjectives almost go without saying, or typing, for that matter. No need to clutter things up with a lot of repetition. I use non-GMO and organic grains whenever possible, at home and at Blackbird Bakery. As chef Marcus Samuelsson put it, "We must all begin to eat with a moral compass." My moral compass points to locally sourced, naturally grown and raised ingredients, of the highest quality, for everything I cook, every time I cook. Organic, natural, real food is not only better for us, it's better tasting and better for the future of our food supply. If you're able to stick with such ingredients

as you make my recipes, as well as recipes you find or make on your own, you'll notice the difference. I've included in the Resources section (page 227) a list of gluten-free, organic, and non-genetically modified flour companies I trust. Throughout this Pantry section, I'll also cite brands I consider dependable.

What holds back many cooks and eaters from joining the natural-foods renaissance is not availability so much as price. There are ways not to spend like a drunken sailor on these ingredients, though. Buy in bulk and with your friends. And remember, the step-up to organic is higher, price-wise, than the step-up to gluten-free, so take it a step at a time. The essentials of the gluten-free pantry are not inexpensive, in comparison with the gluten-bearing alternatives, but they're core constituents of the recipes you'll be adopting; you're not using a whole lot of any one of these special flours, so remember—a little goes a long way.

Now, my students' second question, often, is, "What tools do I need that I don't already have in my kitchen?"

That's pretty easy to address: Strictly speaking, you won't need any tools you wouldn't find in a decently equipped kitchen. But I am a big fan of one thing many cooks do without: the digital scale.

Gluten-free pantry items for the most part have one attribute in common: They're sold in bags, or boxes, or bulk and require measuring. The science of gluten-free does serve you better if it's approached with precision. I weigh ingredients just as often as I scoop them into teaspoons, tablespoons, and cups.

Bear in mind that measuring can be a tricky business. The different flours, meals, and starches in my recipes vary considerably in weight relative to volume. For example, ¼ cup of potato starch weighs 40 grams, while the same measure of tapioca flour weighs a mere 26 grams. That difference in density carries through into what we make with these flours.

But flours also have to work in certain *volumes*, not just weights, relative to liquids and fats; otherwise, textures go out of control. Weighing out flours will, in the long run, keep you well within the desired margin of error, but be sure to fluff starches and flours with a fork as you measure, as they can really get packed into measuring cups, and then spoon-level the measured quantity. When you begin doing recipe conversions of your own, do start with volume measurements and then weigh what you've measured, and record both quantities. Thinking in terms of both weight and volume will serve you as a useful tool, in making my recipes and in your own adaptations.

(A cross-referenced chart of measures and weights, for all the staples listed in the pantry and included in the recipes, appears at the back of the book, as an appendix.)

So, let's get back to my students' original question: What are the *essential* ingredients to stock, the gluten-free pantry's true make-or-breaks? It starts with a short list of my four must-haves.

BATTER UP! THE BLACKBIRD BAKERY ALL-STAR TEAM

The range of flours available to use in gluten-free baking and cooking gives us a very different perspective from the ethos embodied by the phrase "all-purpose." Each of the flours that goes into your pantry you'll choose for a certain set of attributes: some, chiefly for flavor, or a combination of flavor and texture; others for their ability to bring cohesion to a batter or dough. Here are the characteristics and quirks of my top four heavy-hitters.

THE FANTASTIC FOUR FLOURS

SORGHUM FLOUR

Basic Data: Sorghum flour is derived from the seed of the grass *Sorghum bicolor*, a relative of sugar cane. Like millet, sorghum is a complete-protein grain, but not as protein rich (coming in at 7.5 percent protein by weight).

Flavor & Texture: Thanks to its mild flavor, sorghum flour complements just about every gluten-free combination imaginable. From cream puffs to cookies, it's a wonder; for baking bread, it's *the* star. The combination of its nutritive and structural properties make sorghum flour a win-win-win for gluten-free baking.

Architecture & Engineering: The granule size is almost the same as that of oat flour, giving a marginally coarse texture that breaks down quickly with the application of liquids and heat. Yielding an ideal consistency and crumb, sorghum out-performs all other gluten-free flours.

Extras: Of all the grains we consume, sorghum flour is the least acid-inducing, making it ideal for people with inflammatory issues like ours. Celiac disease correlates highly with severe deficiency in zinc; happily, sorghum is bursting with that element.

GLUTINOUS RICE FLOUR

Basic Data: Don't let this name mislead. There is no gluten in *Oryza sativa*, aka glutinous rice, or in the flour milled from it. A more suitable adjective would be "gluten-like," thanks to its high percentage of amylopectin, a major component of starch. The term *glutinous rice* is a catchall for various rices of the sticky and sushi types, grown and prized in East Asia. The flour this rice yields is the finest textured of rice flours.

Flavor & Texture: Glutinous rice flour is white and nearly odorless (but if you wave a handful under your nose, I swear you'll get just a whiff of toasted rice). The texture is feathery light. You'll note glutinous rice flour among the ingredients for practically every recipe in this book. And it's my go-to flour for rolling out tart and pie crusts, as it won't affect the texture of the dough. In creating your own recipes and adaptations of favorites, use glutinous rice flour with confidence!

Architecture & Engineering: An alchemical reaction takes place when glutinous rice flour granules are combined with the flour of a complete-protein grain like sorghum or millet. The result? The perfect crumb. For baked goods like cakes, you'll wonder why anyone bakes with anything that's got gluten in it. And a bit of poetic justice here: A good cake needs to be low in gluten, so the cake is cakey and not bready. Cake comes out even better without any gluten at all! These virtues make glutinous rice flour blends the closest thing I've discovered yet in taste, texture, and appearance to all-purpose wheat flour.

Notes of Caution: It's said that sweet rice flour is the same as glutinous rice flour, but it sure doesn't seem the same to me. Sweet rice flour is less fine in texture. I'm not territorial about my recipes, but when one calls for glutinous rice flour, trust me, you'll be happiest with the result if you use glutinous rice flour. I should add, though, that I don't recommend it for thickening sauces. (We all have our shortcomings.)

BROWN RICE FLOUR, SUPERFINE

Basic Data: Brown rice flour is derived by multiple, fine millings of brown rice and is pale sandy blond in color.

Flavor & Texture: This flour has the nutty flavor of brown rice, with a super-smooth texture, and is ideal for lending its golden hue to pastries, muffins, cookies, and breads.

Architecture & Engineering: Unlike traditionally milled brown rice flour, which is coarse, the superfine variety is silken smooth and will not leave your finished product with a grainy finish. Like glutinous rice flour, it helps produce a moist, delicate crumb, but doesn't have glutinous rice flour's gift of cohesion.

Notes of Caution: It's on the pricey side, relative to other gluten-free ingredients. Happily, the full-bodied flavor of brown rice flour lets a little go a long way, so you can use it economically. It's more perishable than most flours, so this one stores best in the fridge.

TAPIOCA FLOUR OR STARCH

Basic Data: We're going underground! Tapioca is itself a starch, derived from the cassava plant, *Manihot esculenta*, also known by the names manioc, *mandioca*, *aipim*, *kamoteng kahoy*, *mogo*, and *yuca*. It's cultivated and serves as a staple in South America, Africa, and East Asia. In America, tapioca flour and tapioca starch are one and the same—some companies market their product as flour rather than starch. The pearl tapioca commonly seen in puddings and Asian "bubble" teas and other beverages is "beads" of the extracted starch.

Flavor & Texture: Tapioca's superfine texture, coupled with its nearly neutral flavor, make this starch a must-have for your gluten-free pantry. I recommend tapioca starch for almost any gluten-free baking application. It adds a delicate crumb to cookies and crusts and a smooth texture to cakes and pies and makes gluten-free fried chicken authentic, honest-as-the-day-is-long fried chicken. In a pinch, when I run out of glutinous rice flour, I use tapioca starch to roll out my pie or tart crusts.

Architecture & Engineering: Less dense than potato starch and flour, but more smoothly binding, tapioca lends a lightness to gluten-free baked goods, and when used as a thickener, gives a creamy quality. Its superior binding quality helps create that perfect crumb for a pie crust.

Notes of Caution: On the shopping front, one thing to be aware of: In countries where cassava is a staple, tapioca-starch producers typically put out "sweet" and "sour" varieties. My recipes call for the sweet type, which is what you'll generally encounter here in the United States. But just in case, check that label, and by no means should you *ever* substitute instant tapioca for tapioca starch. Just think "bad plastic surgery" and the visual alone will keep you on the right path.

MVP: GUAR GUM

Gluten is a little protein with huge bonding power; I call it the "magic rubber band" of traditional baking. Gluten enables that cool pizza guy to spin the dough on the tip of a finger without breaking it, lets cakes and breads rise to towering heights, and helps popovers pop and yet stay tender. No matter what kind of leavening you combine with a gluten protein, the gluten will expand and contract without breaking. It's almost infinitely elastic. And this makes traditional baking both versatile and, well, not exactly easy, but simpler.

Elasticity is the most difficult challenge of baking without gluten. A gluten-free dough, going it alone without employing something to do the work of the magic rubbery gluten, crumbles and comes apart in a grainy heap, or implodes into an impenetrable mass. We've tossed out the rubber band, so now what? Enlist a thickening agent that doubles as an emulsifier and a volumizer. My number-one draft choice: Guar gum.

Basic Data: Guar gum is derived from the guar bean, *Cyamopsis tetragonoloba*. The gum varies in color based on purity (in descending order) from pale slate to muddy gray or pale pink-beige. "Gum" is something of a misnomer, because what we use, and find available in our stores, is a powder.

Flavor & Texture: Guar gum's superfine texture makes the powder slippery to the touch; its faintly earthy aroma in raw form vanishes once you've incorporated it into your baked goods and other foods. This miracle of gluten-free cooking adds volume, structure, and elasticity without making anything rubbery.

Architecture & Engineering: High in soluble fiber, guar gum is a very powerful and natural ally to have in your gluten-free kitchen. The chemical structure of guar gum is that of a blooming arbor or a treetop, so it is literally engineered to rise to the occasion.

Extras: The guar bean and its gum are recognized for their ability to lower blood-sugar levels, reduce serum cholesterol, and aid in prevention of heart disease.

Notes of Caution: If you're allergic to legumes as well as gluten, then guar gum is clearly not your choice in this department. Fear not! Find alternatives on page 222.

STAFF OF LIFE: MORE FLOURS, MEALS, AND STARCHES

Much as I'd love to write up *every* gluten-free flour, meal, and starch, doing so would double the size of this book. Instead, I've limited this review to only the ingredients used in the recipes. Two things to remember about these ingredients: their impact on your thinking as a craftsman in the kitchen and their effects on the results you get. I always tell my students to view these ingredients as the parts necessary to making an exotic meal. You may not recognize all of them, but you'll be blown away by the results they produce. My focus is the ingredients' physical characteristics—color, texture, odor, flavor— and how these traits are actualized in handling and cooking.

"Texture" and "consistency" are words often used interchangeably, but I use the first for the feel of an ingredient, on its own, and the second for the feel the ingredient produces in the stages of a recipe, in both the uncooked and cooked forms of the food. Texture is the primary distinguisher, for our purposes, of what's a meal, flour, or starch (that list running in descending order of coarseness). Corn gives us a natural example. Cornmeal is rough and has a grain; corn flour is ground finer, to a powder; and cornstarch is processed into a cakey starch that clumps together.

ALMOND FLOUR

Basic Data: Not to be mistaken for almond meal, almond flour is, in a nutshell, just blanched almonds (i.e., their skins removed) and ground fine. Its color, varying from brand to brand, ranges from pale sand to light dirty blond.

Flavor & Texture: The almond's mildly sweet flavor, free of the hints of bitterness of some nuts, lends itself perfectly to baking and cuts the edge off stronger-tasting flours like buckwheat and millet. Its intrinsic butteriness, meanwhile, does wonders for textures throughout the range of baked-good consistencies. I add almond flour to everything, from bars, layer cakes, cupcakes, and cookies to quick breads. Texture, also varying brand to brand, runs from coarse, even mealy, to very fine, almost like white all purpose flour. Coarse almond flour is great for a pastry crust, but not what we want for a French macaron, as the beautiful, smooth-domed surface winds up lumpy. (That's more like an Italian almond cookie, which is a lovely confection, but not an authentic macaron.)

Architecture & Engineering: As almond flour has no natural constituents that help it bond, it needs to collaborate in most baked goods with other flours or bonding-and-elasticizing ingredients. (You'll find the skinny on those on page 220.)

Extras: Almonds help baked goods stay moist without seeming wet. And if you are looking to give a boost of concentrated food value to your gluten-free baked goods, almond flour is one of the best options you've got. High in vitamin E, folic acid, and unsaturated fats, this nut is lauded as a "super food" for its perfect balance of macronutrients and micronutrients beneficial to heart and brain health. (Those French and Italian bakers are onto something.)

Notes of Caution: Sadly, due to its texture, I can't recommend almond flour for yeast-risen doughs, laminated doughs like puff pastry, or finer-textured batters like those for crêpes and choux paste.

BUCKWHEAT FLOUR

Basic Data: Here, too, don't let the name mislead you; buckwheat is no relative of regular wheat. It is a relative of rhubarb and sorrel. Dark brown with flecks of black, buckwheat produces a flour that's grayish, sometimes with a slight blue cast. It's visually the most distinctive of all gluten-free flours.

Flavor & Texture: The flavor, likewise, is in a class by itself: earthy, with a rotund, nutty base note. Buckwheat adds a prized tenderness and delicacy to baked goods, a famous instance being the delectable blini, caviar's most classic vehicle. The grain's masculine flavor makes it a perfect addition to quick breads, and a tablespoon or two will make your gluten-free sourdough something to talk about. These characteristics also make buckwheat a distinguished addition to savory gluten-free cooking.

Architecture & Engineering: The flour is slightly coarse, what I call "medium fine," as its granules aren't as hard as those of, say, white rice flour. Buckwheat's granules soften quickly and give a consistency to the finished product that's anything but grainy—quite the opposite! Mucilage, a complex carbohydrate found in buckwheat, absorbs water and makes buckwheat flour somewhat sticky. This "weak bond" of gluten-free physics helps hold things together, but just barely. To compensate for the limited connectivity of mucilage, my recipes and blends calling on buckwheat flour also include a tablespoon or two of tapioca starch or glutinous rice flour, plus a provider of elasticity.

Notes of Caution: Buckwheat's earthy taste can, in the wrong proportion, incline toward bitter.

CORNSTARCH

Basic Data: Cornstarch, according to Harold McGee in his book *On Food and Cooking*, is what the grain of the corn plant yields "when the germ, hull, and seed proteins . . . have been removed."

Flavor & Texture: Nearly odorless, bright white in color, and superfine in texture, cornstarch is one of the most versatile ingredients in the pantry. It's my thickener of choice for sauces and even pastry cream. A wonderful addition to batters for gluten-free bars, cookies, and cakes, cornstarch renders a pie crust gorgeous and flaky but only when used in conjunction with other gluten-free flours.

Architecture & Engineering: Starch molecules are always looking to get together. This makes starches effective thickeners and means a little can go a long way. A modicum of cornstarch can play a decisive role without significantly impacting flavor or appearance. Part of what's miraculous about cornstarch is that it's light in feel, yet dense (in weight-to-volume ratio, only potato starch and potato flour top it). Heft a box of cornstarch and you'll see, or scoop up a handful of the loose stuff and squeeze: It clumps right together, almost like a snowball.

Notes of Caution: Many brands of commercial cornstarch are produced from genetically modified grain, which has been subjected to radiation, and the starch is processed with harsh chemicals. Most corn grown in the United States has also been bred to be high in sugar. My picks among non-GMO brands are Rapunzel and Let's Do Organic (see the Resources section, page 227). Cornstarch doesn't serve gluten-free breads well and isn't the thing to use to roll out dough, as it forms a rubbery outer coating. If corn allergy is an issue, go with a combination of potato starch and tapioca starch, in equal parts, as your substitution.

HAZELNUT MEAL

Basic Data: In one sense, hazelnut meal is analogous to almond flour: It's a ground nutmeat. But in this case, the nut is roasted and its skin is retained, making the meal a dark brown, with the copper of the skins popping through.

Flavor & Texture: A wonderful way to add moisture and flavor to almost any baked good, this is my pick for flourless chocolate cakes, for *baci*, the Italian hazelnut macarons held together with amaretto ganache, and as an occasional addition to decadently rich desserts. Hazelnuts' substantial flavor and fragrance speak of the autumn, but I keep some around all the time, stored in the freezer (a good way to avoid the holiday-season price spike). I also roast and grind them myself (a blender, chopper, or food processor works well), as the flavor is so much more fully retained if the roasted, ground nuts are used fresh. (Think coffee.)

Architecture & Engineering: Hazelnut meal, like almond flour, has no natural constituents that help it bond, so it needs the aid of flours and elasticity agents.

Notes of Caution: The seasonal character and pronounced flavor of hazelnut makes this, for most of us, not a meal for everyday use.

MASA HARINA

Basic Data: Back to corn! This is corn flour, including (unlike cornstarch) both the kernel and the germ of the corn. Made into a paste, the corn is then flash-dried to yield a flour. The aroma recalls fresh cornbread, right out of a cast-iron skillet. Minuscule flecks of yellow in off-white give the flour a variegated visual appeal.

Flavor & Texture: Masa harina adds a moist crumb to your baking, making every bite more tender than the last. I use it to make tortillas, tamales, or tortilla chips, or as a flavor enhancer in biscuits, tart crusts, empanadas, dumplings, cobblers, and even savory soufflés.

Architecture & Engineering: The smooth but dense texture makes the flour clump easily; it can hold together, but not with elastic effect or quality.

Notes of Caution: As masa harina clumps easily, be sure not to pack it into measuring cups. It's not recommended for sponge cakes, layer cakes, custards, puddings, or (because corn takes on a bitterness in the presence of yeast) for donuts and yeast-risen doughs.

MILLET FLOUR

Basic Data: Millet is a high-protein grain (22 percent protein by weight). Nicknamed "the little giant" and long a staple in Africa, millet contains the essential amino acids and all the carbohydrates the human body requires. Millet grain and flour are a medium-hued yellow, going toward blond.

Flavor & Texture: Millet has a distinctive, nutty flavor. I love to use it in gluten-free bread, popovers, pancakes, some cookies, and even in gnocchi. It's an ideal candidate for savory gluten-free cooking and the best substitute (when you need one) for sorghum flour.

Architecture & Engineering: Millet flour has a medium graininess and gives a fine, moist crumb. Refrigerating a millet dough overnight breaks down the granule's coarse shell and teases out the grain's natural elasticity. After this cold rest, when heat is applied, the effect, along with that heavenly crumb, is of a creamy, custardy texture. If you can't do sorghum, this is the flour I recommend most as a substitute.

Notes of Caution: Millet flour is perishable and needs to be stored in an airtight container in the fridge.

OATS AND OAT FLOUR

Basic Data: Oats are the naturally gluten-free seed of the grass *Avena sativa*. The oats we're accustomed to eating have been rolled into flat disks and are a variegated beige, and the flour derived from them is a toasty brown.

Flavor & Texture: Oat flour's light aroma reminds me of hay barns and moments in farmhouse kitchens and country general stores. Oat flour is a wonderful way to add flavor and varied texture to breads, while fine-rolled oats make a lovely addition to quick and yeast-risen batters, like cookies and muffins.

Architecture & Engineering: Oat flour has a surprisingly moist, thick texture, and its large, smooth granules enable it to give a dough or batter considerable body.

Extras: Oat bran famously helps lower cholesterol, and oats have a high ratio of fat-digesting enzymes, which help indigestible carbohydrates absorb toxins so the body can flush them out.

Notes of Caution: Commercially, oats are often milled on equipment in which gluteny grains have been processed. It's necessary to seek out oats that are handled in dedicated gluten-free facilities to avoid cross-contamination. If even gluten-free oats do not agree with you, substitute oat flour with millet flour. As versatile as oat flour is, I can't recommend it for finer pastries, and I don't use steel-cut oats, the "Irish" kind, in baking (but I do love them as a porridge on cold mornings). See the Resources section (page 227) for the best brands to trust.

POTATO FLOUR

Basic Data: Potato flour is derived from pulverized and cooked potatoes and is off-white in appearance, more pinkish-cream than eggshell.

Flavor & Texture: The flavor and aroma are pronounced. Some describe potato flour as pungent, but I think that's a little prissy. Potato flour is extremely fine in texture, silkier than most above-the-ground flours.

Architecture & Engineering: By far the most dense of the flours. (As with potato starch, its smooth, light texture can be deceiving.)

Notes of Caution: With its density and big flavor in mind, use potato flour sparingly, especially in combination with anything delicate, and be sure to adjust seasonings with this taste-bud heavy hitter.

POTATO STARCH

Basic Data: Yep, it's the extracted starch of the potato, analogous to cornstarch in its relation to the source staple. Stark white and much lighter in flavor than potato flour, it's easily distinguished from other starches in your pantry.

Flavor & Texture: Extremely fine in texture—the finest of all the gluten-free starches and flours—potato starch feels silky and slippery cool to the touch. It makes tart crusts flaky, cake crumbs springy, and fried foods crispy.

Architecture & Engineering: With the highest density of all the starches, potato starch has wonderful thickening power. It also doesn't congeal when a sauce cools, as cornstarch does, which can be a plus, just not for sauces.

Notes of Caution: Potato starch easily gives rise to a rubbery, dense texture, so it should be used with discretion. It's not the thing to use to roll out any kind of dough, for the reason noted with cornstarch. The non-congealing property makes this starch less desirable for thickening puddings, custards, and pastry creams. In sauces, too, it can have a tendency to get viscous and stringy.

CONSISTENCY IS EVERYTHING

The trickiest part of living and cooking gluten-free, perhaps the most contentious as well, is finding the magic rubber band that works best for your body *and* for what you cook. Because many people have to navigate around multiple food allergies, and can't use guar gum, I'll list some alternatives known to work.

There are two classes of ingredients commonly used in place of gluten to give that "magic rubber band" effect:

First, hydrocolloids: A hydrocolloid is a substance that forms a gel with water and influences how liquids flow. Used in small amounts, a hydrocolloid keeps a salad dressing from separating in the bottle and helps hold a variety of gluten-free products together. Some hydrocolloids add volume; others don't. Of the two involved in gluten-free cooking, guar gum does; xanthan gum doesn't.

Second, fiber: Fiber comes from the cell walls of plants, and in cooking provides structure to combine ingredients. I'm a bit wary of the old adobe-brick analogy, but think of the straw that holds that mud together. Fiber can be pretty rigid. There are two types: insoluble (wheat bran, psyllium, cellulose) and soluble (konjac, fruit pectin). Both work to thicken things up and can make things dense and heavy if used in excess.

My personal favorite, guar gum, I've covered already, with its All-Star teammates. Here are some alternatives:

KONJAC POWDER

Basic Data: Konjac fiber powder is derived from the root of the konjac plant, *Amorphophallus konjac*, which is native to subtropical Japan, China, and Indonesia. This is pure soluble fiber and therefore sugar-free (as opposed to konjac glucomannan, a sugar derived from the root).

Flavor & Texture: Konjac power is white and odorless, with a superfine texture and little to no taste.

Architecture & Engineering: Konjac has ten times the thickening power of cornstarch; just 1 teaspoon will gel a whole cup of water. It essentially functions like a starch and thickens extremely quickly when heat is added. The result is a consistency similar to that obtained with fruit pectin (from which preserves,

marmalades, and *gelées* get their viscosity). It's wonderful for all types of sauces, custards, puddings, and pastry creams.

Substitution Ratio for Guar Gum: ¼ to 1. For every 1 teaspoon guar gum, use just ¼ teaspoon konjac.

Notes of Caution: Konjac can be a little problematic when added to baked goods. Use too much and your muffins will shake more like Jell-O rather than spring like a muffin should.

PSYLLIUM HUSK POWDER

Basic Data: Psyllium husk powder is a soluble fiber made from the outer coating of the seed of *Plantago ovate*, an herb native to India. The powder's color varies from brown-black to light brown.

Flavor & Texture: Psyllium husk powder has a strong flavor and a medium-fine texture.

Architecture & Engineering: In contact with water, psyllium husk fiber swells, forming a gel that helps hold moisture in gluten-free baked goods as well as providing some cohesion and elasticity.

Substitution Ratio for Guar Gum: ½ to 1. If a recipe calls for 1 teaspoon guar gum, use ½ teaspoon psyllium husk powder.

Notes of Caution: Psyllium husk powder will give baked goods the plant's distinctive husky flavor. To offset that, increase the quantities of extracts and other flavorings in the recipe. Use psyllium in moderation so as not to get dry baked goods. And while you're at it, drink plenty of water (the fiber is a natural laxative).

Now, I feel obligated to give some time to two magic-rubber-band substitutes I don't look on with favor.

SLURRIES

"Slurry," in the culinary vocabulary, means a starch-water amalgam that becomes gelatinous. The mix of cornstarch or flour and water that people use to thicken a gravy is a kind of slurry. In contemporary gluten-free baking, slurries are most commonly made with ground seeds, generally flax or chia, and have to stand at least a couple of hours before they're ready for use. Some cooks swear by slurries, but this kind of magic rubber band takes time to prepare, and the performance isn't consistent enough for everyday use. For me, it's less about time or fine-tuning than that gluten-free foods made with slurries often look what I call melty.

XANTHAN GUM

Not to trash talk anyone's elasti-mulsifier of choice, but . . . well, as far as I'm concerned, the less said about xanthan gum, the better. There are some compelling reasons to buy this hydrocolloid, but they are political and nutritional rather than culinary: Not a lot of guar beans are grown in the United States, whereas our production of xanthan gum is huge.

Basic Data: Xanthan gum is a hydrocolloid derived from a toxic bacterium, *Xanthomonas campestris*. The common name is "black rot," since that's what it produces on broccoli and leafy vegetables. The bacterium is grown in laboratories on everything from wheat and high-fructose corn syrup to dairy foods and soy. Since our labeling laws do not require xanthan gum manufacturers to disclose what they grow their black rot on, the gum you just paid a good price for may not even be gluten-free. (Read on; it gets worse.)

Flavor & Texture: As a bonder-elasticizer, xanthan gum does work. I avoid eating foods made with it, so I speak from limited experience, but xanthan gum is infamous for the "dirty sock aftertaste" of many commercial gluten-free products.

Architecture & Engineering: Xanthan gum is used in multiple industries for its ability to augment the viscosity of fluids. Like guar gum, it keeps salad dressings from separating.

Substitution Ratio for Guar Gum: At least this is easy: 1 to 1.

Notes of Caution: Where do I start? The FDA took more than a decade to approve xanthan gum as safe for human consumption, though the product was developed under the auspices of the U.S. Department of Agriculture. Recent studies show symptoms identical to gluten exposure in gluten-intolerant and celiac sufferers following ingestion of xanthan gum. More alarming yet is the number of infants and children fed xanthan gum now presenting with compromised immune systems, necrosis, or tissue death. And if you've got an allergy to soy or dairy, xanthan gum's a good thing to avoid.

KEEPING IT LIGHT

Leavenings work biologically or chemically, but either way, they do the same thing: give off carbon dioxide. They produce different textures and flavors, but the big practical difference is speed. The biological kind takes its time, so a dough made with this sort of leavening needs to rise before baking. Chemical leavenings produce carbon dioxide in high gear, making quick breads feasible, and work in batters that are more liquid.

GLUTEN-FREE YEAST

Yeast is a live, naturally occurring, microscopic fungus that consumes sugar and produces carbon dioxide. This CO_2, building up inside dough as thousands of tiny bubbles, makes the dough rise and gives the resulting bread its light, airy feel. The wonderful aroma in a kitchen as bread is rising is, in part, the rich smell of yeast going to work.

Yeast, the traditional biological leavening, goes back to time immemorial. In commercial form, it's usually sold as active, or highly active, dry yeast, which is granular but dissolves quickly in liquid. In some markets, it's occasionally still sold in moist cakes, but dry yeast is now pretty much the standard.

I'm afraid to say that we do need to check to see that our yeast is gluten-free, too. Fleischman's and Red Star are; Rapunzel grows its yeast on malt, produced from barley, so it's better to avoid that brand. I've listed more brands in the Resources section (page 227).

BAKING SODA

Baking soda, sodium bicarbonate, reacts with acids to produce carbon dioxide—doing what yeast does, but non-biologically. Baking soda can be used on its own if a batter contains enough acid to precipitate the chemical reaction. Buttermilk, lemon juice, chocolate,

light and dark brown sugar, and molasses can all provide the acid component to make a soda-leavened
batter rise.

BAKING POWDER

Baking powder is baking soda with the acid built right
in (usually in the form of cream of tartar, a by-product
of the tartaric acid produced in winemaking). The two
active ingredients are usually suspended in an inert
medium like cornstarch. The reaction takes place as
soon as the compound is wet, and proceeds briskly,
so the rising can happen right in the oven (and will
happen right in the bowl if you don't move fast).

Double-acting baking powder gives an initial
release of carbon dioxide that bubbles up and makes
a batter expand within minutes of being added, followed by a second rising in the oven.

In gluten-free baking, you'll get the best results
with cakes and most quick breads by using baking
powder. The trick is getting the ratio correct in your
adaptations, which of course depends on the kinds
of flours used and their densities. Too little baking
powder and your baked goods will be under-risen
and dense; too much and your cakes will bubble
over—and then collapse anyway! Too much will also
influence flavor, adding a bitter, alkaline taste.

Then there's this little secret, which is not a leavening
but . . .

GLUTEN-FREE MERINGUE POWDER

Meringue powder is a mix of dried egg whites, gum
arabic (a natural sap from two species of acacia tree),
cornstarch, citric acid, cream of tartar, and the mineral
silica. Meringue powder has a superfine texture and
clumps together easily. Its color ranges from white to
a pale ochre.

Though it's typically used to make meringues and
specialized icings, gluten-free meringue powder is a
great volumizer for a yeast dough. The acids and the
egg whites help a gluten-free dough to rise up beautifully and avoid collapsing once it's out of the oven.

(And remember, egg white plays well with guar gum.)

Meringue powder has a very sweet bouquet, which
can impact the flavor profile of bread. As you'll see in
my recipes, a little does the trick.

Not all meringue powders are gluten-free, so check
labels. "Modified food starch" means possible gluten,
so if in doubt, stay away. (Yep, more on this in the
Resources section, page 227.)

SUGAR, SPICE, AND OTHER THINGS NICE—AND SALT, TOO

Not my All-Stars, but these last few items are every
bit as much mission-critical in my gluten-free kitchen.
Find quality sources for all of these in the Resources
section (page 227).

SALT

Salt is an imperative in making gluten-free bread. In
traditional baking, salt strengthens the effects of the
gluten protein, so an over-salted bread is rubbery
(and an unsalted dough produces a strange-textured
bread). Luckily for gluten-free cooks, salt enhances
the strength of guar gum, too. So using it increases
the elasticity of a dough, the texture of the baked
product, and the gorgeousness of the loaf.

So, what kind? For me, this one's pretty simple: For
baking and general cooking, I stick with the kosher
kind. It's had all iodine removed, so you may need
another source of that for your thyroid, but it's one of
the purest salts you can get.

SUGAR

Sugar is an ally to the gluten-free baker. Sugars help
hold moisture and, by feeding yeast or providing
a bit of acidity, aid the leavening agent. Also, being
somewhat sticky, sugar helps hold things together.
Getting the right rise is not nearly so simple without
sugar to do a good part of the work, so we can use
the assist.

The thing to bear in mind with sugars is that they
operate across a very full spectrum of flavors, textures, and colors. From the least to the most refined:

Granulated White Sugar

Granulated white sugar, or refined pure cane sugar, is almost pure sucrose, with the other components of the cane juice removed. Using granulated white sugar is advantageous in any recipe delicate enough in flavor and color that you don't want to shift the flavor profile or the color by using a darker sugar. White sugar does help achieve a look we often want in cookies, cakes, and pies—whether it's a smooth surface, a slight translucence, or a slightly less cohesive crumb. When you don't need the fuller acidity of the molasses in brown sugar, refined pure cane sugar Is what you want. Caster or superfine sugar is a granulated white sugar with a consistency between confectioners' sugar and regular granulated sugar. It dissolves quickly and is ideal for making custards and pastry creams.

Confectioners' (Powdered) Sugar

The most refined sugar. Ground ten times, to be finer in texture than "superfine," it's right for the most delicate baked goods: meringues, icings, and simple syrups. It dissolves fully in liquid, without needing to be heated, and is virtually zero-impact on delicate textures, like those of macarons.

EXTRACTS, ESSENCES, AND FLAVORINGS

These are *the* elements that best harmonize the flavors of batters and doughs and are especially important in gluten-free baking. You can include dozens of extracts in your arsenal, but you'll be just fine with vanilla and almond. Some vanilla extracts contain additives that are not gluten-free, so be sure to check the label.

SPICES

Spices are second only to extracts in working to harmonize the varied flavors we bring together in gluten-free cooking. Spices are inherently gluten-free, so enjoy them! (When using blends or seasoning mixes, which may have non-spices worked in, do check those labels.)

Dark & Light Brown Sugars

Light and dark brown sugars get their color and flavor from residual cane juice or molasses that gets separated, in refining, from white sugar, then reintroduced. The cane juice or molasses adds flavor and boosts acidity more than white sugar to help a chemical leavening. There's also a specific texture range brown sugars deliver. An oatmeal cookie made with brown sugar is more tender and "bendy," whereas the same recipe made with white sugar will get glassy; brown-sugar cakes (like my Chocolate Mayonnaise Cake, page 157, or a gingerbread) have just the right crumb, which will stick together when pinched, and the sugar has a way of deepening and complementing the main ingredient. Finally, brown sugars have built-in moisture (that's why they turn into a rock if the bag or canister is left unsealed), and that moisture goes right into your baked goods.

RESOURCES

ANCIENT HARVEST
www.ancientharvest.com

AUTHENTIC FOODS
www.authenticfoods.com

BOB'S RED MILL
www.bobsredmill.com

BLUEBELL ICE CREAM
www.bluebell.com

FLEISCHMANN'S YEAST
www.fleischmannsyeast.com

GUITTARD CHOCOLATES
www.guittard.com

GF HARVEST
www.glutenfreeoats.com

HONEYVILLE
www.honeyville.com

NOW FOODS
www.nowfoods.com
(especially for guar gum)

NUTIVA
www.nutiva.com

PENZEY'S SPICES
www.penzeys.com
(especially for vanilla extract)

RED STAR YEAST
www.redstaryeast.com

SAVORY SPICE SHOP
www.savoryspiceshop.com
(especially for spices and black onyx cocoa)

SUR LA TABLE
www.surlatable.com

TITO'S HANDMADE VODKA
www.titosvodka.com
(hands down the best vodka that happens to be gluten-free)

WILLIAMS-SONOMA
www.williams-sonoma.com

BIBLIOGRAPHY

Allard, Harriet. *The Household Searchlight Recipe Book*. 1932. *The Household Magazine*, Tokepa, Kansas.

Beranbaum, Rose Levy. *The Bread Bible*. 2003. W.W. Norton Company, New York.

Crocker, Betty. *Century of Success*. 1979. General Mills, Inc., Minneapolis, Minnesota.

Friberg, Bo. *The Professional Pastry Chef*. 2002. John Wiley & Sons, Inc., New York.

McGee, Harold. *On Food and Cooking: The Science and Lore of the Kitchen*. 1984. Scribner, New York.

Pepin, Jacques. *La Technique*. 1976. Pocket Books, New York.

WEIGHT & VOLUME EQUIVALENTS

ALMOND FLOUR/MEAL

1 tablespoon	6 g
¼ cup	22 g
⅓ cup	30 g
½ cup	44 g
1 cup	90 g

SUPERFINE BROWN RICE FLOUR

1 tablespoon	8 g
¼ cup	27 g
⅓ cup	40 g
½ cup	62 g
1 cup	125 g

BUCKWHEAT FLOUR

1 tablespoon	10 g
¼ cup	27 g
⅓ cup	37 g
½ cup	61 g
1 cup	114 g

CORNSTARCH

1 tablespoon	9 g
¼ cup	30 g
⅓ cup	44 g
½ cup	63 g
1 cup	122 g

GLUTINOUS RICE FLOUR

1 tablespoon	8 g
¼ cup	28 g
⅓ cup	39 g
½ cup	57 g
1 cup	115 g

HAZELNUT MEAL

1 tablespoon	6 g
¼ cup	22 g
⅓ cup	32 g
½ cup	45 g
1 cup	92 g

MASA HARINA

1 tablespoon	7 g
¼ cup	26 g
⅓ cup	36 g
½ cup	50 g
1 cup	110 g

MILLET FLOUR

1 tablespoon	8 g
¼ cup	29 g
⅓ cup	37 g
½ cup	58 g
1 cup	117 g

GLUTEN-FREE OAT FLOUR

1 tablespoon	6 g
¼ cup	21 g
⅓ cup	30 g
½ cup	45 g
1 cup	93 g

POTATO STARCH

1 tablespoon	11 g
¼ cup	42 g
⅓ cup	57 g
½ cup	88 g
1 cup	176 g

POTATO FLOUR

1 tablespoon	12 g
¼ cup	40 g
⅓ cup	57 g
½ cup	85 g
1 cup	172 g

SORGHUM FLOUR

1 tablespoon	8 g
¼ cup	26 g
⅓ cup	36 g
½ cup	54 g
1 cup	111 g

TAPIOCA STARCH

1 tablespoon	8 g
¼ cup	26 g
⅓ cup	35 g
½ cup	54 g
1 cup	110 g

TEFF FLOUR

1 tablespoon	11 g
¼ cup	32 g
⅓ cup	45 g
½ cup	68 g
1 cup	140 g

INDEX

ACKNOWLEDGMENTS

First and foremost I would like to thank everyone who supported my Kickstarter campaign in 2012, especially Paul Caruso, enabling me to complete the research and development for this book. I am both humbled and honored to have over one hundred friends and strangers (see below) believe enough in me to give. Thank you all.

To my incredible son, Leo, for believing in Mommy, even when I didn't play Legos with you long enough. May this book be your book, too, as you were my inspiration so we can help all the gluten-free children together.

To my love Joseph Stallone, whose brilliant mind and loving heart wouldn't let me quit. To my agent, Nena Medonia, for placing my book in a noble home. To my editors Holly Dolce, Jess Taylor, and Ivy McFadden, for believing in my vision and helping breathe it to life. To Danielle Young for the beautiful design and layout. To the immensely talented Knoxy, for her pleasure-seeking photographs, and to Ariel Godfrey for her styling. To Kristen Piegza, my lead baker at Blackbird Bakery, who impresses me daily with her work ethic and perfectionism. I thank you every day, even when I forget to say it.

On the home front, I thank my parents, Tom and Carol Hassell, for putting up with all the missed dinners so I could complete this book. I wish to especially thank my father for making me build that 1963 Rambler engine when I was sixteen, as I'm convinced it taught me the mechanics of life. Love and thanks to my brothers and sisters, Jeanne, Mark, Amy, and Jon. To Tim Morgan for helping me live the answer, I am forever grateful. Mom and Pops Stallone, and Max and Kiera, so much love to you all.

To those who stood by me through the thick and thin: Traci Goudie Tracy Ganske, Caysi Jean Burns, Tess Masters, Amie Valpone, Laura Striese, and Taryn Fixel; I adore you all. To Alyssa Jo Keltner for being my guide when I needed one most, *om mani padme hung*.

For Denise at Core Power Yoga for keeping me in line and my body fit!

From Kickstarter: Thank you to Paul Caruso, Sally Candee, Chris Hamberlin, Jessica Aberthal, David Wheeler, Florence Noel, Heather Jacobson, Laura Thoms, Shef, Meg Stacks, Mary Miller, ebanbakery, Liliyana Greer, Lisa Hickey, Belinda Hare, Paula Foore, Andrea Villareal, Nancy Coplin, Dan Royzycki, David Bartholow, Jack Watson, Holly Thompson, Miles Compton, Judy Bolin, Chuck Burns, Nick Alt, Rachel Jahnke, Ashley Garmon, Daria DiTorro, AnnMarie Olson, Elizabeth, Randi Klett, Steve Farmer, Brian, Rachelle King, Charissa, Elizabeth Craig, Barbara, Natalee Thronburgh, Carrie Clarke, Vicki Palmer, Joseph Stallone, Jon Hassell, Sean Berry, Meghen Hiller, Jan Mirkin-Earley, Cory Hughart, Perrydotto, Wendy Castleman, Merrit Meade, Laura B. Russell, Laura Streise, Jane Pinto, Tabatha Conarko, Graham Frandson, Bridget Bauer, Carol Hassell, JoAnn Meyers, Jeffrey Carrier, Tiffany Sun, Becky Getter, Leigh Ward, Michelle Fandrich, Meghan Jones Turley, Claire, bacchus, Susan Bollinger, Blair Richardson, Brad Ehney, Danielle Thomas, Christopher Weidmark, Steve, Danielle Elliot, Laurie Gallardo, Liliyana Greer, Amanda Gentzel, Cory, Alyssa Jo Keltner, Diane Carr, Rosalba Andrade, Jessica Murnane, Karin Haberlin, Nathan Binford, Alfred Gray, Cherri Robbins, Mistine O'Connor, Holyone, Heilla, Robin Behrstock, Rebecca Peters, Catherine Oddenino, Jennifer Barreca, Sarah B., Emily Dye, Aaron Seifert, Lila Tenenbown, Jennifer Harris, Mary Jane Mendell, Jessica Guzman, Caitlin Tyler, Tony Tringale, Ali Slutsky, Elliot Kralj, Ken Ciancimino, Ann Richardson, Paula Tyler Standridge, Jenna Kitley, Maureen, Jack Watson, and Marion Cimbala. I am still here because of you.